# Hydronarratives

Hydro

© 2022 by the Board of Regents of the University of Nebraska

A version of chapter 3 originally appeared as "Extractive Fictions and Post-Extractive Futurisms: Energy and Environmental Injustice in Appalachia," *Environmental Humanities* 11, no. 2 (2019): 402–26. The poems "A Mother Near the West Virginia Line Considers Public Health" and "F Word" by Julie Spicher Kasdorf and Steven Rubin are from *Shale Play: Poetry and Photographs from the Fracking Fields* (Pennsylvania State University Press, 2018), 90–91; permission conveyed through Copyright Clearance Center, Inc., and republished with permission of Pennsylvania State University Press: A division of the Pennsylvania State University Libraries and Scholarly Communications. A short section of chapter 4 was originally published as "Imagining a Green New Deal through Climate Fiction" in *Edge Effects: A Digital Magazine*, February 21, 2019.

All rights reserved

The University of Nebraska Press is part of a land-grant institution with campuses and programs on the past, present, and future homelands of the Pawnee, Ponca, Otoe-Missouria, Omaha, Dakota, Lakota, Kaw, Cheyenne, and Arapaho Peoples, as well as those of the relocated Ho-Chunk, Sac and Fox, and Iowa Peoples.

∞

Library of Congress Control Number: 2022947338

Set in Lyon Text

# narratives

Water, Environmental Justice, and a Just Transition

MATTHEW S. HENRY

University of Nebraska Press / Lincoln

For Jessica

# Contents

| | | |
|---|---|---|
| | List of Illustrations | ix |
| | Acknowledgments | xi |
| | Introduction: Storying Water and Justice | 1 |
| 1/ | Decolonizing Drought: Indigenous Collective Continuance in the Lower Colorado River Basin | 25 |
| 2/ | Freedom Dreams for Flint: Imagining a Just Transition beyond Racial Capitalism | 57 |
| 3/ | Extractive Fictions and Post-Extraction Futurisms: *Energy, Water, and Environmental Justice in Appalachia* | 85 |
| 4/ | On the Wrong Side of the Levee: Sea Level Rise Narratives in the Decade of the Green New Deal | 113 |
| | Conclusion: Imagining a Community-Driven Just Transition in Wyoming | 147 |
| | Notes | 159 |
| | Bibliography | 191 |
| | Index | 211 |

# Illustrations

| | | |
|---|---|---|
| 1 / | Hohokam Garden reproduction | 49 |
| 2 / | Municipal water piping near Hohokam Garden reproduction | 49 |
| 3 / | *Su:dagi Haicu A:ga (Water's Story)* by Marcus, Butler, and Manuel | 51 |
| 4 / | Model wearing Tracy Reese's Flint Fit Collection | 80 |
| 5 / | *Greetings from Flint* mural by Emily Ding | 82 |
| 6 / | *Sunflower Children* mural by Emily Ding | 82 |
| 7 / | AMD & Art Park blueprint | 107 |
| 8 / | AMD & Art Park holding pond | 107 |
| 9 / | *Chroma S4 Chimaera* by John Sabraw | 109 |
| 10 / | Green New Deal poster for Flushing Meadows Corona Park, Queens | 145 |
| 11 / | Green New Deal poster for the Public Garden, Boston | 146 |
| 12 / | Flyer announcing Imagining Wyoming's Future contest | 155 |

# Acknowledgments

This book emerges from work I did as a graduate student at Arizona State University, which is located on the occupied lands of the Akimel O'odham and Piipaash peoples. I transformed the that work into a full-length manuscript while at the University of Wyoming, which is located on the ancestral and traditional lands of the Cheyenne, Arapaho, Crow, and Shoshone peoples. White settlers stole these lands, violated treaties, and killed, forcibly removed, oppressed, and sought and continue to seek to erase Native peoples and cultures. This acknowledgment refuses the assumption that Indigenous peoples have been erased or eliminated by the settler state. It also recognizes that land acknowledgments are but one step in a broader effort to support Indigenous sovereignty and the return of land. As a settler descendant it is my hope that the words in this book have been written in the right relationship with these lands and their peoples.

This book would not be possible without the ongoing and generous support of my graduate school mentors Joni Adamson and Claudia Sadowski-Smith. I am forever indebted to them for their guidance and for showing me how to be an ethical, engaged scholar and citizen with a generosity and patience rare in higher education.

I am deeply grateful to the Haub School of Environment and Natural Resources, the School of Energy Resources, and the Department of English at the University of Wyoming for financial and institutional support to complete this project during my time as a scholar in residence from 2019 to 2021. To Melinda Morgan: Thank you for giving me a chance to succeed as a new faculty member at the University of Wyoming. I extend my gratitude to Scott Henkel and the Wyoming Institute for Humanities Research for sustained support of this project during and beyond the faculty research fellowship workshops in 2020. An additional thanks to the Association for the Study of Literature and the

Environment for the opportunities to share ideas and grow as a scholar over the years at the always invigorating biennial conferences. I thank José Casas for generously providing me with an unpublished script of *Flint* and Stacy Levy and John Sabraw for their willingness to discuss their incredible environmental reclamation art projects in Pennsylvania and Ohio, respectively.

To Kenneth Ladenburg, Travis Franks, and José Sebastian Terneus: Thank you for your endless willingness to workshop drafts and talk through ideas presented in this book, and for providing much-needed moments of levity during a challenging process. Finally, to my family: Thank you to Jessica, my person and partner in everything, for sacrificing so much to support this work over these last many years; to Rowan and Asher, my children, who constantly remind me why sustainable, equitable futures are worth fighting for; and to my parents, Joel and Kelley Henry, for their support, of both the moral and the childcare variety, as I worked to finish this project.

# Hydronarratives

# Introduction

*Storying Water and Justice*

In March 2017 a coalition of community and national organizations including the Standing Rock Committee, Hip Hop 4 Flint, and the Hip Hop Caucus hosted the Water Is Life Expo at the McCree Theater in Flint, Michigan. The three-day event, featuring musical performances, workshops, and talks by activists, was organized by Oglala Lakota activist and rapper YoNasDa LoneWolf and supported by Black Lives Matter, the Indigenous Environmental Network, and other national organizations. The event was meant to draw comparisons between the lead water crisis in Flint, Michigan, and Indigenous opposition to the Dakota Access Pipeline (DAPL) in Standing Rock, North Dakota. In 2014 residents in Flint, a low-income, majority-Black city an hour north of Detroit, experienced a sharp drop in water quality after the city switched its water source to the nearby Flint River. After months of denial by local and state officials, outside researchers determined that corroding pipes had caused elevated lead levels in the water, sparking an ongoing public health crisis that remains in many ways unresolved today. In 2016 Indigenous Water Protectors gathered outside the Standing Rock Reservation to oppose the pipeline's planned route beneath Lake Oahe on the Missouri River, citing concerns about the potential impacts of spills on the traditional lands and primary water supply of the Standing Rock Sioux Tribe. The protests were thrust into the national spotlight after police and private security forces violently attacked Water Protectors with rubber bullets, tear gas, and attack dogs as they peacefully demonstrated, sparking public debate about the ongoing violence of settler colonialism. In an interview leading up to the Water Is Life Expo, LoneWolf described both crises as a "war on our water."[1]

Through its name alone, the Water Is Life Expo united both struggles under the banner of "Water Is Life," an activist mantra that emerged during the height of the Standing Rock protests as "Mní Wičóni" (Lakota). Moreover, the comparative nature of the event offered a space for the type of generative storytelling and cultural expression that has long been a critical part of environmental justice activism. In Flint and Standing Rock, one primary medium of expression has been hip-hop. As Saginaw Anishinaabe scholar Kyle T. Mays notes, tracks like Detroit-based Anishinaabe rapper SouFy's "Pay 2 Be Poisoned," written specifically about Flint, speaks to shared experiences of oppression in a white supremacist settler state, punctuated by the line "Black labor plus red land equals white gold."[2] Likewise, Black and Indigenous hip-hop artists and groups like Taboo from the Black Eyed Peas, Prolific the Rapper, and A Tribe Called Red have all responded to events at Standing Rock by calling attention to the DAPL as the logical culmination of centuries of land theft and oppression. While these particular artists were not present at the Expo, the event represented one of many coalition-building efforts between community activists in Flint and Standing Rock that "present alternative narratives—even renewed possibilities—of solidarity between Black and Indigenous people, acknowledging differences and commonalities."[3]

Elevating such narratives is critical to ongoing water justice struggles in Flint, Standing Rock, and beyond. Such struggles represent a fight over "the color of water"—that is, the racialized dimensions of natural resource policy in the United States.[4] A recent study by the U.S. Water Alliance and nonprofit group Dig Deep shows that race and poverty are primary predictors of barriers to clean water access throughout the country.[5] In April 2019 President Trump signed the seven-state Colorado River Drought Contingency plan into law despite a consensus view that planned cutbacks will be inadequate to address expected shortages due to a long-term drying trend that has been partially attributed to the river's many large dams.[6] In California's Central Valley, where the felt impacts of drought have been especially severe, the legacies of segregation during a mid-twentieth century influx of Black farmworkers persist into the present, leaving now predominately Latinx farmworker communities to grapple with crumbling water infrastructure and dry wells.[7] April 2019 also marked five years since lead was first detected in Flint's water. Flint is not unique: We now know lead-contaminated water poses risks in other majority-Black cities like Newark, New Jersey, and Baltimore,

Maryland.[8] A 2018 report issued by the National Resources Defense Council estimates that 30 million people get their water from systems that violated the Environmental Protection Agency's (EPA's) Lead and Copper Rule between 2015 and 2018.[9] Across Kentucky, Ohio, and West Virginia—the heart of Appalachian coal country—130,000 EPA drinking water rules have been violated over the last two decades, underscoring a growing water crisis associated with fossil fuel extraction in impoverished pockets of the rural United States.[10] Elsewhere, climate-related coastal flooding disproportionately impacts low-income communities and communities of color. Patterns of displacement and mortality evident in the wake of Hurricane Katrina in 2006, when four of the seven hardest hit neighborhoods in New Orleans were at least 75 percent Black, have been evident in more recent disasters like Hurricane Harvey in Houston and Hurricane Maria in Puerto Rico in 2017.[11] The legacies of segregation and the maldistribution of capital necessary for disaster preparedness, along with climate adaptation policies that ignore the racialized dynamics of coastal development, have rendered Black and Indigenous communities especially vulnerable to climate-related sea level rise.[12]

Current water crises in the United States stem in part from the collective failure to transition to less consumptive resource use paradigms. In many ways, we have reached an impasse of water-fueled modernity in the age of global climate change. Scholars in the burgeoning subfield of the energy humanities have often spoken of the "impasse," the endemic ontological inertia preventing a system-wide transition from fossil fuels to renewable energy. Despite broad consensus that fossil fuels are a primary driver of greenhouse gas emissions and a warming climate, they remain integral to the very fabric of capitalist modernity.[13] The same can be said for water. A form of conventional energy (hydropower) as well as a critical input for agricultural production, global food systems, industry, and municipal use, water is arguably just as important as fossil fuels to the functioning of the global capitalist system. Water is also utterly critical to life on earth, literally powering the greater integrated biosphere by keeping essential, life-enabling elements like carbon, hydrogen, and nitrogen in constant circulation.[14] But over the past two centuries, these processes have been critically disrupted by human activity in support of economic development. Dams, reservoirs, canals, irrigation networks, and water-intensive enterprises such as raw materials extraction and processing have reduced seasonal discharge rates on major rivers, depleted aquifers, and reduced freshwater availability globally.[15] Much of the planet is steeped in a "crisis of cheap water," whereby easily accessible freshwater has begun to disappear, extractive efforts have intensified, and water commons have become increasingly enclosed by state and private interests.[16] In coastal regions, an unwelcome *abundance* of water in the form of increasingly intense storm-related flooding has generated a growing class of climate precariat. Many of what sociologist Saskia Sassen has called global cities, those mega-metropoles and financial hubs critical the functioning of the global economy, are now best described as what Ashley Dawson calls extreme cities, their continued existence contingent on keeping rising seas and intensifying storm surges at bay.[17]

The story of water in the United States is one of systemic disruption and social injustice. But this story is not new, nor does it foreclose the possibility of just, sustainable futures. On the one hand, the felt impacts of many contemporary water crises can be traced to the extractive logics of a capitalist system that has always relied on the differentiation of human value such that some groups are rendered necessarily disposable as a precondition for accumulation.[18] By the descriptor *extractive*, I mean ideologies, discourses, and institutions used to justify and further "capitalism's fundamental logic of withdrawal," the derivation of profits from communities and ecosystems without corresponding reinvestment.[19] Such logics frequently inform natural resource extraction and governance, a primary focus of this book. In practice, a natural outgrowth of capitalism's extractive logics is the emergence of sacrifice areas: communities or regions considered expendable in pursuit of some exclusionary notion of a greater good. This we might call the expendability thesis of capitalism. Determinations of who or what is considered expendable are frequently justified by discursive constructions of a so-called greater good—economic development, energy independence, national security, scientific knowledge, and so on.[20] Environmental studies scholarship has provided a wealth of terms to explain this phenomenon, from Raj Patel and Jason W. Moore's conception of cheap lives to describe how the forces of capital reduce the costs of doing business by offloading them on the colonized, the poor, women, and Indigenous communities to Rob Nixon's notion of unimagined communities displaced by megadams and other large-scale development projects in the Global South.[21] In such formulations, capital accumulation hinges on "the power to decide whose lives matter and whose do not."[22] When it comes to water, questions about what is considered "good," and whose lives matter, remain contested.

Sacrifice zones, unimagined communities, and cheap lives are maintained by narratives of inclusion and exclusion. Wealth inequality, as an inbuilt feature of capitalism, is one way human expendability is expressed, giving rise to what Joan Martin-Alier has described as the environmentalism of the poor, a collective struggle from below against the world-destroying forces of capital.[23] So is racial difference—the relations of production have always been racialized. As Black radical scholar Cedric Robinson wrote in *Black Marxism*, as "the development, organization, and expansion of capitalist society pursued essentially racial directions, so too did social ideology."[24] Buttressed by the forces of capital, the ideologies of white supremacy and settler colonialism drove the water crises in Flint and Standing Rock. Each should be viewed as constitutive of racial capitalism, a system that derives profits from the differentiation of human value within the logic of white supremacy and historically expressed through slavery, colonialism, and their legacies in institutional racism—all of which play an outsize role in environmental crises in the twenty-first century.[25] Settler colonialism scholar Jen Preston uses the apt and adjacent term *racial extractivism* to describe the central conceit of a settler colonial project that uses land theft and resource exploitation as a means to achieve racially exclusionary ends.[26] In this view, the Flint water crisis can be connected to decades of racialized austerity politics and the devaluation of Black communities as "surplus" and as trial grounds for increased privatization of social services in the neoliberal era.[27] Similarly, as Indigenous scholars like Nick Estes (Lakota) and Kyle Whyte (Potawatomi) have shown, the DAPL is an infrastructural manifestation of U.S. settler colonialism, whereby the ongoing legacies of Indigenous erasure are evident in the institutional prioritization of white wealth through broken treaties, land privatization, and natural resource extraction.[28] Both Flint and Standing Rock are uniquely representative of water justice struggles in the United States. They have also served as powerful sites of resistance against dominant narratives that render Black and Indigenous communities devalued, cheap, and sacrificial.

Just as the social ideologies that underpin capital depend on strong narrative foundations, their disruption or transformation depends on strong *counter*narratives that strive for a more inclusive greater good. Focusing on distinct but overlapping instances of water injustice in the United States, this book argues that narrative interventions are necessary for a just transition, a concept rooted in the U.S. labor and environmental justice movements to describe an alternative economic paradigm predicated on sustainability, economic and social equity, and climate resilience. Just transition frameworks vary, but at bottom refuse the extractive logics of capitalism and repudiate capital's expendability thesis of accumulation. As indicated in the title, this book is concerned with narratives, or *Hydronarratives*: stories and cultural representations that imagine just water futures. Hydronarratives can be discerned in literary fiction, film, music, photography, museum exhibits, public art, landscape architecture, and other media that amplify silenced environmental epistemologies, that story frequently erased histories of exclusion and violence, and chart a transition to a more just, equitable world. Amidst the global rise of the climate justice movement, demand for a just transition has become a rallying cry for frontline and fenceline communities most impacted by climate change and energy transitions. Cultural spaces have long been sites of reflection, refraction, and rupture of dominant narratives and power structures. Accordingly, writers and artists have long been a critical part of the U.S. environmental justice movement, calling attention to individual and collective traumas, struggles, and successes and alerting audiences to complex, multilayered histories of injustice.[29] Beyond a diagnostic purpose, moreover, the arts can be radically generative. As Julie Sze reminds us, cultural productions are uniquely positioned to "compose a counterhegemonic soundtrack for a restorative environmental justice politics grounded in solidarity."[30] Storytelling, through a range of media, can help link the individual to the collective, revealing shared experiences and empowering groups and communities to identify shared goals—all critical for overcoming doom-and-gloom environmental narratives centered around trauma, catastrophe, and inertia.[31] This book is concerned with how creative responses to water-related environmental injustices combine to form new narratives that support an approach to environmental decision-making driven by a recognition of past injustice and trauma and a commitment to reparative processes, programs, and policies—that is, a just transition.

### New Narratives for a Just Transition

What might a just water transition look like? In Flint a partial settlement with the state of Michigan in August 2020 awarded plaintiffs more than $600 million, with more than 80 percent earmarked for impacted children and special education services. Activists note, however, that remuneration alone is inadequate to address long-term health and community impacts.[32] Furthermore, Flint residents remain frustrated that most state and city officials who had been indicted for criminal charges reached plea deals and avoided jail time.[33] Litigation over the DAPL ended in 2022 after the Supreme Court declined to hear a case challenging a Standing Rock Sioux's legal victory invalidating a federal permit and requiring the pipeline to undergo a comprehensive environmental review. But Water Protectors have also demanded federal recognition of the pipeline's illegality as a violation of the 1868 Fort Laramie Treaty, the protection of tribal water sources, and a halt to the expansion of U.S. fossil fuel infrastructure. No such demands have been met.

These demands critically sync with reparations-based theories of justice such as reparation ecology, a concept Patel and Moore use to describe a process centered around the recognition of discursive and epistemological constructions that drive systemic injustice and a commitment to reparative processes that are neither strictly monetary nor final, but rather involve "the imagining of nonmonetary redistribution" as an ongoing process.[34] Sze draws on the notion of reparation ecology to develop the relatively undertheorized concept of restorative environmental justice. As an explicit counter to the extractive logic of capitalism, *restorative* evokes an orientation that is "explicitly decolonial and integrative" and, moreover, draws on concepts central to restoration ecology—the recovery and regeneration of degraded ecosystems—to capture the most important contributions of the environmental justice movement: "critical consciousness and a focus on histories and storytelling."[35] Both reparation ecology and restorative environmental justice foreground the necessity of recognizing histories of trauma and oppression as the basis for future-oriented planning. I view the concept of just transition as an example of how a theory of reparation ecology and a framework for restorative environmental justice might look if operationalized. As a set of processes, principles, and procedures grounded in a long history of localized struggles, just transition offers a critical nexus whereby principles of restorative justice—along with distributive and procedural justice—might be subsumed.[36]

To understand how narrative and storytelling can support efforts to imagine and realize a just transition, it is important to consider the origins of the concept. Just transition frameworks have deep roots in organized labor and environmental justice activism in the United States. After a flurry of environmental laws were passed beginning in the 1970s, from the National Environmental Policy Act (NEPA) to the federal Superfund law, increased regulatory pressure on pollutive industries threatened widespread job losses. Labor unions like the Oil, Chemical, and Atomic Workers (OCAW), which had long been vocal about the environmental impacts of its members' work, began advocating for social safety net programs to match heavily subsidized cleanup efforts at contaminated work sites. A dearth of aid programs for displaced workers led OCAW leader Tony Mazzocchi to ask, "Why do we treat dirt better than workers?"[37] Representing OCAW, Mazzocchi worked alongside Barry Commoner, an ecologist who married concerns about chemical contamination and public health, in the spirit of Rachel Carson, with labor activism. Mazzocchi and Commoner argued that labor and environmental organizers ought to proactively form coalitions to develop labor-friendly, community-driven plans for a sustainable, equitable future. Led by Mazzocchi, OCAW joined the Labor Institute in the early 1990s to advocate for a Superfund for Workers, a four-year guaranteed income for displaced workers modeled after the GI Bill, a product of FDR-era reforms that provided education, healthcare, and financial support for veterans reentering the civilian workforce after World War II. The name of the plan was later changed to just transition. The proposal included worker retraining and community support along with broader efforts to plan a more environmentally friendly approach to industrial production to ensure the long-term viability of industry jobs.[38] Just transition platforms are presently supported by several labor organizations, including the BlueGreen Alliance and the Labor Network for Sustainability. Though not part of the AFL-CIO's (American Federation of Labor and Congress of Industrial Organizations') official platform, the late president Richard Trumka expressed support for just transition principles when discussing climate change.[39]

In the 1990s just transition principles became central to alliances between labor and environmental justice groups in opposition to the North American Free Trade Agreement (NAFTA), which was viewed as weak on labor and environmental protections.[40] The advent of environmental justice in the U.S. emerged within the context of a broader movement for racial equity and increasing recognition that low-income communities and communities of color are disproportionately impacted by toxic waste dumping and industrial siting. Watershed events include the 1982 sit-in organized by the NAACP in Warren County, North Carolina, to protest the siting of a toxic landfill adjacent to majority-Black neighborhoods; the 1987 publication of *Toxic Wastes and Race in the United States*, a report commissioned by the United Church of Christ Commission on Racial Justice establishing a correlation between toxic waste siting and communities of color; and the First National People of Color Environmental Leadership Summit in 1991, which produced the 17 Principles of Environmental Justice that continue to inform activism today. Alliances between grassroots environmental justice and labor organizations in the 1990s, then, emerged from broad but overlapping concerns about social, environmental, and economic equity in the United States. Likewise, they represented a significant departure from the predominately "woods and waters" focus of mainstream environmentalism that, since the 1970s, had largely elided issues of social and economic equity in favor of the protection of iconic species and scenic areas.[41]

Just transition frameworks take two distinct but overlapping forms today. First, transition is often discussed in mainstream environmental discourse in terms of energy—specifically, the economic, technological, and policy measures necessary to facilitate a shift toward low- or zero-carbon energy systems. In this context, just transition describes proposed social safety net programs like worker retraining, economic diversification initiatives, and other assistance programs to support workers and communities that are economically dependent on fossil fuel extraction but faced with uncertain futures in a changing energy landscape.[42] Just transition frameworks that animate the U.S. environmental justice movement, on the other hand, outline a more capacious, social justice–centric vision to emphasize the importance of countering structural inequalities *as a basis* for action. Such understandings of a just transition inform much of this book. According to the Climate Justice Alliance (CJA), a coalition of seventy grassroots environmental justice organizations founded in 2013, "Just transition is a vision-led, unifying, and place-based set of principles, processes, and practices that build economic and political power to shift from an extractive economy to a regenerative economy. This means approaching production and consumption cycles holistically and waste-free. The transition itself must be just and equitable; redressing past harms and creating new relationships of power for the future through reparations. If the process of transition is not just, the outcome will never be. Just transition describes both where we are going and how we get there."[43] Key to these processes is an emphasis on redress and reparations. In this framework, policy paths necessary to ensure an equitable transition are highly contingent on geographical and cultural context and require community buy-in, agency, and empowerment. CJA membership includes a diverse range of organizations, from the Energy Justice Network and the Alliance for Appalachia to the Indigenous Environmental Network (IEN) and the National Family Farm Coalition. The group outlines eight principles for a just transition including the charge that efforts "must actively work against and transform historic social inequities based on race, class, gender, immigrant status, and other forms of oppression" and "reclaim capital and resources for the regeneration of geographies and sectors of the economy where these inequities are most pervasive."[44] The IEN adds to this framework, calling for a just transition that involves both "the rejection of market-based mechanisms that allow the quantification and commodification of Mother Earth's natural resources and processes" and also the "healing process of understanding historical trauma, internalized oppression, and decolonization leading to planting the seed and feeding and nurturing the Good Way of thinking." The IEN outlines a markedly decolonial vision for a just transition, viewing it as a process that "affirms the need for restoring indigenous lifeways" by recognizing cultural sovereignty and Indigenous knowledges.[45]

Commitment to redress and reparations is central to climate justice policy proposals like the Green New Deal (GND). House Resolution 109, the resolution for the GND introduced to the U.S. House of Representatives in February 2019, commits to "stopping current, preventing future, and repairing historic oppression of indigenous peoples, communities of color, migrant communities, deindustrialized communities, the poor, low-income workers, women, the elderly, the unhoused, people with disabilities, and youth."[46] Cosponsored by Representative Alexandria Ocasio-Cortez of New York's 14th congressional district and Senator Ed Markey of Massachusetts, and supported by the youth-led political group the Sunrise Movement, the GND outlines an ambitious plan to decarbonize the economy while simultaneously addressing rising inequality by investing in clean energy jobs and green infrastructure. As its moniker indicates, the GND is broadly derived from President Franklin Delano Roosevelt's 1930s New Deal, a package of economic policy reforms and jobs programs that pulled the United States out of the Great Depression by initiating large public works projects. While the GND does not explicitly address issues of water injustice, Senator Elizabeth Warren of Massachusetts outlined her vision for a Blue New Deal during her 2019–20 presidential campaign. As a set of programs and policies designed to protect ocean health and support vulnerable coastal communities, the Blue New Deal also includes plans for reforming the National Flood Insurance Program; drought management, in tandem with tribal governments, in regions like the Colorado River Basin; and enhanced enforcement of the Clean Air and Clean Water Acts, along with reinstatement of the 2015 Clean Water Rule. The proposal encouragingly centers around social, environmental, and economic justice prerogatives of the GND and arguably lays the blueprints for a water-focused just transition.[47]

Despite the encouraging expansion of just transition discourse and policy proposals, however, the planning and implementation of a just transition necessitates more than thoughtful policy design—it demands new narratives. After all, one of the original goals of just transition advocacy in the labor movement was to shift the terms of the debate to consider more thoughtfully how labor is valued in relation to healthy environments—to break the classic "jobs versus the environment" impasse.[48] The false choice between jobs and the environment is reflective of the broader systemic impasse of capitalism versus the climate advanced by climate justice advocates like Naomi Klein, who insist that the two are mutually exclusive.[49] These radical arguments aim to debunk mainstream narratives touting the emancipatory potential of free-market capitalism and the attendant emphasis on privatization, deregulation, and individual entrepreneurial spirit. It is precisely because it is easier to imagine the end of the world than the end of capitalism that we need new stories, new narratives, and new counternarratives for a just transition.

### Narrative Research in Humanities and Social Sciences

Environmental humanities scholars and practitioners have long argued that humanistic modes of inquiry such as discourse analysis, historical research, and literary and cultural criticism can offer deep insight into human motivations, values, and beliefs driving environmental decision-making.[50] Those working in ecocritical literary and cultural studies, environmental history and philosophy, religious studies, and other subfields have shown how environmental and cultural narratives are shaped by and constructed across language, text, and media and have the potential to engage the imaginative and sensory capacities of readers and viewers, shaping the way they think and act.[51] Though by nature anthropocentric, the environmental humanities and its subfields critique the epistemological dualisms of anthropocentrism (e.g., nature versus culture, human versus more-than-human, ecology versus economy) that underpin many of the social ideologies (i.e.,—colonialism, capitalism, anti-Black racism, patriarchy) driving our most pressing environmental crises. As such, the rise of the environmental humanities has given occasion to rethink what it means to be human and to challenge the Anthropocene as a concept that overemphasizes human agency at the species level while ignoring human difference, nonhuman agency, and the differentiation of human value within the parameters of capitalism.[52] Across the field, there is a growing consensus that "interest in geological stratification threatens to displace attention to social stratification."[53] In particular, the field of ecocritical literary and cultural studies has long been concerned with environmental and social justice issues due to its close alignment with the field of American studies, which "has offered a capaciousness in which to rethink categories of the 'human'" through questions about race, class, gender, and citizenship.[54] Pathbreaking environmental humanities scholars like Joni Adamson and Julie Sze have written extensively on the environmental justice literature, or cultural representations that explore environmental issues in terms of social and economic justice and human rights.[55] Critical, here, is the charge that environmental justice issues, which had hitherto fallen under the purview of the social sciences, "must be understood historically and discursively" rather than through a singular focus on public policy.[56] Moreover, literary texts and other cultural representations can "convert into image and narrative" what Rob Nixon has called the slow violence of environmental degradation afflicting the world's poorest and most vulnerable inhabitants. As such, stories can render visible for a broader audience the sociocultural dimensions of environmental crisis.[57]

It is not always clear, however, how to draw a direct line between audience awareness and real-world impact. Take, for example, the genre of climate change fiction, which includes literary, filmic, and other artistic responses to the global climate crisis. Scholars and critics have argued that climate fiction plays an important role in raising public awareness of climate change and "allows a kind of scenario-*imagining*, not only about the unfolding crisis but also about adaptation and survival strategies."[58] But as Matthew Schneider-Mayerson and other practitioners of empirical ecocriticism have shown, this does not necessarily correlate with action. Empirical ecocriticism can be described as a social sciences approach to narrative analysis that combines the type of textual analysis that is typically the province of the humanities with empirical research on the efficacy of environmental narratives. The latter is often achieved through social scientific methodologies such as conducting interviews, convening focus groups, and administering surveys.[59] Through this approach, researchers have shown that while audiences do tend to have significant affective responses to environmental narratives and increased awareness of social and environmental injustices hidden from the public eye, awareness does not necessarily result in activism or other forms of civic engagement, especially when narratives evoke responses such as fear, helplessness, and dread.[60]

Beyond raising awareness, the narrative focus of the environmental humanities shares important commonalities with narrative analysis in community-driven, participatory research in the environmental social sciences. Such methodologies are critical for understanding how cultural representations not only raise awareness but also prompt action through participatory governance. Thus, my use of *narrative* in the title of this book also evokes the use of narrative methods in climate change adaptation research. In futures studies, narrative methods help bridge the gap between scenario planning and action.[61] Scenario planning involves the generation of multiple alternative futures that help organizations make long-term plans when facing present uncertainties.[62] In the social sciences, scenarios function as descriptions of hypothetical futures that result from toggling critical factors to produce varying outcomes, thereby revealing roadmaps for best-case or worst-case futures. Scenarios represent an alternative to forecasts or predictions, for they acknowledge and anticipate unforeseen trends. Scenario planning has increasingly been adopted in the fields of climate adaptation and policy, encompassing a range of approaches including researcher-driven, participatory, and hybrid processes that speculate on or work to delineate factors necessary for desired future outcomes.[63] Scenarios are especially useful for thinking about climate adaptation because they accommodate the consideration of how human values and beliefs drive environmental change and decision making.[64] While typically data-driven, scenario planning shares kinship with humanities modes of inquiry and scenarios are often likened to "an outline of the plot of a dramatic work, script of a motion picture or a television program."[65] This is comparable to views on cultural representations of climate change as examples of scenario *imagining*: Scenarios can function as a form of speculative storying to plan for a range of possible futures, often with real-world implications for policy and governance.

But scenario planning has limits. Often researcher- rather than community-driven, it sometimes fails to translate into policy development and implementation.[66] By contrast, narrative methods accommodate participatory processes and are thus more conducive to justice and equity. Narrative research typically involves conversational interviews with community members structured by open-ended questions designed to understand how they story experiences or events.[67] The coproductive nature of narrative research is often viewed as optimal for fostering participatory governance and decision making and, like scenario planning, is informed by humanistic modes of inquiry including narrative theory and the fields of narratology, literary studies, and film and media studies.[68] The use of narrative theory in climate adaptation research can yield insight into seemingly disparate sociocultural dynamics impacting a community's adaptive capacity. Moreover, storytelling can be viewed as data itself, rather than just a means to collect data, and because researchers privilege the enactment of narrative over the passive reception of storytelling, narrative methods can foster a more coproductive process wherein community values drive action.[69] Drawing on context-specific stories gleaned during the scenario-planning process can render scenarios more believable to local constituencies, thus rendering communities more amenable to change and improving adaptive capacity. Attention to narrative and storytelling as data garnered through participatory research can counter more "extractive" research methods, prompting a community-driven approach to policy development and implementation. This represents a significant departure from policy studies, which tend to view narrative as subjective, unreliable, and untranslatable into usable data.[70] Again, this resonates with environmental humanities research, which considers how human values, beliefs, thought systems, and even the imagination serve as obstacles to or opportunities for collective change.

Cultural representations play an important role in changing dominant narratives and are well-positioned to support the planning and implementation of just transition processes and policies by recognizing histories of erasure and exclusion and elevating diverse ways of knowing often omitted from policy design. In this book, cultural representations—literary fiction, film, photography, public art, and other media—emerge as evidence of efforts to support, challenge, or otherwise produce cultural narratives that reflect the values within a given community. As a researcher, I am interested not only in narratives that challenge the expendability thesis of capitalism, but in those that emerge from communities resisting state-sanctioned environmental violence. In this respect, I am careful to avoid an extractive approach to cultural analysis by elevating perspectives from writers, artists, and activists hailing from the affected communities on which *Hydronarratives* focuses. This book is concerned with how cultural representations function to produce *counternarratives* that invite us to reconsider how human values and belief systems shape environmental decision making. Moreover, the cultural representations I consider throughout this book are not merely diagnostic or critical but also generative. They offer epistemological roadmaps for community-driven visions of a just transition. *Hydronarratives* makes the case that storytelling prompts a form of scenario-*imagining* that permits both the adjudication of past injustices and the conception of sustainable, equitable futures. As the Petrocultures Research Group insists in their collaborative essay collection *After Oil*, an equitable energy transition is impossible without "changing how we think, imagine, see, and hear"—a task best met by engaging with literary texts, visual art, performance, and scholarship.[71] In the same spirit, this book argues that multigeneric engagement is key to the epistemological shift necessary for just water transitions.

## Just Water: Expanding the Energy Humanities

This book is about water, but my evocation of fossil fuels throughout this introduction is deliberate. Methodologically, *Hydronarratives* is in part inspired by the energy humanities, an interdisciplinary subfield that attends to contemporary environmental problems by considering energy through the prism of culture. The energy humanities has been critical for understanding how energy has "influenced our relationships to our bodies, molded human social relations, and impacted the imperatives of even those varied activities we group together under the term 'culture.'"[72] By prompting reflection on modernity's deep cultural attachments to fossil fuels, the subfield is, at bottom, concerned with delineating ontological and epistemological obstacles preventing a transition—what I describe above as the impasse—in the age of global climate change. Over the last two decades, there have emerged rich and diverse approaches to mapping the aesthetic and discursive legacies of petroleum and other fossil fuels in cultural representations.[73] Such work can be viewed within a broader corpus of scholarship on petrocultures or energy culture, which takes as its subject "the social imaginaries brought into being by the energies of fossil fuels."[74] Others have delineated alternative energy histories to explore issues like energy production and access, dependence, and political economy.[75] The field's oil-centricity, however, has rendered it vulnerable to charges of what historian Christopher Jones calls petromyopia. After sampling nearly one hundred energy-focused peer-reviewed articles in humanities journals, Jones determined that more than half focused on oil—five times more than any other discrete energy source—despite the fact that it constitutes less than one third of global energy production. To remedy this, he not only suggests a shift in focus to energy sources like coal, natural gas, and even food, he also insists on "alternative framings of energy studies" beyond the field's current fuel-specific focus.[76]

*Hydronarratives* operates in this alternative space by taking water as its subject, both as a commodity and as a material element marked by human activity. Cultural analyses of fossil fuels can similarly be applied to water and large-scale water systems. Each chapter in this book presents a case study exploring how the socioecological impacts of large-scale water systems and their failures stem from the extractive logics of a capitalist system animated by social ideologies of human and ecosystem expendability. Each chapter also considers how creative responses to these crises challenge the expendability thesis of capitalism by forging counternarratives that imagine sustainable, equitable futures. To be sure, I use the term *large-scale water system* loosely. I am interested, on the one hand, on approaching water as a discrete form of extractable energy. Chapter 1 considers large dams in the southwestern United States as infrastructural expressions of settler colonialism and the logic of Indigenous erasure, which persists in regional hydropolitical discourse amidst ongoing, severe drought in the Colorado River Basin. On the other hand, Chapter 2 explores how crumbling municipal water systems, like the one in Flint, have emerged as expressions of racial capitalism and the politics of austerity and abandonment in communities of color, while Chapter 3 considers how regional watersheds serve as proxies for the depredations of extractive capital in rural Appalachia. All three—the Colorado River Basin, Flint, and central Appalachia—constitute geographies of sacrifice wherein expendability is defined by Indigeneity, Blackness, and rural poverty. The fourth and final chapter of this book takes more liberties with the notion of the modern water system, focusing on the impacts of sea level rise and coastal flooding on communities on "the wrong side of the levee" and disenfranchised by climate-friendly urban planning efforts that are largely conceived to prioritize the interests of racialized capital.[77] A shared theme throughout each chapter is the notion that because large-scale water systems reflect the social ideologies of capitalist modernity, so too does the distribution of their negative social, environmental, and economic impacts—and the contours of resistance.

Surprisingly, until recently there has been little monograph-length scholarship focused on cultural representations of water injustice. One exception is Hannah Boast's brilliantly conceived *Hydrofictions: Water, Power, and Politics in Israeli and Palestinian Literature*. Noting the exception of the hydrological turn of the ocean-focused blue humanities, Boast notes a puzzling dearth of water-focused ecocritical literary and cultural studies scholarship. In response, *Hydrofictions* takes an interdisciplinary approach to explore Israeli and Palestinian hydrofiction—that is, literary fiction that offers insights into the "social circulation" of water, "the ways in which it is produced [as a resource] through a lengthy chain of social and cultural processes."[78] As I do in this book, Boast takes inspiration from the energy humanities, particularly Indian writer Amitav Ghosh's notion of petrofiction, or literature that addresses the entangled cultural, political, and environmental dynamics of oil. Likewise, Boast sees similarities between oil and water as both critical to the functioning of capitalist modernity and "produced by and productive of social power."[79] Using a hybrid postcolonial–settler colonial ecocritical approach and incorporating insights from science and technology studies, anthropology, and political ecology, Boast surveys a body of Israeli and Palestinian hydrofictions to argue that what many view as a conflict over land is, in fact, largely defined by struggles over water, which remains central to claims of Israeli and Palestinian nationhood. In doing so, she situates the Palestinian fight for water justice within a global movement that includes activism in Flint and Standing Rock. Elsewhere, scholars in the world-ecology school have drawn on Jason W. Moore's notion of cheap nature to explore how literary fiction and other cultural representations allow us to apprehend the socioecological impacts of raw materials extraction. Sharae Deckard, for instance, has turned to world literature to explore how "the 'cheap food' central to 'cheap nature' is founded not only in 'cheap oil' but also in 'cheap water.'" Citing Marx's notion of the metabolic rift—the alienation, under capitalism, of humans from natural processes that form the basis of life—Deckard describes the crisis of cheap water as a consequence of extractive capitalism, in which the replenishment of nutrients (water) is subjugated to the imperatives of economic growth, creating a "rift in the hydrological cycle."[80] These ecological regimes, she concludes, both mimic and determine social and class structures, driving the exclusionary dimensions of the "neoliberal hydrological regime."[81]

*Hydronarratives* builds on this work and charts new paths forward at the intersection of the environmental humanities, critical environmental justice studies, and an emergent hydro humanities, as expressed in environmental cultural studies scholarship, like Boast's, concerned with hydro-social relations. A central argument in this book is that cultural representations support a politics of resistance and resilience to water injustice as a function of capitalism's extractive logics. While the mechanisms by which geographies of sacrifice and the extractive logics of capitalism emerge are manifold, so are sites of contestation. Macarena Gómez-Barris, writing of *extractivismo* in Latin America, refers to "the extractive view," the process by which the (settler) colonial project "render[s] territories and people extractible ... through a matrix of symbolic, physical, and representational violence."[82] In response, Gómez-Barris examines how "submerged perspectives" in the form of decolonial, aesthetic, and performative practices, have emerged in opposition to large-scale development projects, including hydropower dams, in Indigenous regions of the Amazon. The cultural representations examined in this book can likewise be viewed as submerged perspectives that resist symbolic and representational violence by calling attention to histories of oppression and envisioning a just, equitable water transition within a U.S. context. Moreover, central to this book is the recognition that just transitions are contingent on uniquely local social, economic, and historical factors, and must be driven by participatory processes and incorporate local knowledge. Therefore, each chapter draws on different but overlapping analytical frameworks to consider how narrative and storytelling can help communities imagine just water transitions.

Chapter 1 explores Indigenous Hydronarratives that resist the settler logic of elimination animating contemporary drought discourse in the southwestern United States. It opens by citing contentious negotiations over the Colorado River Drought Contingency Plan in 2019 in Arizona, where the Gila River Indian Community threatened to withdraw from the plan—likely dooming it—over the introduction of a state bill that aimed to nullify the community's water rights in favor of non-Indigenous farmers. The bill, and the rhetoric used in support of it, can be viewed as a continuation of the settler logic of elimination, the material and discursive erasure of Indigenous peoples through dispossession and disavowal. Drawing on theories of settler colonialism advanced by Potawatomi scholar Kyle Whyte, Lakota historian Nick Estes, and others, I show how the settler logic of elimination has long inflected hydropolitical discourse in the western United States and has, in fact, been supported by literary, artistic, and media representations that erase Indigenous presence and agency. I trace the persistence of eliminatory discourse from the late nineteenth century to the current, ongoing mega-drought, critiquing the work of John Wesley Powell, Marc Reisner, speculative climate fiction writer Paolo Bacigalupi, photographer Edward Burtynsky, and media coverage of drought between 2012 and 2016. In response, I analyze a handful of Indigenous cultural representations including Leslie Marmon Silko's novel *Gardens in the Dunes*; the Pueblo Grande Museum and Archaeological Park in Phoenix, Arizona; and Indigenous public art projects in central Arizona. Each support what Whyte calls collective continuance, a model of Indigenous social resilience characterized by interdependence and reciprocity between humans and nonhumans, systems of responsibilities, and adaptability to shifting environmental conditions. Also implied by the term is Anishinaabe scholar Gerald Vizenor's notion of survivance, which describes how Native peoples may resist narratives of victimhood or disappearance. Silko's novel, the Pueblo Grande Museum, and the public art featured in this chapter resist totalizing narratives of settler conquest and underscore the importance of participatory governance to ensure a just water transition in the Colorado River Basin.

As with large-scale water systems inhabiting the western United States, other resource regimes exhibit the extractive logics of an exploitative capitalist system. Yet here, too, water can be viewed as central—if not as the object of extractive processes, then as a proxy for communities perceived as more or less expendable within the arithmetic of capital. Within the logic of U.S. cultural and political hegemony globally, clean water has long been symbolic of societal sophistication, while contaminated water represents "a symbolic and material manifestation of... inferiority."[83] But amidst a worsening climate crisis and the accelerated neoliberalization of public life in the United States, endemic water insecurity can increasingly be ascribed to a racialized politics of abandonment in places like the Navajo Nation, where one third of households lack access to running water, and Flint. Chapter 2 approaches the Flint lead water crisis as a natural outgrowth of racial capitalism, a process that relies on the exploitation of "surplus" Black people and communities to support economic growth primarily to buttress white wealth. Drawing on the work of Laura Pulido and critical race scholars like Cedric Robinson and Robin Kelley, the chapter considers how just transition frameworks address environmental racism and the ways storytelling and narrative imagine just transition as an explicitly reparative process. I turn to Michigan playwright José Casas's ethnographic, documentary-style play *Flint*, which draws on and dramatizes interviews with city residents to explore the water crisis from the perspectives of those most impacted. *Flint* frames the city's water crisis as a material discursive formation rooted in a long history of anti-Black governance and draws on individual testimony to insist that "Flint Lives Matter." The chapter also highlights community-driven efforts to counter prevailing narratives of Flint as poor, Black, abandoned, and crumbling, including the Flint Fit fashion-art collaboration between fashion designer Tracy Reese and artist Mel Chin and the Flint Public Art Project.

The politics of abandonment are also visible in rural, largely white communities in the heart of coal, oil, and gas country. This is evident, for example, in recent efforts by the Trump administration to gut regulations like the 1972 Clean Water Act and rules regulating coal ash storage associated with coal mining.[84] Chapter 3 examines creative responses to two socioecological legacies of fossil fuel extraction in Appalachia: rampant water contamination and worsening economic precarity. In addition to worsening stream and groundwater contamination associated with fossil fuel industry negligence, a large portion of job losses in the U.S. coal industry have occurred in the region due to mechanization and declining production.[85] In this chapter, I consider how local writers, poets, photographers, and artists are prompting communities to imagine "post-extractive" futures in Appalachia. In particular, I focus on what I call extractive fictions, a term derived from Ghosh's petrofiction, to describe cultural representations that challenge a deep-seated cultural attachment to extraction in communities dependent on the global energy economy.[86] The first half of the chapter analyzes Ann Pancake's novel *Strange as This Weather Has Been* and local art critical of mountaintop removal coal mining; Jennifer Haigh's fracking novel *Heat and Light*; and *Shale Play: Poems and Photographs from the Fracking Fields*, a collection of poetry and photographs by Julia Spicher Kasdorf and Jeff Rubin that documents the impacts of fracking in central Pennsylvania. Each reveals how water contamination and rural poverty result from the same processes, wherein stereotypes about Appalachia as backward, inhabited by the racialized white "hillbilly" other, has rendered the communities vulnerable to exploitation by fossil fuel interests. The second half of the chapter highlights two environmental reclamation art installations in former coal communities: the Acid Mine Drainage and Art Park built atop an abandoned mine in Vintondale, Pennsylvania, and John Sabraw's "toxic art" project in Corning, Ohio. Both projects use reverse-extractive processes, featuring innovative water filtration systems that remove iron oxides, the result of acid mine drainage, from nearby streams. Each project also features memorial aesthetics—murals, interpretive walking paths, and photographs—that pay homage to the region's coal heritage. Conceived in collaboration with local communities, both projects imagine a just transition from a pollutive past to a post-extraction future.

The fourth and final chapter considers representations of sea level rise in speculative climate change fiction and film to explore different visions of a Green New Deal. Rob Nixon has written of neoliberalism's watery metaphors such as the "trickle-down effect," the concept of "global flows," and the old adage "a rising tide lifts all boats," all mobilized in support of unfettered free-market capitalism.[87] Such rhetoric not only ignores the fact that neoliberalism drives rising carbon emissions (and sea levels) and income inequality, it also supports prevailing views that capitalism can fix the climate crisis, giving rise to a bevy of false solutions that, at best, entrench social inequities while guarding the interests of capital. Two sea level rise narratives, Kim Stanley Robinson's 2017 novel *New York 2140* and Benh Zeitlin's 2012 film *Beasts of the Southern Wild*, respond to this impasse by articulating divergent but overlapping politics of climate justice in coastal regions threatened by rising seas. For example, Robinson's novel envisions a GND-style economic revolution, it largely ignores the racialized dimensions of climate vulnerability in a future New York City submerged under 50 feet of water. *Beasts*, on the other hand, asks readers to consider life on the so-called wrong side of the levee in the Louisiana Bayou, where Indigenous communities and communities of color are often victims of flood control infrastructure designed to protect wealthier, whiter communities. Each urges us to consider the broader risk of a representational co-optation of the GND by competing interests in ways that reinforce racial and class exclusion much the way the original New Deal did.

The conclusion examines a major theme of *Hydronarratives*: that for transitions to be just, they must emerge from participatory, community-driven processes and must accommodate and elevate marginalized or previously silenced voices. In thinking about just transition as a theory of social change, I consider challenges facing the energy-dependent state of Wyoming, where much of this book was written. How is it possible to imagine a just transition in a place where cultural and political inertia have resulted in decades of stubborn resistance to change? What underserved constituencies can be engaged and activated, and how? I reflect on numerous efforts underway in response to a worsening climate crisis, a declining coal industry, shrinking state revenues, and accelerated youth out-migration, with a particular focus on my experience engaging communities and teaching environmental justice within a just transition framework at the University of Wyoming.

# 1 /

## Decolonizing Drought

*Indigenous Collective Continuance in the Lower Colorado River Basin*

In January 2019 the Gila River Indian Community (GRIC) in central Arizona threatened to withdraw from the seven-state Colorado River Drought Contingency Plan (DCP). This was a big deal: 25 percent of the water Arizona receives from the Colorado River flows through the community as part of the Central Arizona Project (CAP) canal system. Per the plan, Arizona had agreed to cut its allocation of Colorado River water by 18 percent should Lake Mead fall below a certain level, triggering the official declaration of a shortage. In such a scenario, the state hoped to partially make up losses with 640,000 acre-feet of water from the community's portion of CAP water in exchange for $90 million in development funds for the community, home to Akimel O'odham and Piipaash peoples. GRIC's threat, which would likely have doomed the DCP, emerged in response to a bill introduced in the Arizona House of Representatives by House Speaker Rusty Bowers. The bill aimed to weaken GRIC's claims to the Gila River in deference to non-Indigenous farmers upstream in Pinal County, most of whom have junior rights.[1] The state's "first in time, first in use" policy dictates seniority and tends to favor tribal interests due to the Winters Doctrine, federal water policy guidelines that grant seniority to tribal entities based on the date a reservation was established.[2] In recent years, GRIC has filed several lawsuits to prevent non-Indigenous farmers from hoarding unused waters from the Gila River, a culturally significant waterway.[3]

Bowers eventually shelved the bill, and the DCP was signed into law on April 16, 2019. But his initial response to critics was telling. Non-Indigenous farmers in the area, he protested, have long been "scratching it out" and he could "not see how anyone [would be] harmed by removing a law that has never been exercised except for vengeance."[4] This represents a remarkable distortion of the historical record. The Akimel O'odham used floodwater irrigation techniques to harness the waters of the Gila for centuries, cultivating a diverse array of traditional crops like corn, tepary beans, squash, and melons, prospering even after their 1859 relocation to the Gila River Indian Reservation southeast of Phoenix.[5] In the mid-1860s, however, white settlers emboldened by the newly passed Homestead Act began settling upstream and diverting water to irrigate their own fields. River flows grew increasingly diminished before reaching the reservation, and tensions arose between settlers and the O'odham. There is evidence that white farmers deliberately diverted and wasted water to deprive reservation farms. With the 1889 completion of the Florence Canal to divert water to settler fields in Florence in Casa Grande, the Gila was effectively transformed into an intermittent stream. Between 1866 and 1918, the reservation's percentage use of the river's waters dropped from 100 percent to less than 30 percent. Traditional O'odham agricultural methods became increasingly untenable. The Indian Service was little help, refusing to codify tribal water rights or expand reservation borders, and there were discussions in the U.S. Senate about the potential removal of O'odham peoples to Indian Territory in Oklahoma.[6] Many O'odham were forced to abandon their fields, moving off the reservation in search of work. Crop failures in the 1890s led to starvation and malnutrition, rendering the O'odham increasingly dependent on federal assistance.[7] The legacies of this abrupt shift from subsistence to dependence have been well-documented, with settler water theft directly contributing to cultural loss and food insecurity. Government food assistance, often composed of processed, low-nutrient foods, is considered a primary factor in high obesity and diabetes rates in the community.[8] After eight decades of litigation, the community was compensated with 653,000 acre-feet of CAP water as part of the 2004 Arizona Water Settlement Act (AWSA), representing a path for the community to resuscitate traditional lifeways. Since the settlement, GRIC has initiated the Pima-Maricopa Irrigation Project with the goal of irrigating nearly 150,000 acres of traditional crops.[9]

The GRIC's offer to give up water to the state during a shortage can be viewed as remarkably generous, especially given that a portion of that water would likely go to vulnerable non-Indigenous farmers in Pinal

County.[10] Bowers's brand of ahistorical grievance politics, framing the community's assertion of hard-won water rights as "vengeance," is illustrative of two conflicting dynamics animating contemporary hydropolitical discourse in the western United States. Tribes had until recently been largely excluded from federal water policy discussions, and tribal involvement in the DCP marked an important turning point in participatory resource governance in the region.[11] This is as it should be: Tribal communities in the Colorado Basin hold some of the most senior water rights in the nation, controlling up to 2.8 million acre-feet per year from the river and its tributaries.[12] Like GRIC, the Colorado River Indian Tribes (CRIT), located along the California-Arizona border south of Lake Havasu, voted to allow off-reservation water leasing and committed to leaving 50 thousand acre-feet in Lake Mead for three years in exchange for $38 million in development funds.[13] During DCP negotiations, tribal governments effectively held veto power over the finalization of a management plan for a river that serves 40 million people and 4 million acres of farmland.[14] Despite this shift, however, regional hydropolitical discourse nevertheless remains inflected by the same rhetoric of Indigenous erasure that has long been used to justify settler colonial domination. Bowers's claims efface a long history of violence and dispossession experienced by Indigenous peoples in the Colorado River Basin. His comments do not stand alone; during AWSA negotiations in 2004, former Phoenix city water manager (and current director of the Arizona Department of Water Resources) Tom Buschatzke, described tribal communities as "threats" to the city's water supply.[15]

The presence of this rhetoric in contemporary hydropolitical discourse can be traced to cultural narratives that uphold what the late Patrick Wolfe called settler colonialism's "logic of elimination," whereby settler power is contingent on the physical elimination and cultural dissolution of Indigenous peoples.[16] Eliminatory logic drives what Kyle Whyte (Potawatomi) describes as settler colonialism's imperative to "transform Indigenous homelands into settler homelands" and erase "indigenous economies, cultures, and political organizations."[17] The lynchpin of settler colonialism in the United States has always been federal land policy, wherein vast swaths of productive Indigenous lands were illegally made available for lease at the expense of forcibly removed Indigenous peoples. Lakota historian Nick Estes points out that 96 percent of privately owned agricultural lands in the United States are owned by white settlers, leading him to situate these processes as a product of racial capitalism, which "use[s] race as a form of rule—to subordinate, to kill, and to enslave others—and [uses] that difference for profit-making."[18] Tracking the persistence of colonial violence and the persistence of moralizing narratives, discursive constructions, and eliminatory rhetoric is critical in a region that will be undergoing a water transition for the foreseeable future due to what experts view as the most severe long-term drying trend in at least the last millennium.[19] The western United States. is facing a critical inflection point for regional water governance, and to ensure a just transition, it is important to call attention to, and counter, settler structures of exclusion.

Decolonizing drought discourse requires counternarratives that resist settler logics of elimination expressed in regional hydropolitical discourse. This chapter considers a range of hydronarratives grounded in Indigenous hydrological knowledges in the southwestern United States, including Laguna Pueblo writer Leslie Marmon Silko's novel *Gardens in the Dunes*, the Pueblo Grande Museum and Archaeological Park in Phoenix, and recent water-focused public art and film created by Indigenous communities in central and western Arizona. Each contributes to what Whyte calls collective continuance, a concept he uses to describe "a society's capacity to self-determine how to adapt to change in ways that avoid reasonably preventable harms."[20] Writing of Anishinaabe cultural and intellectual traditions, Whyte describes collective continuance as a form of social resilience characterized by interdependence and reciprocity between humans and nonhumans; systems of responsibilities, wherein "reciprocity is systematized"; and migration, which he uses to broadly describe a societal adaptability to shifting environmental and social dynamics.[21] The notion of migration describes how systems of responsibilities "are not grounded on stable or static relationships with the environment" but are instead inherently flexible and adaptive to emergent socioecological conditions to ensure social continuity.[22] Whyte further explains that "the ways in which responsibilities are organized into interdependent systems facilitate the adaptive capacity of collective continuance," particularly because such systems are built upon trust and quality of relationships, diplomacy, and redundancy. Redundancy is especially critical, referring to "having multiple options for adaptation when changes occur." Using the example of Anishinaabe traditions of wild rice harvesting in the Great Lakes region, Whyte explains that this could include having multiple areas from which to harvest rice or the distribution of agricultural expertise intergenerationally and variously amongst tribal leadership to ensure the maintenance of traditional knowledges.[23]

As a material discursive formation, settler colonialism produces conditions conducive to environmental injustice because, Whyte argues, it "is a social process by which at least one society seeks to establish its own collective continuance at the expense of the collective continuance of one or more other societies." In this formulation, collective continuance is not exclusive to Indigenous societies but is a more broadly applicable theory of social resilience in which the U.S. settler state—characterized by unsustainable, socially and racially exclusionary relationships with the environment—possesses a low degree of collective continuance.[24] As Whyte explains, the concept of collective continuance shares kinship with Anishinaabe scholar Gerald Vizenor's notion of survivance, a combination of survival and endurance whereby native peoples "foster an active sense of presence" and renounce "dominance, tragedy, and victimry."[25] For Whyte, survivance "connotes continuity through constant change."[26] The renunciation of dominance, tragedy, victimhood—all tropes key to the perpetuation of settler colonialism's eliminatory logics—suggests the degree of agency and self-determination critical to a society's capacity for collective continuance. As I show below, the processes and policies that have historically shaped water policy in the western United States emerged from the settler logic of elimination. The persistence of those logics in contemporary drought discourse can be ascribed to dominant ways of storying western water that largely ignore histories of Indigenous dispossession associated with large dam projects, which have not only disrupted hydrological cycles—thus contributing to drought—but also Indigenous collective continuance in the Colorado River Basin. To foster an active sense of presence amid the region's water transition and to ensure the continuation and enhancement of participatory governance, it is critical to call attention to histories of violence that are often elided or erased in dominant discourse.

## Drought and Colonialism in the Colorado River Basin

In 1878, after a decade of surveying expeditions in the western United States, geologist and explorer John Wesley Powell published his *Report on the Lands of the Arid Regions of the United States*. In it he detailed a careful plan for settling the region west of the hundredth meridian, an area stretching west of an imaginary north-south line bisecting Oklahoma's western border with the Texas panhandle. Because the region received less than 20 inches of annual rainfall, Powell doubted that irrigation could make agriculture viable on more than a tiny fraction of the vast landscape. He was skeptical of distributing water according to political borders and neat, 160-acre gridded parcels of land as mandated by the Homestead Act. He urged a cautious and cooperative approach to settlement, viewed western lands as a commons, and argued that state borders should be drawn according to watershed boundaries. Otherwise, he argued, "many droughts will occur; many seasons in a long series will be fruitless; and it will be doubted whether, overall, agriculture will prove remunerative."[27] Powell's reasoned but tepid estimation of the region's economic potential invited widespread ridicule from politicians and land speculators. The idea of federally regulated water and a slow, practical approach were no match for American optimism and a nation eager for capitalist expansion.[28] In 1902 the Fifty-Seventh Congress of the United States passed the Newlands Reclamation Act, establishing the U.S. Bureau of Reclamation (USBR) to oversee the construction and operation of large-scale water infrastructure for irrigation, municipal supplies, and hydropower in the western United States. In 1922 the Colorado River Compact was signed, clearing the way for the construction of fourteen major dams on the river and encoding water allocations for four Upper Basin states (Colorado, New Mexico, Utah, and Wyoming) and three Lower Basin states (Arizona, California, and Nevada).[29] Notably, neither Mexico nor the five Indigenous tribes living adjacent to the river were party to the compact.[30]

It is no exaggeration to say that western North America as it presently exists would not be possible without the settler water resource regime, supported by the damming, storage, and diversion of Colorado River water. Fed by snowmelt trickling down from La Poudre Pass in Colorado's southern Rocky Mountains, the river is critical to agricultural production and urban growth. Around 70 percent of the Colorado's annual flow is used for irrigation and the river basin grows around 15 percent of the nation's produce.[31] The river has also been a catalyst for urban growth, supplying primary sources of municipal water to Las Vegas, Los Angeles, Phoenix, San Diego, and Tucson as well as Mexicali and Tijuana.[32] But the phrase "as it presently exists" also refers to the extent to which large-scale water storage and diversion infrastructures have also contributed to drought. The Colorado has only reached its natural outlet in the Gulf of California a handful of times since the 1963 completion of Glen Canyon Dam near Page, Arizona. Upstream diversions for agriculture and industrial use have slowed flows to a trickle in the 75-mile stretch of river south of Morelos Dam on the U.S.-Mexico border. An increasing body of evidence has shown that the Colorado's decline, and the regional drought more broadly, can be attributed to large dams and groundwater extraction. Dams and reservoirs have also had a net negative impact on regional hydrological processes and water availability and have been linked to an increase in greenhouse gases, as reservoir drawdowns have been observed to release massive amounts of methane into the atmosphere, contributing to global warming and potential drought feedback loops.[33]

The quest to "reclaim" the arid landscapes of the western United States—whether through Powell's notion of careful planning and wise use or through the large-scale, technocratic approach of the USBR—has been central to the U.S. settler colonial project. That the current drought can be partially attributed to such efforts suggests the epistemological failure of large-scale water management as a technocratic extension of Manifest Destiny, an ideology against which Powell, for all his prescience about drought, was not immune.[34] Despite Powell's canonization within environmental circles as a forward-thinking conservationist, his commitment to the settler civilizing mission influenced his views on natural resource governance. In his 1878 report, he repeatedly advocated for Indian removal or the curtailment of Indigenous land use practices to ensure settler prosperity. In his 1885 presidential address to the Anthropological Society, "From Savagery to Barbarism," he categorized native peoples as savages—the bottom of a racist, deterministic societal hierarchy—and derided what he viewed as their "petty agriculture" and unsophisticated use of water.[35] In fact, the very notion of reclamation, bureaucratized with the establishment of the USBR, represented a high-minded rhetorical justification for both Indigenous erasure and large-scale water diversion, storage, and delivery projects. Roderick Nash famously wrote in *Wilderness and the American Mind* (1967) of the evolution of wilderness as a social construct in the Anglo-American imagination, rooted in Judeo-Christian associations of wilderness with wild, pagan, untamed nature that existed in a "fallen" state. For the eighteenth-century frontiersman, to "redeem" nonhuman nature through human technological ingenuity into a pastoral paradise akin to Eden was viewed as a spiritual and moral imperative.[36] Historian Marc Reisner later wrote in *Cadillac Desert* (1985) that during the so-called reclamation era of large dam construction, "greening the desert became a kind of Christian ideal."[37] USBR engineers, aiming to fulfill that ideal, viewed themselves as performing "hydrological miracles," proof of humans' absolute dominion over nonhuman nature.[38] An ethos of conquest through technological ingenuity drove the reclamation era in the western United States, resulting in the construction of nearly 500 dams responsible for delivering water to 31 million people, irrigating 10 million acres of farmland that produces 60 percent of the nation's vegetables and a quarter of the nation's fruit and nuts, and providing more than 40 billion kilowatt hours of electricity annually over the last 10 years.[39]

The USBR, often working in tandem with the Army Corps of Engineers and regional and state agencies, extended the eliminatory logic of previous land-use policies designed to encourage the "reclamation" of Indigenous lands by incentivizing white settlement. The damming and diversion of rivers for irrigation was key for the implementation of the Homestead Act which has had lasting impacts on the exclusionary dimensions of federal land policy. White families gained possession of nearly 250 million acres of Indigenous lands under the law, which was made arable with federally subsidized water and irrigation systems. Today a quarter of U.S. adults directly descend from white settlers who benefited from the act. Because "access to Indigenous water was crucial for securing the ownership of Indigenous lands and generating wealth from these lands over generations," Estes explains, "it informs present disparities, which boil down to a single axiom: land is wealth and water is wealth."[40] This axiom was made manifest through the 1877 Desert Land Act, an amendment to the Homestead Act that allocated federal funds for irrigation, and the 1887 Dawes Act, which subdivided Indigenous lands into small irrigable plots in exchange for large, as-yet-unirrigated swaths of tribal land. The latter was implemented to encourage assimilation (as a precondition for citizenship) through private property ownership and a thinly veiled attempt to disintegrate traditional Indigenous land use practices while redistributing native lands to white settlers.[41]

This dynamic shifted during the reclamation era to include the willful creation of sacrifice zones on Indigenous lands. Estes characterizes the reclamation era as a time during which "Indigenous land was desired merely so that it could be wasted—covered with water." This conveniently served to sever Indigenous ties with lands, waters, and ecosystems—in other words, to advance the eliminatory logic of the settler state.[42] Following the 1944 Pick-Sloan Plan, the USBR collaborated with the Army Corps of Engineers to build a series of earthen-rolled dams for irrigation, hydropower, and flood control on the Missouri River in North Dakota; the plan represented a "twentieth-century Indigenous apocalypse."[43] Pick-Sloan dams displaced tens of thousands of Dakota and Lakota peoples from productive river bottom lands in the Missouri Basin, violating the 1868 Fort Laramie Treaty and serving as a direct precursor to the 2016-17 opposition to the Dakota Access Pipeline in Standing Rock, North Dakota.[44] These policies and processes can be viewed as emblematic of what historian Ian Tyrell calls a settler theory of value, a resource governance paradigm used to advance a racially exclusive approach to nation-building with the goal of "achieving economic efficiency through a regime of technocrats" and to privilege "an expansive Anglo-Saxon race."[45] In this view, federal land and water policies, deeply entangled and contributory to the eliminatory logic of the settler state, are critical to the process of "racial extractivism," wherein colonialism and racial othering materially and discursively support, and serve as moral justification for, extractive processes.[46] In short, water governance in the western United States has always been driven by the parallel violence of environmentally destructive water extraction processes and the eliminatory, racist policies of the settler state.

Dominant narratives that champion large-scale water infrastructure as morally necessary to "reclaim" an arid western landscape for the benefit of white settlers, and which overwrite Indigenous cultural landscapes, have long been supported by cultural and media representations. Jane Griffith uses the term *dam/ning* to describe "how tactics used to preserve White settler memory, history, and claims to land and water seemingly appear to affirm Black and Indigenous lives but in fact veil violence." Writing of Hoover Dam, which occupies the traditional lands of Southern Paiute, Hualapai, Mohave, Hopi, and Zuni peoples, Griffith argues that large dam construction was not only a technological and economic endeavor, but also a *cultural* project in support of racialized conceptions of property rights.[47] In the early twentieth century, media representations of large dam projects served as ad hoc public relations campaigns driving a narrative of American technological prowess. Simultaneously, they tended to disregard Indigenous cultures and perpetuate myths of cultural decline. This cultural work of dam/ning was supported by writing, art, and print media that romanticized a universalized "disappearing" Indigenous culture, framed Indigenous water use methods as "primitive," and discounted Indigenous ways of knowing. During the construction of Hoover Dam, the USBR employed artists to reinforce settler claims to Indigenous land. Allen Tupper True decorated dams with artwork by "borrowing" heavily from what he viewed as Indigenous aesthetics derived from "art originally collected and annotated by anthropologists such as Gladys A. Reichard and institutions such as the American Bureau of Ethnology and the Peabody Museum."[48] True characterized his art as "pioneering innovation" using what he often described as "primitive" or "ancient" influences.[49] Moreover, during the construction process archaeologist Mark Harrington held a series of pageants at the dam site, intended to entertain a largely white work force, that depicted the "rise and fall of Indian culture." Promotional pamphlets portrayed caricatures of native peoples next to a completed dam to emphasize a "disappearing [Indigenous] past" and a "promising" future for white settlers.[50]

This eliminatory logic persists in more recent cultural representations that continue to view western water issues through the settler colonial gaze. This is even true for water narratives that otherwise espouse a broad environmentalist agenda. Reisner's *Cadillac Desert* is one example.

Documenting decades of engineering hubris, economic opportunism, and political maneuvering necessary to conquer and "develop" the western United States, *Cadillac Desert* offers a revisionist history of settlement efforts driven by greed and a desire to control nonhuman nature. As Reisner famously quipped, "in the West... water flows uphill toward money"—an indictment of the federal government's tendency to support water infrastructure projects for short-term benefits, regardless of long-term ecological or economic viability.[51] *Cadillac Desert* is often viewed as required reading for understanding western hydropolitics, and even scientists agree that it anticipates with alarming accuracy the region's present-day water challenges.[52] But its coverage of Indigenous issues is woefully incomplete. Reisner only once alludes to Manifest Destiny as a possible, rather than definitive, ideological ethos of the Reclamation Act.[53] His most sustained engagement with the issue of Indigenous dispossession can be found in three pages (of more than five hundred) explaining the impacts of the Pick-Sloan Plan.[54] Elsewhere, Reisner indulges in the tired myth of the "vanishing Indian," insisting on the disappearance of the Hohokam, ancestors of the O'odham who harnessed the waters of the Salt River to irrigate their vast fields in the Phoenix Valley for thousands of years.[55] Reisner also ignores the O'odham's rich agricultural history extending into the late nineteenth century, claiming that "most of the Indians of the Southwest were hunter-gatherers when whites arrived."[56] His extensive coverage of the Arizona-California water wars and political battles over usage of the Salt-Verde-Gila watershed also exclude the legacies of settler water theft in the region, including those experienced by the Gila River Indian Community.

*Cadillac Desert* is but one historical account, but its stature as what many consider an enduring critique of unsustainable development in the western United States demands scrutiny.[57] Between 2014 and 2016, a particularly intense period of the current megadrought, the book was frequently cited as required reading for those keen to place the drought into historical perspective. Environmental journalist Mark Hertsgaard claimed that "no book illuminates [the historical factors driving drought] better than *Cadillac Desert*."[58] Reisner's book topped "10 Books about Drought: A Reading List for Parched Southern Californians" in the *Los Angeles Daily News*, and John Fleck, director of the University of New

Mexico Water Resources Program, included it in a blog post as one of two books critical to understanding water in the West.⁵⁹ In recent speculative climate change novels like Claire Vaye Watkins's *Gold Fame Citrus* (2016) and Paolo Bacigalupi's *The Water Knife* (2015), *Cadillac Desert* plays an explicit role in fictional renditions of dystopian, drought-beset futures in Los Angeles and Phoenix, respectively. Reisner's influence can be traced to his conclusion in *Cadillac Desert* that technological overreach will lead to societal collapse. Watkins lists Reisner's book as a key influence in the acknowledgments for *Gold Fame Citrus*, which follows a pair of climate refugees coping with social strife and encroaching desertification in a desiccated future southern California. *Cadillac Desert* is central to Bacigalupi's *The Water Knife*, which depicts states and cities engaged in armed conflict over rights to Colorado River water. A hydrologist in the novel dubs *Cadillac Desert* "the bible when it comes to water."⁶⁰ Unfortunately, Bacigalupi exploits Indigenous dispossession as a cheap plot device when protagonists discover in an archive nineteenth-century tribal water rights that are "senior to God" and represent guaranteed water security for whichever state possesses them.⁶¹ Bacigalupi does not engage meaningfully with broken treaties, unenforced water laws, or forced removal, choosing instead to construct his dystopian thriller around the possibility of settler civilizational collapse.

While both novels received widespread and largely positive press, they unfortunately view water through the settler colonial gaze by construing a drought-beset future as primarily harmful to settler society. As dystopian scenario-imagining exercises, they fall within a broader corpus of media representations of drought that exhibit a similarly myopic rhetoric of apocalypse. For example, dams and reservoirs have become favored locations to visually document drought. Between 2014 and 2016, photo-essays published in the *Los Angeles Times*, the *Atlantic*, *ProPublica*, and elsewhere feature bathtub-ringed reservoirs, landlocked docks, dusty riverbeds, beached buoys, grounded speedboats, and cracked, desiccated shorelines.⁶² Likewise, Canadian photographer Edward Burtynsky aestheticizes drought in his acclaimed collection *Water* through images of the Colorado River Delta region. Shot by aircraft from far overhead, photos like *Colorado River Delta #2* depict the river's main channel as sclerotic, its thinning, venous tributaries forking through a vast, salt-crusted floodplain.[63] To be sure, Burtynsky's accompanying documentary *Watermark* features a brief interview with Inocencia González Sáinz, tribal elder of the Indigenous Cucapá peoples who, historically dependent on tilapia and mullet fisheries in the river's delta, have been severely impacted by upstream diversions and contaminated runoff. But the film remains largely committed to the voyeurism typical of disaster porn, frequently cutting to footage of a half-buried rowboat in a dusty-beige stretch of trash-littered channels near the main stem of the river as Sáinz attempts to explain the river's decline.[64] The film does nothing to contextualize the many reasons for the crisis faced by Cucapá peoples, such as the 1944 U.S.-Mexico Water Treaty that led to the construction of Morelos Dam in Yuma, Arizona, which stifled flows south and increased salinity levels south of the border.[65] Currently, 90 percent of the river's water is diverted before reaching Mexico, while the remaining 10 percent is largely being used for manufacturing in Mexicali and Tijuana. Cucapá peoples, long dependent on the river's fisheries and waters for agriculture, have found it increasingly difficult to maintain traditional lifeways, a tragedy worsened by the Mexican government's efforts to foster ecological recovery in the region through a complete ban on fishing in the delta.[66]

Burtynsky's work and other examples of visual documentation of drought exhibit a striking critical aloofness by insisting on the newness of a crisis that represents yet another instantiation of what Whyte refers to as the cyclical history of colonialism. The climate apocalypticism espoused by some scientists and academics and in the popular media often ignores the fact that Indigenous peoples have long been experiencing what their "ancestors would have characterized as a dystopian future" caused by white settler encroachment.[67] To ensure a just transition, cultural narratives about water in the western United States must be expanded and revised to acknowledge settler violence against Indigenous lands and waterways. The persistent violence of erasure, long supported by a broad range of cultural representations that buttress broader cultural narratives, was evident in the rhetoric used by Arizona House Speaker Bowers during 2019 DCP negotiations. Indigenous writers and artists, however, continue to counter these processes by imagining a just water transition through literary fiction, art, and other media. Below, I analyze a range of Indigenous cultural representations that work to advance *counter-narratives* that adjudicate past injustices and strengthen capacities for collective continuance in the lower Colorado River Basin.

### Dam/ning in *Gardens in the Dunes*

An under-studied portion of Leslie Marmon Silko's novel *Gardens in the Dunes* fictionalizes the construction of Parker Dam on the Colorado River along the California-Arizona border near Parker, Arizona. Completed in 1938 to divert water to an increasingly populous southern California for agricultural and municipal use, the dam in Silko's novel represents a form of colonial violence. When the river is diverted in the novel, Indigenous farmers living on the CRIT Reservation downstream, already once displaced from their homelands, are forced into "carrying water on their backs uphill to their fields of corn and beans, until they were defeated by the evaporation and the heat."[68] One of the novel's protagonists, Sister Salt of the fictional Sand Lizard people, struggles to care for sacred datura and wild purple asters that "wilted if she did not carry them buckets of water every day."[69] These scenes take on added resonance when read against the current drought, redolent of a now infamous 2014 incident in which residential wells in East Porterville, California, ran dry. An unincorporated area in the historically agricultural San Joaquin Valley, East Porterville has no municipal water system and residents have long depended on groundwater pumping. Between 2012 and 2014, a combination of historically low precipitation levels and groundwater overdraft by nearby commercial farms significantly lowered the water table, and flows on the Tule River, which runs through the heart of Porterville, were barely measurable. The town, which is nearly 80 percent Latinx and home to many migrant fieldworkers, had to rely on donated bottled and tanked water delivered door-to-door by churches, nonprofits, and the county.[70] By 2015 the groundwater crisis had spread to other parts of the valley, setting off a water truck boom in which growing portions of the valley began to rely solely on water imported from other parts of the state.[71]

Read retroactively, Silko's depiction of "tough water"—to adapt journalist Michael Klare's use of "tough oil" to describe petroleum reserves that are increasingly difficult and risky to extract—invites us to reject the

East Porterville crisis as authoritatively emblematic of drought in the West.[72] Instead, *Gardens* explores how large dam projects and Indian removal policies worked in tandem to disrupt Indigenous collective continuance in the Colorado River Basin. The CRIT Reservation was established near Parker in 1865 for tribes historically residing in the Colorado River Basin, initially Chemehuevi and Mohave peoples. Hopi and Diné (Navajo) peoples were later relocated there. Residents of CRIT were encouraged to take up subsistence farming using irrigation water siphoned from the river. But because soil on the reservation site downstream was poor and irrigation proved ineffective, they found themselves economically marginalized and significantly worse off post-removal.[73] USBR-commissioned dams completed upstream in the 1930s worsened things. Parker Dam, featured in Silko's novel, was built to generate hydropower and divert water to Los Angeles via the 242-mile-long Colorado River Aqueduct, and central Arizona via the 336-mile CAP canal.[74] The localized impacts of damming have been significant and widespread, including dwindling downstream flows, diminishing native fish habitats, rising water temperatures, increasing siltification, and contamination from erosion and irrigation runoff.[75] Silko's novel places these impacts into historical context, depicting the immediate impacts of large dam construction on Indigenous lifeways that occurred long before the Porterville crisis and framing drought not merely as a climatic phenomenon affecting settler society, but as a logical outcome of settler colonialism.

Social and environmental justice have been persistent themes in Silko's fiction, especially in novels like *Ceremony* (1977) and *Almanac of the Dead* (1990) in which she highlights the effects of, and Indigenous resistance to, uranium mining and damaging trade liberalization policies in the U.S. southwest, respectively. *Gardens* is best known for its exploration of the cultural and ecological significance of Indigenous ethnobotanical knowledge. The novel follows Indigo and Sister Salt, two young Sand Lizard sisters who learn from their elder, Grandmother Fleet, to plant and maintain thriving gardens of corn and amaranth in a hidden canyon along the Colorado River before being forced into boarding schools on the CRIT Reservation. After the sisters are detained and separated by Indian police, Sister Salt escapes and takes up residence in a riverside camp downstream from the dam site near Parker while Indigo falls into the care of Hattie and Edward Palmer, a wealthy white couple who take her on an extended tour of the eastern United States and Europe. During her travels, Indigo visits several different gardens, where her experiences frame a long history of global seed cultivation and exchange as well as the Euro-Western practice of biopiracy, the exploitation of indigenous plants and botanical knowledge for commercial gain. Joni Adamson argues that the novel's emphasis on the cultural significance of certain "medicine foods" like amaranth helps highlight Indigenous contributions to global food traditions, represents a form of resistance to the Euro-Western theft of ethnobotanical knowledge, and provides critical historical context for global food sovereignty movements. In the novel the Sand Lizards' cultivation of amaranth represents a form of resistance against the colonial repression of Indigenous knowledges dating back to when Spanish conquistadors prohibited Aztecs from growing or cultivating the culturally important crop.[76] The novel's focus on gardens has also been viewed as a targeted critique of colonialism and imperialism, particularly "by pointedly contrasting nineteenth-century gardening aesthetics and ideologies with the Sand Lizards' subsistence farming" and emphasizing the "ecological sophistication" of Indigenous floodwater irrigation methods that allow the Sand Lizard people to thrive in arid lands.[77]

The novel's critique of settler water governance complements more overt themes of food sovereignty and the importance of ethnobotanical knowledge to imagine how the maintenance of Indigenous collective continuance will be critically important to ensuring a just water transition as regional drought conditions worsen. In the novel's under-explored Sister Salt sections, Silko contrasts the Sand Lizards' approach to water use, predicated on reciprocal relations with desert ecosystems, with the extractive logic of Parker Dam and the growing boomtown of Parker. The Sand Lizards are likely based on the Hia C-ed O'odham, or "Sand People," a subgroup of the Tohono O'odham.[78] Once nomadic, inhabiting a broad swath of the Sonoran Desert, the Hia C-ed O'odham are presently integrated into the larger Tohono O'odham nation near Tucson and are actively seeking federal recognition. Approximately 1,000 people claim direct ancestry to the subgroup.[79] The Hia C-ed O'odham long relied on desert plants such as *Pholisma sonorae*, also known as sand root or sandfood, a perennial flowering plant that grows in sand dunes and from which the group received the anglicized designation "Sand People" or "Sand Papago."[80] Oral histories suggest they migrated with regularity to agricultural sites where desert crops, such as amaranth, were grown using floodwater or spring-fed irrigation methods.[81]

Silko's fictionalized Sand Lizards maintain collective continuance through a sustainable, reciprocal approach to water management to cultivate plants in their desert gardens. Desert plants are viewed as kin, given individual nicknames as the people tend to them in the gardens, and harvest ceremonies are organized around offerings to honor desert rains and fauna. The Sand Lizard agricultural model also applies during periods of drought, during which the people depend on a sacred natural spring guarded by Grandfather Snake, a cousin of the Sand Lizard. "All desert springs have resident snakes," Grandmother Fleet warns the girls, emphasizing that "if people killed the snakes, the precious water disappeared."[82] Sand Lizard gardening practices exhibit a central feature of Whyte's notion of collective continuance: kinship with nonhuman entities and the notion that "nonhumans have their own agency, spirituality, knowledge, and intelligence."[83] As such, Sand Lizard lifeways are predicated on interdependence, systems of relationships, and adaptability to shifting environmental conditions such as seasonal drought—all elements of collective continuance necessary for social and ecological resilience amidst settler encroachment.

Sand Lizard lifeways in *Gardens* mirror those of the Hia C-ed O'odham, which are illegible within the logic of capitalist modernity. Both engage in a dynamic form of nomadism, engaging in what Whyte refers to broadly as migration and adherence to a seasonal round system of governance that permits the fluidity of social, cultural, economic, and political systems according to seasonal resource availability.[84] This system contrasts with the extractive logic of the Parker Dam, the *raison d'etre* of which is to harness and export the river's water to support agriculture and urban development hundreds of miles away without efforts to maintain or replenish the river basin's finite water resources. The imported economy of Silko's fictional Parker resembles that of a typical Western boomtown or "man camp" situated adjacent to mines, railroads, and other sites of strategic economic or military significance and mobbed with nervous, fortune-seeking hopefuls. Sited adjacent to the bustling dam site where only "the sound of coins seemed louder than the sounds of the earth-moving machines," Silko's Parker features a casino, saloons, and mobile, wagon-based brothels.[85] The town's commercial apparatus caters to a mostly male, mostly Anglo labor force. Sister Salt's male companion, a freed slave named Big Candy, earns a fortune making home-brewed beer using groundwater extracted from the desert.[86] When California and Arizona eventually clash over the river's diversion from Parker to Los Angeles in a fictional rendition of the region's infamous water wars, it is characterized by the dam's site supervisor as "all politics and money."[87]

In *Gardens*, the clash between two disparate approaches to water use proves initially devastating for the Sand Lizards as well as the inhabitants of the CRIT Reservation downstream. When Sister Salt encounters the dam site for the first time, it is as if she has happened upon a corpse: "[She] was shocked at the destruction she saw below: the earth was blasted open, the soil moist and red as flesh. The construction workers appeared the size of flies crawling over the hills of clayish dirt. The river had been forced from her bed into deep diversion ditches, where her water ran angry red. Big earth-moving machines pulled by teams of mules uprooted groves of ancient cottonwood trees. Off to the west, the workers were digging a huge ditch to carry river water all the way to Los Angeles."[88] The exposed flesh of the dam site, its decomposition helped along by droves of workers like "flies crawling," tells a story of violence that Sister Salt gradually pieces together as she makes her way downstream. Later she finds "silver-green carp belly-up, trapped in water holes in the empty riverbed" and "datura plants and wild purple asters on the riverbank suddenly left high and dry" before awakening one morning to find the river "unrecognizable—rechanneled and trapped into narrow muddy chambers outside its old bed," the trees "ripped out and plowed into mounds of debris, where their roots reached out plaintively like giant skeleton hands."[89] The river's diversion evokes the death of a relative, the desert anthropomorphized into the skeletal remains of a once-vibrant ecosystem. The river's death serves not only as a vivid analogy for the ecological violence of settler colonialism, but also the disruption of Sand Lizard collective continuance punctuated by the loss of traditional flora and fauna. Later, when Indigo reconnects with Sister

Salt, she attempts to reproduce Sand Lizard gardens by planting beans, peas, and amaranth on the reservation near the banks of the river. But the rising waters of Lake Havasu—created by the completion of Parker Dam—drown the plants and many homes on the reservation, prompting the sisters to return to the abandoned Sand Lizard gardens in the desert.[90]

In 1935, when President Roosevelt dedicated Hoover Dam 150 miles upstream from Parker, he praised it for "its contribution to the health and comfort of the people who live in the Southwest."[91] By "people," of course, he meant predominately white settlers. Such exclusionary rhetoric embodies Griffith's notion of "dam/ning," explored earlier in this chapter as a settler colonial process related to water extraction that "stimulates the growth of some life and curtails others, all under a banner of harmless progress." But damn/ning has a second meaning, according to Griffith, denoting "strategies used to thwart and undermine settler-colonial violence, dehumanization, displacement, and land theft."[92] For example, when hundreds of local native peoples were enlisted to perform in dam site archaeologist Mark Harrington's pageants eulogizing their "disappearance," they collectively bargained, by threat of strike, for competitive wages and fair treatment. Griffith characterizes these actions as forms of survivance. Likewise, affected Indigenous peoples downstream opposed the dam's construction through testimony and threatened direct action.[93] In *Gardens*, Sister Salt and her Chemehuevi companions, twins Maytha and Vedna, similarly resist colonization by escaping reservation boarding schools and asserting their independence and economic sovereignty. Saddened by the sight of impoverished peoples on the reservation, confined to tin shacks and resorting to drinking, gambling, and fighting, Sister Salt and her companions steal supplies and establish their own laundry camp on the banks of the river downstream from the dam site, making a fortune as sex workers and washing clothes for dam laborers.[94] While this *could* be viewed as one of many violent legacies of colonialism, Sister Salt in particular takes enthusiastically to sex work with white settler laborers at the dam site, even eventually bearing a child. This is an inversion of the Native captivity narrative. The three women move freely amongst white male bodies and are remunerated for their work, eventually raising enough money to move onto the reservation downstream in an attempt to return to a semitraditional form of subsistence farming.[95] This, too, represents a form of survivance, a resistance of externally imposed victimry and assertion of presence and agency.

In the novel's concluding pages, Indigo and Sister Salt return to the desert gardens in their homeland to find their gardens destroyed and the guardian of their sacred spring, Grandfather Snake, killed by intruding settlers. The sisters' presence prompts recovery: tending to their gardens as they once had, the gardens flourish once again, and Grandfather Snake's daughter takes up residence next to the sacred spring.[96] While the Colorado would be dammed eight more times after the completion of the Parker Dam, *Gardens* foresees the regenerative potential of collective continuance. In seemingly impossible circumstances, Sister Salt adapts by participating in the informal economy of Parker to support herself as she maintains Sand Lizard relationships and systems of responsibilities with the desert gardens, which she and her sister are eventually able to restore using traditional agricultural knowledge. Ultimately, *Gardens in the Dunes* offers a potential roadmap for a just transition in the Colorado River Basin: a heightened attention to the violent legacies of U.S. settler colonialism, especially those associated with large water infrastructure and water governance policies and processes; recognition of Indigenous sovereignty as a counter to deeply entrenched logics of elimination; and strategies for the maintenance of collective continuance. In doing so, *Gardens* buttresses decades-long tribal water rights battles and victories in the region, including AWSA in 2004 and, more recently, the central roles played by the GRIC and the CRIT in DCP negotiations in 2019.

### Curating Collective Continuance

In his 2011 book, *Bird on Fire*, Andrew Ross designates Phoenix as "the world's least sustainable city."[97] The book explores obstacles to and opportunities for sustainable growth in Phoenix during the long tail of the Great Recession, while the city faces new challenges associated with climate change. Ross ultimately concludes that technical and economic solutions will have a limited effect if not accompanied by social and political transformation. It is difficult to argue with this assessment; insofar as water governance in the West has always been driven by a deep-seated belief in human transcendence over nonhuman nature, perhaps no location can be considered more of an affirmation of this belief than Phoenix. The city is quite literally founded on the performance of what Reisner called hydrological miracles performed by federal planners. The CAP, which travels over 300 miles from Lake Havasu to Phoenix and Tucson, pumps water 1,250 feet *uphill* to reach its destinations.[98] It has an annual capacity of 2.8 million acre-feet of water, representing Arizona's full allocation of Colorado River water as stipulated by the 1922 Colorado River Compact, and right now, nearly a quarter of Phoenix's water comes from the Colorado and over a third is siphoned from the heavily dammed Salt and Verde Rivers, in both instances distributed through a labyrinthian network of canals via the CAP and the Salt River Project, respectively.[99] The CAP has enabled Phoenix to maintain a guise of livability despite annual rainfall totals averaging a mere eight inches.[100] During droughts, water pumped from the Colorado keeps golf courses green, swimming pools full, and lawns thriving throughout greater Phoenix while other cities in the region must ration water supplies.[101] Yet because of the CAP, and federal water subsidies awarded to the city in support of economic growth, city water rates have remained incredibly low; at one point in 2010, the cost per 100 gallons of water was less than half that of Seattle.[102]

But the CAP is not fully representative of a long history of human water management in the Phoenix Basin, which dates to well before the Akimel O'odham tended their fields on the banks of the Gila River. The Hohokam, ancestors of the both the Akimel and Tohono O'odham ("Desert People") who inhabited the region well before settler arrival, began developing irrigation farming as early as 300 BC and effectively harnessed the waters of the Salt River, as well as the Gila and Verde Rivers to the southwest. At their peak, the Hohokam functioned as a sophisticated state-level society comprised of forty thousand inhabitants, four thousand square miles of farmland, and one thousand miles of irrigation canals. There has been some debate about reasons for their decline, though most agree that a combination of overpopulation due to an influx of migrants, coupled with prolonged drought and a series of unprecedented floods, led to their dispersal over the course of the fourteenth or fifteenth centuries. While some have viewed the Hohokam's decline as a cautionary tale of the ecological risks of resource overuse and mismanagement, the fact that the Hohokam built and maintained a successful, irrigation-based pseudo-state for nearly two thousand years implies a relatively sustainable approach to water management considering the scale and severity of current regional water crises arising just a century after the initiation of large dam building in the western United States.[103] Descended from the Hohokam, the O'odham are likewise water innovators: while the Akimel O'odham used Hohokam canals to water their fields in the nineteenth century, the Tohono O'odham used floodwater farming, irrigating their crops by harnessing sporadic flash floods and storing water in catchment basins.[104]

The Hohokam pueblo ruins at the Pueblo Grande Museum and Archaeological Park in Phoenix offer a rich setting to consider the city's dependence on settler water infrastructure and the collective continuance of the valley's Indigenous communities. The pueblo persists along the city's border with Tempe and is bracketed to the east by the Hohokam Expressway, to the north by the South Mountain Freeway, and to the south by the dry bed of the once free flowing but now heavily dammed Salt River. Along the southern edge of the site, visitors can view a CAP canal linking the city's East Valley to the Agua Fria River downstream from New Waddell Dam and Lake Pleasant, where excess water from the Colorado is stored as part of the Agua Fria Recharge Project.[105] For the Hohokam, the site was politically prominent and strategically significant, serving as a crucial checkpoint controlling the diversion of water from the Salt River to a main irrigation canal carrying water to hundreds of fields throughout the valley. Visitors to the site can view an indoor museum and explore a walkable outdoor archaeological site, where a self-guided tour reveals an enormous platform mound, a ball court, and unused remnants of a larger canal network, much of which has been appropriated by the CAP to distribute water to suburban Phoenix.[106]

Pueblo Grande's archival account of the region's vital Indigenous histories draws important connections between the eliminatory dimensions of settler reclamation efforts, environmental change, and Indigenous dispossession. It does so, however, through an unintentionally critical curatorial approach. Curation typically evokes the notion of a strategically assembled exhibit comprised of objects arranged to provoke a cognitive or behavioral response. Museum studies scholars have hailed the public museum as a space well-positioned for public engagement around climate change and environmental justice; as Jennifer Newell, Libby Robin, and Kirsten Wehner explain, museums promote dialogue between people, objects, and stories and catalyze a form of "material storytelling" that allows "objects to live again."[107] Despite a formal curatorial approach that can be described as educational rather than political, Pueblo Grande manages to engage in a form of material storytelling that reminds visitors of the city's settler history, the eliminatory water policies that serve as the basis for its existence, and the active presence of Indigenous peoples in central Arizona.

For example, when I visited the park in March 2016, the gallery abutting the main museum space featured the work of local photographer Wayne Norton entitled *Desertscapes*. According to the artist's statement, the exhibit was intended to "question Man's treatment of the desert." It featured familiar, sepia-tinted imagery of drought-induced climate dystopia in the western United States: fenced-off canals, dry riverbeds, grounded speedboats, and abandoned desert subdivisions. Photos were complemented by wall-painted quotations from white environmental writers like Reisner and Edward Abbey warning of the follies of large dams and reservoirs. No Indigenous writers were quoted, no Indigenous peoples were pictured, and the exhibit largely advanced a dominant narrative of drought as a harbinger of an exclusively settler dystopia. When viewed alongside the more historically earnest museum space, *Desertscapes* results in striking cognitive dissonance, imbuing Pueblo Grande with a politics of resistance against Indigenous erasure. Against the prescriptive aesthetics of *Desertscapes*, which can be viewed as a Reisner-esque critique that erases Indigenous presence, the museum mirrors Silko's historiographical approach in *Gardens*. Near the museum's exit space, visitors are presented with a question prominently displayed on a sign: "Did they disappear?" The answer is a resounding "No," as the museum displays various theories on the decline of the Hohokam corroborated by Akimel O'odham oral narratives and by archaeological evidence that traces O'odham lineage to the present. The pueblo remains, the canals remain, and the site celebrates this heritage and a form of collective continuance that works to offset or challenge visions of apocalypse that largely function to eulogize the decline of settler society.

During the short outdoor walking tour at Pueblo Grande, one finds frequent, unwelcome reminders of Phoenix's dependence on water extracted, imported, and delivered through a largely hidden municipal water system. Interrupting otherwise carefully curated scenes of Hohokam daily life, these disruptions are most poignant at the site of a replicated Hohokam garden that, a nearby sign explains, would have been watered by a small lateral canal connected to the main Hohokam canal, which linked directly to the Salt River (see figs. 1–2). The reproduction of the garden is well-executed: green shoots emerge in neat rows from dark, moist topsoil. But the eye is drawn, instead, to copper piping jutting rudely from the ground at the far end of the garden plot, its perpendicular valve lever in the off position, temporarily stifling the flow of water in an underground network of pipes siphoning water from the Colorado River hundreds of miles away. Parallel to the garden, the recreated lateral canal remains dry, an unintentionally critical metaphor for the violent legacies of large dams as a central feature of the U.S. settler colonial project. As such, the replica Hohokam garden, watered by modern, pipe-fed municipal water systems, narrates a succinct history of settler water governance in the western United States. Perhaps inadvertently, Pueblo Grande implores visitors to consider the palimpsestic overlay of settler resource regimes that have failed, after all, to erase Indigenous lifeways in the lower Colorado River Basin. Through material storytelling, the museum demands a similar type of cognitive work as *Gardens*. It prompts reflection on past injustices, emphasizes the continued presence of Indigenous lifeways, and—due to the site's location in the heart of Phoenix during a climate-driven megadrought—invites viewers to imagine a socially equitable and culturally inclusive water transition.[108]

Recent water-themed public art exhibits in the Phoenix area likewise work to story Indigenous collective continuance. In 2018 the Arizona Community Foundation, a philanthropic organization, held a prize competition called the Water Public Art Challenge. The organizers selected five teams of artists from a field of sixteen that, according to the competition's description, "honored the legacy of the Hohokam peoples, whose vast irrigation system and agricultural society laid the foundation" for life in the valley. Two winning teams were noteworthy. The first, calling

1. Hohokam Garden reproduction. Pueblo Grande Museum and Archaeological Park, Phoenix, Arizona. Courtesy of Pueblo Grande Museum, City of Phoenix.

2. Municipal water piping next to Hohokam Garden reproduction. Pueblo Grande Museum and Archaeological Park, Phoenix, Arizona, 2016. Photo by author.

themselves The Continuum, was comprised of O'odham artist Thomas "Breeze" Marcus, Dwayne Manuel, and Jacob Butler. Their project, entitled *Su:dagi Haicu A:ga (Water's Story)*, featured an informational panel and four hand-painted timeline murals depicting Hohokam irrigation and water-use techniques, highlighting the centrality of water to the O'odham cosmology and telling the "story of water" and its impacts on southern and central Arizona over time. The installation also included a glass case featuring traditional tools used to dig canals and plant crops as well as hand-etched seashell artwork originating from an O'odham site in Baja, Mexico, and still worn today to honor ancestral connections and the water on which the O'odham depend.[109] According to Marcus, the exhibit was meant to call attention to his peoples' "experience of losing the water to the dams and how it has affected tribes by losing the ability to grow our own food, causing the government to distribute processed

3. *Su:dagi Haicu A:ga (Water's Story)* by Thomas "Breeze" Marcus, Jacob Butler, and Dwayne Manuel. Mill Avenue, Tempe, Arizona, 2019. Photo by author.

foods to Native Americans that resulted in the diabetes epidemic."[110] The exhibit advances a striking mixed-media narrative of settler water theft and food injustice, some of the worst legacies of settler colonialism in central Arizona. It also reminds passersby of the *presence* of the O'odham, descendants of the Hohokam, despite an overbearing settler infrastructural overlay.

The siting of *Su:dagi Haicu A:ga (Water's Story)* (see fig. 3) was especially striking, as it was displayed at the base of the now-defunct Hayden Flour Mill in downtown Tempe, several hundred yards from Tempe Town Lake, the reservoir created when a dam was installed on the Salt River in the early 2000s. The mill was established by Charles Trumbull Hayden

*Decolonizing Drought* 51

(who also founded the city of Tempe and Arizona State University) and is designated on the National Register of Historic Places. It also helped facilitate the rise of Tempe as a major economic suburb of Phoenix. As a young trader from Connecticut, Hayden was inspired by *acequias* in New Mexico, exalting Edenic gardens he encountered near Santa Fe in the 1850s in grandiloquent poetry, watered by "canals of clear, pure rippling water," echoing the sentiments of many enterprising white settlers in the late nineteenth century seeking to "reclaim" arid lands.[111] In 1870, under the authority of the Homestead Act, he claimed lands south of Hayden Butte near present-day downtown Tempe and water rights from the Salt River to support the Hayden Milling and Farming Ditch Company. Hayden employed Mexican and Akimel O'odham laborers to dig a canal to divert water from the Salt to power his grist mill and water wheat fields to the west.[112] While geographically removed from the white settler communities depriving the Akimel O'odham of Gila River waters to the southeast, Hayden was nevertheless ideologically invested in the same colonizing impetus to tame the desert through large-scale irrigation.[113] He passed this legacy on to his son, Charles, who went on to serve seven terms in the United States Senate as a major supporter of large scale water projects in the Colorado River Basin and was a key architect of the CAP. *Su:dagi Haicu A:ga (Water's Story)*, situated in the shadow of the crumbling flour mill on Tempe's busiest street in full public view, insists on a deeper history, emerging from the cultural and topographical superimposition of settler epistemologies to affirm O'odham collective continuance.

A second group, the Water Heritage Collective, also received support for its project *Portal to the Past*, a sculpted gate and guided information markers at the entrance to the Pueblo Grande Museum from the CanalScape, a recently completed 12-mile multiuse trail system along the Grand Canal. One member of the group, Zarco Guerrero, is a sculptor of Acjachemen (Hashimen) descent and has long been active in the local native and Latinx art scenes. For the project, he designed a cut metal gate to mark the entrance to the park honoring Hohokam irrigation and ethnobotanical knowledges. The gate features two serpents representing the Gila and Salt Rivers and detailed depictions of Sonoran Desert flora and fauna. The exhibit was inaugurated in October 2019 and included events and programming encouraging visitors to take a guided tour to learn more about and acknowledge Indigenous cultural and agricultural contributions and traditional irrigation methods passed from the ancestral Sonoran Desert people to their present-day descendants.[114] Like Pueblo Grande, the exhibit's location is notable. The CanalScape trail traces the Grand Canal, which was built as part of a larger network of canals superimposed over Hohokam canals in the late nineteenth century by Jack Swilling, a contemporary of Charles Trumbull. These canals laid the groundwork for the Salt River Project, a public water and electrical utility in Phoenix that was supported by low-interest loans following the 1902 Reclamation Act.[115] *Portal to the Past*, like *Su:dagi Haicu A:ga (Water's Story)*, affirms the ongoing presence of Indigenous communities in the Phoenix Valley and works to dispel a common misconception, perpetuated in many settler historical accounts, of the Hohokam's "disappearance."[116]

Along the California-Arizona border, the Colorado River Indian Tribes have also sought to decolonize drought discourse and promote collective continuance by creative means. Starting in 2015, CRIT began commissioning a series of films exploring Indigenous knowledges and tribal histories. This includes the 2016 mini-documentary *Beyond All Boundaries*, which documents the tribes' longstanding efforts to assert rights to Colorado River water and to affirm their position of strength in regional water negotiations. The film is especially poignant considering the tribes' role in DCP negotiations in 2018-19. The first half of the 30-minute film explores the water history of the CRIT Reservation, which (re)gained water use rights to the Colorado following the 1963 Supreme Court Decision in *Arizona v. California*. The film features interviews with tribal lawyers, elders, and tribal chair Dennis Patch, and it importantly reframes water issues from the perspective of an empowered tribal entity. In an interview, Patch insists that the CRIT tribal council views the tribes as an equal and important "part of the solution for the southwest [water] problem." But the film also highlights the tribes' struggle against encroachment of other forms of land use, including the Genesis Solar Energy Project, which was fast-tracked by the Obama administration despite vehement opposition by CRIT due to the site's location on tribal lands. The project was completed in 2014 near Ford Dry Lake (which is currently dry due to drought) and west of the CRIT Reservation in California. It was controversial because during the construction process, Mohave cultural artifacts were unearthed and damaged or destroyed by construction equipment. Federal authorities later permitted the objects to be reburied in their original locations per the wishes of CRIT and the Mohave peoples, and the film features poignant footage of this taking place beneath vast desert solar arrays. By featuring a combination of Indigenous knowledges and legal and political discussions surrounding the project, the film situates water issues within the larger context of tribal sovereignty, land rights, and the regional energy transition.[117]

Together, each of the cultural representations considered in this chapter can be viewed as contributing to a broader cultural counternarrative that insists that regional stakeholders consider past injustices—settler water theft and the disruption of Indigenous collective continuance—in the face of an ongoing water transition. By decolonizing dominant water narratives that frequently elide such histories, these representations have the potential to broaden perspectives and challenge diverse audiences to apprehend the ongoing cultural and environmental violence of settler water resource regimes. In *Bird on Fire*, Ross points to GRIC's court victory, the 2004 Arizona Water Settlements Act, as an example of the ways in which environmental and social justice struggles can provide a viable path to sustainability. He ultimately implores stakeholders to think beyond "green gizmos"—technology-driven solutions intended to benefit a wealthy few—and begin to think of sustainability in terms of "innovating healthy pathways out of poverty for populations at risk."[118] Literary fiction, museum and public art exhibits, and documentary film can do this work by adjudicating the ongoing violence of settler colonialism and imagining just water transitions. They can demand that readers and viewers imagine equitable water futures that emerge from the acknowledgment of, and redress for, past injustices by challenging dominant cultural narratives that elide histories of Indigenous dispossession in the lower Colorado River Basin. At bottom, such cultural representations serve as critical correctives for dominant hydropolitical discourse that tends to favor policy, economic, and technological solutions that are often articulated in the same technocratic vernacular that fueled settler water extraction efforts in the western United States in the mid-twentieth century.

This is true, for example, of initiatives such as Arizona State University's Future $H_2O$ program, which "helps create the future through solutions-oriented research and implementation partnerships with the world's biggest corporations, NGOs, transboundary multinationals, venture funds and public institutions." While Future $H_2O$ aspires to "advance new narratives of water abundance" rather than the self-defeating rhetoric of scarcity—an admirable discursive shift, to be sure—the initiative ultimately advances a type of top-down, technocratic vision for water solutions that can be traced to the ethos of "reclamation" that drove the development of the western United States in the mid-twentieth century.[119] This vision has been confirmed by the initiative's director, John Sabo, who in a 2016 op-ed in the *Arizona Republic* entitled "7 Ideas that Will Change How We Look at Water" argued for drought solutions that included an emphasis on big data; the integration of food, water, and energy technology; and desalination, among other ideas.[120] While technological, economic, and policy solutions are critically necessary, they are often ill-equipped to support coproductive approaches to environmental problem-solving that foreground community needs and cultural sovereignty. Silko's *Gardens in the Dunes*, the Pueblo Grande Museum, and the handful of public art exhibits featured in this chapter represent starting points for imagining a just water transition in the lower Colorado River Basin.

# 2 /

## Freedom Dreams for Flint
*Imagining a Just Transition beyond Racial Capitalism*

An August 2019 Michigan NPR story responded with skepticism to widespread claims on social media that the majority-Black city of Flint still lacked clean water. Those claims were misleading, the article insisted, because two years of tests had revealed the lead concentration levels in Flint's water to be well below the federal limit of 15 parts per billion. Due to the crisis, Flint's municipal water system had become of the most closely monitored in the United States and had been bolstered by a new lead and copper rule passed at the state level in 2018, rendering Michigan's drinking water standards the strictest in the country. Therefore, the article claimed, Flint's water quality was better than a handful of Michigan cities; tens of thousands of service lines had been inspected and thousands of pipes had been replaced in the city since 2016, and water quality was continuing to improve. Despite these efforts, the article conceded, mistrust persisted in Flint. Many residents still opted for filters and bottled water even after the state ended free distribution in 2018, and the long-term public health impacts of lead exposure, especially in children, remained unknown.[1] The perhaps unintended message of the article's "well, actually" framing is that thus far reparative measures in Flint had failed. Despite new laws, infrastructure upgrades, and testing protocols, the Flint water crisis was still unfolding. Even if claims that "Flint still doesn't have clean water" were *technically* untrue, they gestured to the fact that achieving reparative justice is a continual process with no clearly demarcated conclusion, especially in scenarios in which the impacts are slow, accretive, and intergenerational.[2] Achieving justice in Flint will be about more than just water.

Any vision for a just transition in Flint must acknowledge how the "color of water"—and, indeed, of democracy—is a product of the racialized dynamics of natural resource governance and policy in Michigan.[3]

Replacing infrastructure and passing legislation are important first steps but remain inadequate. So is the settlement with the state of Michigan that, in August 2020, awarded plaintiffs over $600 million, with 80 percent earmarked for impacted children and special education services. Residents and activists have noted that remuneration alone is not enough to cover long-term health and community impacts and have expressed frustration that many state and city officials who had been indicted for criminal charges reached plea deals and avoided jail time.[4] A politics of reparations in Flint can take several forms. For example, Patel and Moore's reparation ecology framework is one place to start, for it articulates an approach to justice that is never final and is not bound to remuneration or technocratic fixes. Instead, reparation ecology demands the recognition of historical, systemic inequities to guide ongoing efforts toward restorative justice including the redistribution of wealth and reconstitution of labor relations and the imagining of equitable futures as a "collective act of liberation."[5] Just transition frameworks arguably represent reparation ecology in practice. The Climate Justice Alliance, a coalition of seventy leading urban and rural environmental justice organizations and community support networks, emphasizes that an equitable transition must be focused on "redressing past harms and creating new relationships of power for the future through reparations."[6] These goals mirror environmental justice platforms espoused by racial justice groups like the Movement for Black Lives, a coalition of more than fifty Black-led community organizations, through an emphasis on "reparations for the wealth extracted from our communities through environmental racism, slavery, food apartheid, housing discrimination, and racialized capitalism."[7]

Narrative and storytelling can function as important conduits through which to imagine a just transition as an explicitly antiracist, reparative process. Following Laura Pulido, I contend that the Flint water crisis should be viewed as the logical outcome of racial capitalism. Because the state is ideologically and structurally bound to uphold this system, typical avenues for attaining reparative environmental justice like advocacy and litigation, which are dependent on the myth of an impartial state, have largely failed to improve prevailing environmental conditions for Black and Brown communities.[8] To understand the Flint water crisis as a feature of racial capitalism, however, requires new narratives that ground the city's experience of environmental racism within a deeper history of racialized austerity politics and the privatization of public debt that is often elided by media accounts of the crisis. The situation in Flint is frequently misrecognized as a product of the very recent past, driven by a handful of poor and negligent decisions made by state officials, some deliberately covered up and in violation of the law, in misguided efforts to rescue a financially strapped city. Timelines pieced together by media outlets like CNN, NPR, the *Associated Press*, and the *New York Times* typically begin in April 2014, when the city of Flint—under the auspices of a state-appointed emergency fiscal manager—switched its primary water source from the Detroit River to the Flint River to save money and return the city to fiscal solvency. This is followed by dizzying accounts of water quality complaints, officials' refusal to acknowledge the problem, scientific studies showing elevated levels of lead and other contaminants in the water, state aid packages acknowledging the issue, an uptick in water-related illness, evidence of a cover-up and negligent decision making from city and state officials, a federal disaster declaration, criminal charges, cleanup efforts, plea deals, more federal aid, and ongoing litigation. Some timelines begin slightly earlier, dating the start of the crisis to Michigan's decision to begin officially overseeing Flint's finances in 2012, but the effect is the same: Most public knowledge of the Flint water crisis is transmitted in the form of recognizable spectacle—press conferences, protests, and high-profile hearings—that belie the extent to which the Flint water crisis is the product of long-standing politics of abandonment.[9]

It is unsurprising that that activists and residents in Flint remain dissatisfied with the reparative measures thus far taken, for they represent short-term responses to long-term problems like segregation, white flight, deindustrialization, and urban disinvestment that go back almost a century.[10] As I showed in chapter 1, narrative and storytelling play important roles of diagnosis and resistance, challenging the extractive logics of an always-racialized capitalism and prompting communities to imagine equitable alternatives. Doing so means not only viewing the Flint water crisis as a symptom of racial capitalism, but also recognizing that existing reparative measures are inadequate and that a just transition requires imagining radically equitable futures driven by efforts to explicitly address environmental racism as a material discursive formation. A just transition that moves *beyond* racial capitalism, then, requires new narratives that work explicitly to abolish the politics of abandonment and Black disposability that drive instances of environmental racism. Cultural responses to the Flint water crisis like José Casas's ethnographic, documentary-style play *Flint* and efforts like Mel Chin and Tracy Reese's Flint Fit fashion-art collaboration and the Flint Public Art Project exhibit remarkable generative potential by foregrounding community resilience in Flint. By humanizing the city and the crisis and testifying to the power of community, each insists that the city is more than an environmental sacrifice zone and, in the words of Flint activists, that "Flint Lives Matter." By considering each within the context of Black radical politics, it becomes clear that storytelling can advance what Robin Kelley calls freedom dreams—visions for emancipatory futures articulated by a collective movement led by Black scholars, artists, and activists he describes as the Black radical imagination.[11] This chapter explores the extent to which freedom dreams support a just transition in Flint, Michigan.

### Racial Capitalism, Justice, and Flint Freedom Dreams

I am not the first to view the Flint water crisis as constitutive of racial capitalism, but here I would like to examine the radical potential for narrative, storytelling, and the arts to imagine sustainable, equitable futures beyond racial capitalism. It has become increasingly insightful to approach environmental justice issues under the assumption that capitalism has both always been racialized and exploitative of racial difference in increasingly sophisticated ways to achieve its ends, namely the enhancement and protection of white wealth and power. The late Cedric Robinson first articulated the notion of racial capitalism in *Black Marxism: The Making of the Black Radical Tradition* (1983) to claim that as the "development, organization, and expansion of capitalist society has always pursued essentially racial directions, so too has social ideology."[12] Robinson's recognition of capitalism as inherently racialized arose from his critique of Marxist theory, which he argued has historically ignored the role of race in class formation in favor of Euro-centric models of history and, as a consequence, discounted a rich tradition of

Black political and social resistance dating to precapitalist Europe. The latter he called the Black radical tradition, which emerged from "the continuing development of a collective consciousness informed by the historical struggles for liberation and motivated by the shared sense of obligation to preserve the collective being, the ontological totality" of Black experience.[13] Robinson traced Black radicalism to slave revolts and maroon communities on the peripheries of the capitalist world system, and elsewhere argued that the roots of socialism lie not in Marxist formulations of proletarian revolution but in collectivities of resistance that emerged from Black radicalism over time.[14] While Robinson delineated the currents of Black radicalism in an early twentieth century Black intelligentsia—with a focus on the work of W. E. B. Du Bois, C. L. R. James, and Richard Wright—he located their work as the product of a politics from below, from plantations to the Black working class, that envisions radically inclusive societies predicated on community and democracy.[15]

In the nearly forty years since the publication of *Black Marxism*, numerous scholars have adapted and expanded on the notion of racial capitalism as an organizing principle of modernity and have traced the evolution of Black radical politics into the present. There has been increasing recognition that "capitalism *is* racial capitalism."[16] Many scholars now share the view that the central conceit of capitalism is, in fact, the construction of difference and the persistence of unequal relations between human groups along the lines of race, class, gender, and other categories.[17] Such "antinomies of accumulation require loss, disposability, and the differentiation of value," and racism serves as a particularly potent conduit through which to channel capitalism's fundamentally exclusionary logics.[18] Overt structures of racial oppression, such as slavery, colonialism, and genocide, are some ways in which such logics have been expressed. So are their aftermaths. Jodi Melamed locates them, for example, in the terms of the "formally anti-racist, liberal-capitalist modernity" of the postwar era—rhetorics of diversity, multiculturalism, colorblindness—that purport to separate racism from the material depredations of capitalism. Melamed shows that antiracist liberalism often amounts to little more than a performative exercise.[19] Jackie Wang maps the contours of "carceral capitalism," a framework that reorients formulations of racial capitalism beyond questions of wage labor to consider how par-

*Freedom Dreams for Flint*

asitic governance and predatory lending, central to the extractive logic of neoliberal capitalism, disenfranchise communities of color. Within this framework, the privatization of public debt and social services and the proliferation of an unregulated lending system converge to extract wealth from people of color. The term *carceral*, here, refers to both social confinement through debt and physical confinement within a prison-industrial complex that profits from the mass incarceration of, violence against, and neglect of communities of color.[20] Such dynamics can be viewed as inherent to the extractive logics of what Françoise Vergès has called the racial Capitalocene, recognizing the connections between the climate crisis and racial capitalism.[21]

As I have argued previously, just transition frameworks stand in direct opposition to the expendability thesis of capitalism, wherein accumulation hinges on the relative disposability of communities along the lines of race, class, gender, and ethnicity. Therefore, it is worth pausing for a moment to consider Laura Pulido's case for incorporating critical responses to racial capitalism in environmental justice scholarship and advocacy. Pulido argues that despite some limited successes, the U.S. environmental justice movement has largely failed to improve living conditions for communities of color because it is overly reliant on state-based avenues for relief. For example, environmental justice lawsuits filed under the Equal Protection clause of the Fourteenth Amendment of the U.S. Constitution and Title VI of the Civil Rights Act have mostly been unsuccessful, and in fact have served to reproduce instances of environmental racism.[22] In short, the environmental justice movement has largely failed to recognize the false impartiality of a state that frequently sanctions environmental racism as necessary for capital accumulation, which relies on the creation of differential value among human groups. If proper functioning of the markets is dependent on environmental racism, then its regulation is ultimately "the province of the state."[23] It is in the state's best interest to preserve the residues of colonialism like land theft, dispossession, and slave labor. This production of difference mirrors patterns of environmental degradation: Just as pollutive industries require "sinks," or places to deposit pollution cheaply and easily in order to maximize profit, capitalism too requires sinks, which includes both land *and* human bodies.[24] In this view, environmental racism should be viewed not as an externality of capitalism but instead as a "constituent element of racial capitalism."[25] As such, environmental racism can be viewed as a form of state-sanctioned violence that functions as a precondition for capital accumulation. To the extent that environmental justice victories can be claimed within such circumstances, the result is often institutional performativity that precludes real, meaningful change.

These dynamics are detectable within the *longue durée* of the Flint water crisis, which can be viewed as a logical outcome of racial capitalism. The crisis can be traced to a decades-old politics of abandonment that casts Black communities as inherently disposable. Flint—once a critical node in the booming mid-century automobile industry and home to several General Motors facilities—is today a Rust Belt casualty of the neoliberal turn in global economic policy, still grappling with the post-1980s outsourcing of manufacturing jobs and plant closures. More than half the city is Black, poverty rates are over 40 percent, and the population has declined by 50 percent over the past forty years, in part due to white flight. A primary factor driving the city's decline, and contributing to the eventual water crisis, is finance capital. Facing dwindling tax revenues, the city increasingly turned to private lenders rather than raising taxes out of fear of alienating business interests. As a result, policy decisions in Flint have prioritized economic growth over public funding for social services and infrastructure. This shifting commitment, evident in the state's unwillingness to maintain basic infrastructure, can be characterized as a "politics of abandonment," which in Flint is evident through the city's failure to replace corroding water pipes, a primary factor in the water crisis.[26] In 2011 then-governor Rick Snyder placed Flint under emergency management and appointed an emergency fiscal manager to solve the city's financial woes, prioritizing fiscal solvency over public services. In 2014 Flint's emergency fiscal manager switched the city's water source from the Detroit River to Lake Huron to save around $17 million. Because the switch was projected to take about two years, the city began drawing water from the historically polluted Flint River for the interim. Shortly thereafter, the Flint General Motors plant complained about the water corroding car parts and the city promptly switched the plant's water source back to the Detroit River.

*Freedom Dreams for Flint*

Complaints from Flint residents, however, were ignored. Despite evidence that Flint River water was corroding pipes and allowing lead and other contaminants to leech into the water—contributing to an array of health problems from rashes to Legionnaires' disease—city officials downplayed, deflected, denied, and covered up the crisis for over a year before allowing the city to return to the Detroit River for water. The state's initial unwillingness to accept responsibility or act to remedy the crisis reflects a politics of abandonment which, as Pulido explains, was possible because Flint's status as a majority-Black city. While the crisis also impacted white residents, their experiences can be ascribed to the fact that the city is "racialized as Black" within market logics.[27] Within the equation of always-racialized capitalism, people of color are viewed as disposable; in the very least, the lives and well-being of Flint residents were "subordinated to the goals of municipal fiscal solvency."[28] Furthermore, it is important to recognize that under Michigan law, emergency fiscal managers are not democratically elected and in fact retain veto power over mayors and city councils on fiscal decision making. Writing of Flint, Wang calls this scenario a "financial state of exception," which entails the suspension of democratic norms in favor of governance that prioritizes the interests of the financial sector.[29] What should be emphasized, then, is that the Flint water crisis emerged from the deliberately uneven distribution of environmental toxicity along racial lines in the service of capital.

To the extent that just transition frameworks advance essentially postcapitalist visions for the future, they should be viewed as potential avenues for attending to racial inequality as a material discursive formation. Just transition frameworks, moreover, can serve as forceful counters to state-sanctioned environmental violence as a precondition for capital accumulation. If traditional paths for redress are incommensurable with a state committed to upholding racial difference, then just transition frameworks can "change how we view the state and our relationship to it."[30] To the extent that Black radicalism can be viewed, according to George Lipsitz, as a "a politics rather than a pigment, a culture rather than a color" led by the Black working class, Black radicalism in the United States today can be located in movements like Black Lives Matter, which emerged in response to the murder of Black Americans at the hands of police.[31] Such movements emerge from the collective experiences of those who "cannot make a separate peace with racial capitalism" in ways Black bourgeoisie figures like Barack Obama, Colin Powell, and others have, representing as they do the culmination of civil rights victories that nonetheless remain the province of a state that sanctions myriad forms of violence as a precondition for capital accumulation.[32] In recent years, efforts have proliferated to "recuperate and recover the Black Radical Tradition and to enliven it in the academy and the community."[33] The tradition can be viewed as both a politics and a critical practice, and new methodologies have emerged for writing about struggle wherein the intellectual is considered part of, rather than separate, from the collective. Moreover, contemporary Black radicalism in its current iterations is more recognizably intersectional; abolition has come to denote the demolition of oppressive systems more broadly. As Gaye Theresa Johnson and Alex Lubin suggest, Black radicalism "refers to demands and articulations of freedom by Black activists, artists, and intellectuals on behalf of everyone's freedom. Black freedom is freedom for all."[34] Resistance in the spirit of the Black radical tradition can be located, for example, in the solidarities forged between Black Lives Matter and decolonial struggles in Standing Rock and Palestine.[35] As with just transition frameworks, Black radicalism as both a politics and a critical practice is fundamentally positioned against the normalization of human disposability.

Narrative and storytelling play an important role in efforts to abolish racial capitalism and ensuring a just transition in communities ravaged by environmental racism. As noted earlier in this chapter, Kelley uses the phrase freedom dreams to describe the radically inclusive, emancipatory visions of Black intellectuals, artists, and activists he situates within the Black radical imagination.[36] A student of Robinson's, Kelley considers how progressive, antiracist social movements have harnessed storytelling, narrative, and the imagination to outline visions for radically inclusive futures. Much as I have argued in this book, Kelley insists that "progressive social movements do not simply produce statistics and narratives of oppression; rather, the best ones do what great poetry always does: transport us to another place, compel us to relive horrors and, more importantly, enable us to imagine a new society."[37] Kelley's reading of post-Reconstruction reparations movements as examples of emancipatory claims advanced within the Black radical imagination is particularly compelling; such movements are never merely about remuneration but rather about social justice and reconciliation through "securing funds for autonomous black institutions, improving community life, and in some cases establishing a homeland that will enable African Americans to develop a political economy geared toward more collective needs than toward accumulation."[38] Kelley cites James Forman's anticapitalist "Black Manifesto," presented at the Black Economic Development Conference in Detroit in 1969, and N'COBRA's wide-ranging reparations plan, presented to the United States Congress in 1987, entitled "An Act to Stimulate Economic Growth in the United States and Compensate, in part, for the Grievous Wrongs of Slavery and the Unjust Enrichment which Accrued to the United States Therefrom." These freedom dreams outline transformative, essentially anticapitalist visions for a radically equitable society wherein reparations would support the establishment of Black-led universities, food cooperatives, think tanks, skills training centers, banks, media organizations, and other institutions. Such visions are also frequently predicated establishing territory for Black self-government. Central to these efforts was the goal of rebuilding and establishing community and democracy.[39]

Freedom dreams articulate visions for reparative justice centered around community. This is a key feature of just transition frameworks that insist on community-driven approaches to environmental decision making. According to the just transition framework and principles outlined by the Climate Justice Alliance, a shift from an extractive to a regenerative economy entails a collective commitment to deep democracy, self-determination, and the prioritization of community.[40] Below, I turn to José Casas's ethnographic, documentary-style play *Flint*, which responds to the water crisis as a crisis of racial capitalism by (1) attending to environmental racism in Flint as a historical discursive formation, (2) critiquing the state's role in upholding systemic racism and therefore thwarting efforts for true reparative justice, and (3) creating the conditions of possibility for reparative justice *beyond* technocratic fixes like legislation, infrastructure repair, and one-time remuneration. While the play itself does not articulate an explicit vision for a postcapitalist society, it calls attention to the color of water in Flint and draws on individual testimony to insist that Flint lives matter. In doing so, it urges audiences to rethink dominant narratives of the water crisis that fail to account for its historical roots and fetishize Black poverty and urban decline. Moreover, initiatives like Flint Fit—the fashion-art collaboration between artist Mel Chin and fashion designer Tracy Reese—and the Flint Public Art Project represent examples of freedom dreams that tell new stories about community that resist the politics of abandonment and expendability and work toward equitable, sustainable futures.

### Flint Lives Matter: José Casas's *Flint*

José Casas's play *Flint* premiered on April 5, 2019, at the Arthur Miller Theater at the University of Michigan's North Campus—exactly five years after Flint residents began complaining about poisoned water flowing from their pipes.[41] A series of related events accompanied the play's ensuing tour, including a symposium to foster dialogue about the crisis and an art exhibit featuring the work of Flint-based artists. The play was performed in Flint two weeks post-debut, and an additional performance was live streamed for Flint residents a week later. An ethnographic, documentary-style play, *Flint* is largely composed of vignetted monologues—some from individuals, some composites—derived from interviews Casas conducted, over the course of three years, with over one hundred Flint residents and others connected to the crisis. Some monologues also draw on public records, quotations from public officials, and news reports. The play was performed by student actors at the University of Michigan, where Casas teaches as an assistant professor in the School of Music, Theatre, and Dance. As Casas notes in an interview, the play and associated events had two goals: to show people that "the common denominators [of the crisis] are class, and this idea of bodies of color being disposable" and also to prompt people to "think about change and what that means to them."[42] Throughout the play, individual monologues tie the water crisis to systemic racism, segregation, poverty, immigration, ableism, and deindustrialization and the politics of abandonment.[43]

Casas's play is not the first documentary-style response to the Flint water crisis, but it is the first to engage with the city's residents meaningfully. Actor-writer Jeff Daniels also wrote a play entitled *Flint* that was performed at the Purple Rose Theater in Chelsea, Michigan, in 2018.

Daniels's play, too, uses the water crisis to talk about issues like racism and postindustrial poverty, and it does so through a fictionalized scenario in which two Flint couples—one white and one Black—reflect on and argue about reasons for the city's decline during the course of a single night.[44] British director Anthony Baxter's documentary *Flint*, narrated by actor Alec Baldwin, takes a chronological look at events leading to and following the crisis, and the Netflix docuseries *Flint Town* explores the many issues facing Flint through the eyes of law enforcement.[45] Casas's *Flint* can be distinguished from this crowded field through its status as a performative ethnography that draws deeply on testimony and observations from those affected firsthand by the crisis. Because it is based on interview transcripts performed verbatim, the play elevates voices and experiences seldom included in official accounts of the crisis— from single Black mothers raising poisoned children to construction workers tasked with demolishing abandoned homes, undocumented immigrants scared to seek relief, and high school seniors facing uncertain futures. Rather than unilaterally assigning meaning to the crisis through fictionalization or chronological storytelling, Casas convenes a breadth of stakeholders and provides a platform for them to respond to the crisis on their own terms, thus avoiding an overly prescriptive tone. Moreover, the play refuses to treat the water crisis as a cause célèbre, the type of cause embraced by politicians and celebrities, sometimes in cynical attempts to score political points or build personal brands. In interviews, Casas has noted that unlike Baldwin and other famous outsiders, he was unsuccessful in securing interviews with public officials like U.S. representative Dan Kildee of Michigan's Third Congressional District (which includes Flint) and former Flint mayor Karen Weaver. While the play does incorporate quotations from Mayor Weaver and others taken from news reports, the play's dialogue is largely derived from the words of ordinary Flint residents. This is arguably *Flint*'s greatest asset, for the conspicuous absence of the state punctuates the play's critique of racial capitalism and refusal to generalize about Flint as a homogenously poor Black city. While environmental racism is framed as the product of the same system that has historically supported slavery, Jim Crow, and ongoing systemic racism, through the words of the community, the play defers to individual experiences of the city's many crises.

*Flint* falls into the category of documentary theatre, which typically draws on interview transcripts, testimony, trials, media reports, autobiography, and other first-order or primary sources and works to reframe real events. Casas, a Chicano playwright from Los Angeles whose work frequently engages with social justice issues, has compared the play to Moises Kaufman's play *The Laramie Project*, which similarly uses monologues to reflect on events surrounding the murder of gay University of Wyoming student Matthew Shepard in Laramie, Wyoming, in 1998. Shepard's death brought international attention to LGBTQ rights and hate crime laws, and it is difficult to imagine that the play—which has been performed for millions of people in dozens of countries—did not have some impact on the eventual passing of the Matthew Shepard and James Byrd Jr. Hate Crimes Prevention Act of 2009. Like *Flint*, *The Laramie Project* consists of monologues based on interview transcripts with community members, though the latter names the individuals interviewed and juxtaposes monologues to construct a chronological narrative of events in Laramie.[46] Thematically, *Flint* also shares similarities with Anna Deavere Smith's Tony Award–nominated *Twilight: Los Angeles 1992*, which explores the uprising in response to the police brutality case against Rodney King. Smith conducted over three hundred interviews and performed all of the play's seventy-two monologues herself.

Documentary theatre takes many overlapping forms, with little agreement upon terms, and here I will not attempt to litigate the generic conventions of *Flint*.[47] Critics generally agree that *The Laramie Project* is an example of ethnodrama and, due to its similarities with *Flint*, I will analyze the latter as such.[48] Ethnodrama involves the conversion of ethnographic research, such as interview transcripts, into performance text that frequently challenges dominant narratives of controversial events by foregrounding diverse and marginalized perspectives. In the creation of ethnodrama, the "interpretive ethnographer"—the playwright and/or performers—"enters those strange and familiar situations that connect critical biographical experiences (epiphanies) with culture, history, and social structure. He or she seeks out those narratives and stories people tell one another as they attempt to make sense of epiphanies or existential turning points in their lives." The term *epiphanies*, here, denotes a subject's or informant's response to events after first-hand experience and reflection. Intended for consumption by both academic and public audiences, open to media coverage and meant to spark conversation and debate, ethnodrama "seeks to tell truth as [its subjects] see it, so as to give them a voice."[49] As such, ethnodrama has emancipatory potential for those involved, for it features "plausible accounts" of events and experiences constructed to through consensual processes, such as interviewing.[50]

Because Casas's *Flint* draws on ethnographic research to story the water crisis, it also evokes the notion of counter storytelling, a strategy first described by Richard Delgado, a founding contributor to critical race theory, to describe a method of storytelling in legal scholarship that foregrounds the experiences of marginalized or silenced communities and challenges "majoritarian" stories or narratives that support dominant social ideologies.[51] Counter storytelling has been examined extensively in education research to better understand how to build more equitable educational experiences. Storytelling is presented in myriad forms, from autobiographical, biographical, and composite (i.e., generated from multiple stories). [52] Such methodology is more broadly representative of the role of storytelling and narrative in critical race scholarship generally, which views each as critical tools for sharing experiences of oppression, challenging majoritarian narratives, and imagining alternative, emancipatory futures.[53] As Delgado argues, stories have the power to challenge the "prevailing mindset by means of which members of the dominant group justify the world as it is, that is, with whites on top and browns and blacks at the bottom."[54] Stories have the power to disrupt this mindset, he continues: "Most who write about storytelling focus on its community-building functions: stories build consensus, a common culture of shared understandings, and deeper, more vital ethics. Counter stories, which challenge the received wisdom, do that as well. They can open windows into reality, showing us there are possibilities for life other than the ones we live."[55]

As ethnodrama, *Flint* presents a rich mosaic of testimonial counter stories documenting individual experiences of structural and symbolic violence. Each monologue in the play challenges the majoritarian narrative underlying racial capitalism: that Black lives are ultimately expendable in the service of capital. A primary theme of *Flint* is the intergenerational trauma experienced by Black families. The play opens with an angst-filled monologue delivered by a father who challenges racist stereotypes about absentee fatherhood in the Black community by tying his family's struggles to Flint's seemingly interminable public health crisis. "Tell 'em this mess ain't over," he pleads with the audience. "Tell 'em it doesn't matter how many movies they make. Tell 'em it don't matter how many politicians apologize. Tell 'em I still got poison in my body . . . that every person in this city they call a nobody still got poison in they body." These opening lines serve as a direct response to claims that Flint's water is now safe to use. They also serve to complicate the father's reflections on poverty and fatherhood. He explains that his two teenage sons have left Flint for Phoenix, Arizona, where they have become immersed in gang life. While he wants to bring them home, he wonders, "What the fuck is there for them in Flint?" Moreover, he has internalized his perceived failure as a father as a function of race, saying "I hate that blackness! I hate bein' that waste of space that people expect me to be! I *am* that nigga that everybody wanna hate!" Here, he recognizes that it is his Blackness that drove his sons away, but not perhaps in the way he thinks; his difficulties as a father are not a function of race nor, as far as we know, a failure at all. Rather, it is his family's Blackness, in a city racialized as Black, that renders him disposable within the equation of capital, robbing him of a comfortable livelihood and his sons of a future in Flint.[56]

*Flint* is, in fact, book-ended by painful reflections on the burdens of intergenerational trauma borne by Black families. The play closes with a wrenching powerful monologue from a Black mother whose family has lived in Flint for generations. She reflects on the gendered dimensions of the crisis: As a Black woman and mother, she is torn between expressing anger at the risk of enacting the "angry Black woman" stereotype or crying, therefore looking weak. "My voice is not being heard," she explains to officials, "because you don't even value me!" She feels helpless as she watches her children fall ill—her seven-year-old has high cholesterol—and grapples with the fact that she was forced to move her family from a 3,000-square-foot house in Flint to a small apartment in the less affordable college town of Ann Arbor, sacrificing hard-earned financial equity and starting their lives over in their forties. Even then, she explains, the crisis continues—her children are traumatized, and she feels compelled to perform her resilience:

**A Mother:** It's all a show. It's all a show; whether it's a minstrel show or a song and dance ... especially for mothers. See, that's the fucking thing. Mothers gotta carry it ... and, you carry the heart, the social welfare of your family in your hands ... in everything that you do. Blackface for your kids. You put on blackface for your church. You put it on for your husband. For your other family members. And, then for your community.... But it's all faces ... to hide the fact that you're hurting! And you know they're hurting and you have to make it like everything is ok because that's what mothers do.[57]

By comparing the pressure to pretend the crisis is in the past to blackface, the mother challenges efforts to relegate the Flint water crisis temporally and spatially. Its impacts are neither limited to the past nor to the city of Flint and, in fact, are distinctly gendered. We now know, for example, that Flint's poisoned water negatively impacted birthrates and likely contributed to a spike in miscarriages of more than 50 percent over pre-2014 levels. Impacts on children born healthy remain to be seen, but there are concerns about long-term implications of lead exposure, including behavioral problems and slowed cognitive development.[58] The play's opening and closing monologues, then, show how the crisis is a product of a politics of abandonment that is literally based on the sacrifice of Black lives and livelihoods.

*Flint*'s deeply personal accounts are complemented by broader critiques of racial capitalism within the neoliberal state. One scene responds to Nestlé Waters North America's exploitation of the situation in Flint as cover for its large-scale, immensely profitable water extraction and bottling operations in Michigan. For context, Nestlé netted $7.4 billion in bottled water sales in 2019.[59] In April 2018 Governor Snyder ended free bottled water distribution in Flint following a series of tests showing safe levels of lead in municipal water systems despite the fact that residents continued to report discolored, foul-smelling water and adverse health effects like rashes.[60] Around the same time, the Michigan Department of Environmental Quality (DEQ) approved Nestlé's request to draw more groundwater—up to 400 gallons per minute—in Osceola County, a few hours northwest of Flint. Besides a $5,000 application fee, the company was obligated to pay nothing more than an annual $200 administrative fee to pump groundwater. Meanwhile, Flint residents were paying some of the highest water rates in the country, sometimes topping $200—more than what Nestlé pays annually in exchange for billions in bottled water sales. A month earlier, Mayor Weaver had announced the resumption of water shutoffs for residents unable to pay their bills even though water quality remained questionable.[61] While Nestlé is technically permitted to extract water for free under riparian rights dating to Michigan's entrance into the union in 1837, the cognitive dissonance evoked a strong reaction in Flint. That a billion-dollar corporation could extract, bottle, and sell water with little to no benefit to nearby communities, especially amid an ongoing water crisis, seemed egregious. More than eighty thousand people agreed during the DEQ's public comment period, but it made no difference.[62] Nestlé's exploitation of the Flint water crisis is indicative of a broader pattern of disregard for low-income communities and communities of color in the company's water extraction efforts. In Ontario, for instance, it was revealed in 2018 that the company was illegally extracting water from Six Nations treaty land where Indigenous communities regularly lack access to clean water.[63] This is arguably a key part of Nestlé's business model—leveraging constructions of racial difference upheld by the neoliberal state in service of the interests of extractive capital.

Weeks later, in what many viewed as an attempt to salvage its public image, Nestlé announced it would donate one hundred thousand bottles of water per week in Flint for sixteen weeks. It should be noted that the population of Flint is around one hundred thousand, which works out to one bottle per resident per week. Accompanying the announcement were three advertisements, including a widely panned thirty-second video advertisement in which Nestlé claimed that "some people have forgotten about Flint, but Nestlé Waters never did."[64] The ad grotesquely casts Nestlé as the beneficent savior of a downtrodden community, depicting crews of workers smiling and handing out cases of water to a line of Black residents who smile back in gratitude. The ad stoops to racial pandering—the narrator is a Black woman—in a shallow performance of feigned recognition. Nestlé is, of course, unable to recognize the roots of the crisis, for they are the literal beneficiaries of a racialized capitalist system. This is reflected, for instance, by the company's refusal to contribute funds to help repair and upgrade the city's municipal water system, a demand many residents and activists have made.[65] In an official response to critics, the company acknowledged merely that "water is an emotional issue, and we appreciate the passion people everywhere have about it."[66] Such condescension elides the company's official position in favor of the commodification of a resource many consider to be a human right. To do anything else would be to pursue ends incommensurable with capital. As Melamed reminds us, "capital can only be capital when it is accumulating, and it can only accumulate by producing and moving through relations of severe inequality among human groups."[67]

Casas's *Flint* criticizes Nestlé's cooptation of the water crisis for an image-boosting public relations stunt that ultimately fails to abolish the "antinomies of accumulation" central to racial capitalism. This is accomplished through a scene juxtaposing the monologue of a water deliveryman set in direct opposition to Nestlé public relations language recited in unison by other actors behind him. The sequence starts with a group of actors chanting "We at Nestlé" with smarmy, corporate grins before the deliveryman alerts the audience to the company's grift: "Nestlé is literally taking millions and millions of gallons of Great Lakes water . . . bottling it . . . selling it . . . making stockholders happy. 240 to 400 gallons per minute. Doesn't even go to Michiganders. When is this going to stop? How is this 'Pure Michigan'? I think it's pure something else." Besides the implied view of Nestlé's performative philanthropy as bullshit, the notion of "pureness"—evoking the state's official tourism slogan—also arguably gestures to the water crisis as the result of institutionalized white supremacy. As the deliveryman continues his monologue expressing perturbation at Nestlé's profiteering, the Nestlé Corporation assures a hypothetical public that they are "passionate . . . [about] ensuring long-term sustainability of Michigan's resources" and that their ad campaigns "are our way of showing the many ways we support Michigan communities." Meanwhile, the delivery man expresses dismay at the ads, calling them insulting and patronizing, wondering, "Where are the numbers on how much profit they have made from selling our water back to the people of Flint? We the citizens of Flint are unable to get water, but you can give Nestlé water for free and force us to buy that back at a premium. Does that seem fair to you?"[68]

Midway through the scene, an actor playing Mayor Weaver emerges to say, "I want to thank Nestlé for their willingness to help the people of Flint. It is a generous donation"—a direct quotation of her official response to Nestlé's May 2018 donation.[69] The play offers a subtle critique of the state as an arbiter of racial capitalism—how can reparative justice be achieved within a system that privileges institutional alliances between the state and the private sector and enables such performative acts of relief? The deliveryman's ensuing, extended response to this impasse is frequently interspersed with the insincere enthusiasm of boilerplate corporate rhetoric:

> **Nestlé Corporation**: We are proud to continue supporting the Flint community.
> **A Delivery Guy**: They say that their business in Michigan has nothing to do with the Flint water crisis, but it does! They may not have changed the water source or put lead in the pipes, but what they are doing shows how unequal the system still is. They see that—
> **Nestlé Corporation**: We at Nestlé . . .
> **A Delivery Guy**: Need to fight and convince them not to charge us for tainted water. They need to fight so that we get medical coverage for the damage that's been done. They need to make a call for justice; hold those who created this situation accountable for their actions!
> **Nestlé Corporation**: Some people have forgotten about Flint, but Nestlé Waters never did.
> **A Delivery Guy**: But, instead . . . they give more water.

The sequence closes with the deliveryman's demand for justice, arguing that instead of profiteering, Nestlé ought to "fight and convince [the city] not to charge us for tainted water. They need to fight so that we get medical coverage for the damage that's been done. They need to make a call for justice; hold those accountable for their actions!" He sadly concludes, however, that "this will not happen." Here, it is acknowledged that clean water is not enough—abolishing capitalism's "antinomies of accumulation" requires a deeper acknowledgment of the material historical forces of racial capitalism.

To be sure, the polyvocality of Casas's *Flint*, which I view as its primary strength, does not permit it to articulate a precise vision for a just transition. But a key subtext that persists throughout is the notion of collective trauma and the emphasis on community as a source of resilience, even as technocratic initiatives ostensibly designed to empower residents fail at the hands of an indifferent state. These concerns are especially evident in a late scene that interweaves monologues from a Black man gardening in his yard and a white sociologist offering metacommentary on obstacles to community recovery in Flint. The scene opens with the gardener digging in his garden and asking, "How do we fix this system?" Reflecting on issues of food insecurity in the largely Black neighborhoods of Flint (he notes that "You don't see a Whole Foods in the hood"), he initially insists that urban gardening has the potential to be empowering: "There is strength in a man getting his hands dirty, the soil slipping through his fingers, knowing he's growing something pure . . . that he's feeding his family. I'm going to grow my own food!" From here, he envisions the power of community gardens creating a "special kind of unity" to "feed our liberation." Meanwhile, the sociologist ruminates in academic language about obstacles to equity in a place riven by the politics of abandonment. Despite the promise of community gardens, he notes, residents face a basic deficit of access to clean water with which to grow food. "Who's going to come and check their soil?" he asks. As with the rest of the play, these monologues are based on interview transcripts, and the exact context of each interview remains uncertain. But it is worth noting that the water crisis has posed unique challenges to existing food justice efforts in Flint such as community gardens and urban agricultural education.[70] The implication, here, is that community-based solutions do not always provide a clear path to justice and self-determination if those communities have been abandoned by the state, which has the role of ensuring the delivery of necessities like potable water. The sociologist in *Flint* admits as much, noting that "clean water is just a proxy" for broader conceptions of justice and equity. Likewise, the gardener ultimately refuses to feign ignorance, acknowledging "the poison running through the roots of these vegetables is the same as the poison running through my veins." Ultimately, the two men arrive at parallel conclusions as they complete their interwoven monologues. While the gardener recognizes that a path forward must include plans for more than just clean water, the sociologist insists that, for the state and others who provide relief, "there needs to be an understanding of how a community is formed and organized and, with that, an understanding of how you relate to others."

Against dominant narratives of Flint as downtrodden, crumbling, and racially and culturally homogenous, the notion of community is potent. How can reparative environmental justice be achieved when the state is complicit in the environmental violence wrought by a capitalist system dependent on the expendability of communities of color? Such complicity certainly forecloses the possibility of adequate relief through traditional avenues like litigation and voting. But it is worth returning to the imaginative elements of Black reparations movements described by Kelley in *Freedom Dreams*. As Kelley writes, "a successful reparations campaign has the potential to benefit the entire nation, not just the black community." This is so because reparations are, at bottom, about renewed investment in schools, housing, infrastructure, civic organizations, and social services—all critical to community health and resilience.[71] *Flint* recognizes the extent to which environmental racism as racial capitalism harms *everyone* in a city racialized as Black, including testimony through monologues from a member of the deaf community, undocumented immigrants, underemployed white working-class residents, healthcare workers, and others. In a monologue from a young Latinx activist, the audience learns that Flint's Latinx community was initially unaware of the water crisis and only through the work of bilingual advocates learned about the poisoning, water shutoffs, and water donation availability. She reflects on the reluctance of *indocumentados* to ask for help due to the threat of deportation from ICE: "Imagine ... just imagine. Having to show proof of citizenship for bottled water?"[72] These fears have been well-documented during the crisis.[73] But later, during a monologue delivered by a middle-aged Catholic Latina woman, the audience learns that residents came together to donate water to her church, which acted as an intermediary to distribute water to *indocumentados*. She describes the reliance on community in a time of need, of "different hues blending into one. No one cared about who was who. No one's religion was better than anyone else's religion. Brown. White. Black. *Ni modo* ... it didn't matter. You had Catholics like me. Muslims. Buddhists. Protestants ... even atheists."[74]

Ultimately, *Flint* is about individuals collectively apprehending the complicity of the state as both a client and enabler of always racialized capital, and thus about activating and building on community ties forged through collective experiences of trauma stemming from systemic expendability. In this way, the play creates the conditions of possibility for audiences to imagine models for reparative justice in Flint that extend beyond technocratic fixes and one-time remuneration. Casas's *Flint* pushes audiences to understand Flint anew; each monologue functions as a counter story that implores viewers to view Flint as a city defined by a history of state-sanctioned environmental racism and, simultaneously, as a site of renewed possibility for emancipation through community-driven policies, processes, and programs.

There currently exist several creative responses to the water crisis that imagine the possibility of a community-driven just transition in Flint. One example is the Flint Fit project, a collaboration between visual artist Mel Chin and Black fashion designer and Detroit native Tracy Reese, best known for designing Michelle Obama's dress worn during the 2012 Democratic National Convention. Flint Fit's website describes the project as a "prototype for action, where Flint's empty water bottles are transformed into thread, thread becomes fabric, fabric becomes fashion, and fashion gets fabricated right back in Flint." Conceived in 2017, the goal of Flint Fit was to "show that empty bottles can become vessels of hope rather than reminders of an unjust crisis."[75] As part of the project, Flint residents and activists were paid to collect ninety thousand plastic water bottles, which were then shipped to a processing facility in Greensboro, North Carolina, where they were transformed into REPREVE yarn—a fiber that gets knitted into a fabric made entirely of recycled plastic by the textiles company Unifi. The fabric was then shipped back to the St. Luke N.E.W. Life Center, a faith-based community organization in Flint that supports survivors of abuse and homelessness through educational programs and skills training. There, residents were paid to sew the fabric into clothing designed by Reese as part of her capsule collection, Flint Fit.

The collection is composed of nine looks, and individual garments are water-inspired, including rainwear and swimwear, and resemble khaki and twill workwear as a throwback to the styles of Flint's manufacturing heyday in the 1940s (see fig. 4).[76] The collection was initially unveiled as part of Chin's broader exhibit, *Mel Chin: All Over the Place*, at the Queens Museum in April 2018. As part of the exhibit, the mannequins wearing Reese's collection were situated around a topographical map of New York's aqueduct system overlain with a rusted metal cast of the Flint River.[77] Likewise, the project included a photo shoot in April 2018 featuring an all-Black modeling cast donning each piece of the collection.[78]

Flint Fit is compelling in that it seeks to transform the detritus of the water crisis—plastic water bottles, manufactured as part of the bottled water industry's extractive logics—into a community development initiative for residents of Flint. The project is an argument against the disposability of Flint residents, and in fact reverses the logic of disposability. The bottles, at least a portion of which were likely donated by Nestlé, represent fleeting and inadequate relief from a private sector that has become an inadequate stand-in for social services that should fall under the purview of the state. As Casas's *Flint* emphasizes, the true value of bottled water donations resides less in their safe use for residents and more in the value of corporate public relations and the performative philanthropy of liberal capitalist modernity.[79] In response, Flint Fit empowered some of the city's most vulnerable residents to upcycle material signifiers of racial capitalism into a fashion-art exhibit that simultaneously calls attention to the city's manufacturing heyday and gestures toward the possibilities of a just transition. The effect was not merely to generate temporary opportunities for employment, nor to call attention to the crisis. Rather, Flint Fit established a model for community self-sufficiency that, in the spirit of freedom dreams advanced by Black reparations movements, refuses the expendability thesis of capital. This is one way to envision a just transition in Flint.

Another way is through the community building efforts of the Flint Public Art Project. Initiated in 2012, the project is a citywide arts program that organizes public events and workshops, sponsors festivals and other public events, and supports local artists with the goal of urging residents to reimagine the city's public image. It can rightly be described as an

4. Model wearing Flint Fit Collection by Tracy Reese. Photo by Philippe Rhodewald.

urban reclamation effort: Much of the artwork it supports, including major mural projects, is completed in vacant lots and on abandoned buildings. The project also collaborates with architects, city planners, and community organizations to revitalize neighborhoods through art and design. Executive director Joe Schipani explains that the primary goal of the project is "to change the narrative of the city from water crisis to art." This has involved partnerships with local artists as well as national and international activist artist collectives like CoLabs and Indecline that specialize in murals and street art. Some of the resultant art exhibits explicit activist tones and commentary on the water crisis, like the *Greetings from Flint* mural produced in collaboration with CoLabs and Indecline (see fig. 5). The mural mimics a mid-century postcard, the word "Flint" in blocky letters inlaid with the stencil silhouette of a weeping child; a wanted poster for former Governor Snyder; a Flint Lives Matter logo topped with a tightened Brown fist; and the iconic Flint water tower overlain with skull and crossbones.[80] But much of the artwork supported by the project avoids deliberate political commentary and instead serves the purpose of community revitalization (see fig. 6). For example, the organization sponsored and oversaw the Mural Project, which involved the completion of 104 murals citywide in 2019. Intended to represent what Schipani described as "rebirth, happiness, and healing" in the city, the effort attracted local, national, and international mural artists, helped beautify worn neighborhoods, and rendered Flint "one of the world's top destinations for street art."[81] Other Flint Public Art Project initiatives include "Free City" festivals, which temporarily reclaim neglected parts of the city, such as the former Chevrolet manufacturing site next to the Flint River, for public use through music, dancing, art, and community connection.[82] In June 2020 the project convened local artists and residents to paint a gigantic Black Lives Matter mural on the city's Martin Luther King Avenue in support of nationwide George Floyd protests.[83]

In a city racialized as Black and riven by state-sanctioned environmental racism, the arts offer a possible template for a community-driven just water transition. This is critical, as the Flint water crisis remains ongoing. Over a hundred lawsuits against the city and the state of Michigan remain pending in court at the time of writing.[84] Activists and residents insist that while remuneration is a start, it is far from enough to address the

5. *Greetings from Flint* mural by InDecline. Flint, Michigan, 2019. Photo by Gary Lewis/picfair.com.

6. *Sunflower Children* mural by Emily Ding. Flint, Michigan, 2019. Photo by Flint Public Art Project.

intergenerational impacts of a crisis and to regain trust in city and state officials. Infrastructural repairs and strict regulatory policy are likewise viewed as inadequate. To achieve true reparative justice requires an ongoing commitment to the redistribution of wealth and political power and an emphasis on policies that recognize community—and the community's relationship to the state. Traditional avenues for relief, such as the courts, are unlikely to succeed given the state's ideological commitments to racial capitalism. Casas's *Flint*, an ethnodrama composed of monologues based on interviews with Flint residents, advances a counternarrative that repositions the water crisis as constitutive of this system and suggests that a just transition in Flint requires exercises in radical scenario imagining articulated by a collective movement of scholars, artists, and activists that work to dismantle *all* forms of oppression. Critical to freedom dreams, such as those outlined by twentieth-century Black reparations movements, is the postcapitalist commitment to the redistribution of wealth and political power and focus on community resilience and self-sufficiency. Flint Fit and the Flint Public Art Project advance narratives of an equitable future for Flint beyond the water crisis. Flint Fit works to dismantle the city's racialized expendability by upcycling crisis-related waste—plastic water bottles—into community-focused art. The Flint Public Art Project empowers residents to reimagine the city's public image and to reclaim its abandoned infrastructure through art, education, and celebration. Such are the makings of freedom dreams for Flint.

# 3 /

## Extractive Fictions and Post-Extraction Futurisms

*Energy, Water, and Environmental Justice in Appalachia*

In Ann Pancake's 2007 novel *Strange as This Weather Has Been*, Bant—a teenager living in the heart of Appalachian coal country in southern West Virginia—surveys a ruined hollow above her family's property after a flash flood. "Anymore," she notes, "it seemed there was too much water or too little, the temperature too high or too low. 'Strange as this weather has been,' people would say.... And [she] knew... the weather was linked to the rest of this mess, but [she] wasn't sure how."[1] The extreme climatic flux to which Bant refers, symptomatic of global warming, can be linked to modernity's continued appetite for fossil fuels. This includes coal extracted from places like West Virginia, home to the highest concentration of active coal mines in the United States.[2] Yet "the mess" to which she refers is not the local manifestation of climate change but instead the human and environmental costs of coal extraction: collapsed impoundment dams, flash floods, coal slurry mudslides, acid mine drainage, forest dead zones, black lung disease, rising unemployment, and crippling poverty.[3] Extraction, in the novel, is not merely framed as the crucial link within a chain of causality in which fossil fuel consumption drives global environmental change. Instead, the novel maps a complex dialectic between environmental change, extractive capitalism, and regional cultural identity. *Strange as This Weather Has Been* is less concerned with unusual weather than with a grotesque climate of environmental and economic precarity in communities that have historically functioned as key nodes in the United States' extractive economy.

Pancake's novel affirms that the legacies of fossil fuel extraction in Appalachia are as evident in the land as in the water. Industrial waste left behind in abandoned, collapsed mines and byproducts from natural gas drilling—hailed as a way to replace jobs lost amidst the slow and steady collapse of coal—frequently leech into community water sources. This includes contaminants like arsenic and lead. Public health crises including liver and kidney issues have been the inevitable effect, but state agency evaluations often result in ambiguous findings, accountability is nearly impossible to come by, and people are afraid to speak out for fear of social ostracization or having their properties condemned. EPA records show that in Kentucky, Ohio, and West Virginia, there have been over 130,000 violations in the last two decades, and more than two thousand water systems have been contaminated—excluding private wells. Some residents are forced to install expensive rooftop runoff systems and store water in cisterns, but often the water is not potable, forcing people to purchase bottled water at an additional cost. Water crises in places like Martin County, Kentucky, have been compared to the situation in Flint. Despite producing millions of dollars' worth of coal, the county has done little to upgrade or repair vulnerabilities in municipal water infrastructure, reflecting a politics of abandonment.[4] The threat of flooding has also increased as altered landscapes have led to altered stream flows and the threat of collapsed impoundment dams. There has been a long history of the latter, including infamous disasters like the 1972 Buffalo Creek Flood in Logan County, West Virginia, which killed 125 people, and the Martin County, Kentucky, coal slurry spill in 2000, which the EPA called the worst ever industrial disaster in the southeastern United States. The likelihood of additional disasters looms.[5]

*Strange as This Weather Has Been* calls attention to both the environmental and social legacies of extractive capitalism, exemplifying what I call extractive fictions—a category of literary texts and other cultural representations that narrativize the socioecological impacts of extractive capitalism and problematize extraction as a cultural practice. Extractive fictions can be viewed as conceptually adjacent to the extractive frame used by literary critics in recent years to examine how world literature registers the cultural and ecological violence wrought by raw materials extraction on the peripheries of what Jason W. Moore calls the capitalist world-ecology. Drawing on world-systems theory, Moore maintains that capitalism is a world-*ecology* (as opposed to a world-*economy*), a process of environment-making dependent on the (un)availability of "cheap nature," or "cheap labor, food, energy, and raw materials."[6] Scholars like Sharae Deckard, Michael Niblett, and others have increasingly approached postcolonial and world literatures from a world-ecological perspective to map the violence of extraction as an ongoing legacy of colonialism in the Global South.[7] This chapter focuses on extractive fictions that reflect the material realities of a single node of the capitalist world-ecology: the central and northern portions of the United States' Appalachian region, particularly energy-rich parts of southern West Virginia and western Pennsylvania. I proceed from what Stephanie LeMenager has called commodity regionalism, an approach to energy studies that "activates vital historical and ecological frames ... such that we can see and sense them."[8] There presently exists a growing collection of scholarship exploring cultural responses to the violence of extraction in "resource cursed" regions like the Niger River Delta.[9] Through an attention to literary texts and multimedia cultural representations, such work maps the internal contradictions of resource-rich areas nevertheless beset by environmental degradation, public health crises, poverty, and social conflict.[10]

Here, I focus on Appalachia because of its originary status in the United States energy economy—the nation's first oil well was drilled in Titusville, Pennsylvania in 1859—and because extraction has long been central to the region's cultural imaginary.[11] Extractive fictions challenge the deep-seated role of extraction as a cornerstone of regional cultural identity in environmental sacrifice zones in central Appalachia. As I argue below, Pancake's novel evokes a sense of ecological grief—manifested by a pathological fear of water contamination and flash flooding—in residents who exhibit strong place-based identities and connections to the landscape. Faced with the combination of rising poverty levels and a sense of economic abandonment, the novel's protagonists begin to question the embeddedness of regional coal culture, prompting some to turn to activism. Similarly, cultural representations of hydraulic fracturing and the presence of natural gas interests in the region challenge what might be termed a post-coal culture of extraction. As I show, texts like Jennifer Haigh's novel *Heat and Light* (2015) and Julia Spicher Kasdorf and Steven Rubin's poetry-photography collection *Shale Play* (2018) insist that debates about fracking pivot on the complex interplay between latent fears about water contamination, cultural identity, and economic precarity. Each, by rendering visible instances of environmental degradation and economic decline associated with energy development in Appalachia, uniquely challenges the firmly established role of extraction as a cornerstone of regional cultural identity and the mythos of fossil fuel development as a path to economic and social progress. In doing so, they lay bare the epistemological failures of extractive capitalism, a mode of accumulation based on the large-scale withdrawal and processing of natural resources.

Because extractive fictions question dominant notions of the "greater good" that have pervaded the Appalachian coal fields for over a century and are often framed in a false jobs-versus-environment dichotomy, they represent an opening to envision and plan for alternative futures. As such, they urge readers to contemplate the possibility of a post-extraction Appalachia and complement existing efforts from local advocacy groups and national organizations and federal state partnerships like the Just Transition Fund and the Appalachian Regional Commission to support a just transition in coal country. Such initiatives tend to focus on sociotechnical solutions like workforce retraining, employment services, new investment in education and infrastructure, and business grants to stimulate innovation and economic diversification.[12] For example, initiatives like the New Economy for Appalachia program, sponsored by the environmental advocacy group Appalachian Voices, has hosted numerous "community visioning sessions" to empower citizens to contribute their ideas on potential paths forward beyond regional dependency on coal extraction.[13] The nonprofit Generation West Virginia focuses on stemming youth out-migration by attracting and retaining a young talent to the state.[14] Narrative and storytelling can support these efforts by urging new forms of scenario-imagining in which equity, sustainability, and quality of life are prioritized. The concluding section of this chapter considers two reclamation art projects in Pennsylvania and Ohio that take critical first steps to support a just transition by storying a post-extraction Appalachia: the Acid Mine Drainage (AMD) & Art Park in Vintondale, Pennsylvania, and artist-activist John Sabraw's toxic art initiative in southern Ohio. Both projects respond to the myriad failures of extractive capitalism through the articulation of what I term *post-extraction futurism*, an artistic approach that combines environmental science and historically situated aesthetics to remediate ecological and social injustices associated with energy extraction. Emerging from collaborations amongst artists, academics, scientists, and local communities, each project literally and metaphorically reverses the impacts of extraction through a combination of innovative water reclamation techniques, visual art, and memorial aesthetics.

Theorizing Extraction

Extraction, by definition, is an act of removal. According to the organizers of EXTRACTION, a cross-disciplinary collaborative research project carried out at the University of California, Santa Cruz, in 2017, extraction "designates capitalism's fundamental logic of *withdrawal*—of value, nutrients, energy, labor, time—from people, lands, culture, life-forms, the elements, without corresponding deposit (except as externalities of non-value in the form of pollution, waste, climate change, illness, and death)."[15] Externalities may also be described as the inbuilt "remainders" of extractive economies, those ravaged landscapes and dilapidated communities left behind by an ever-itinerant instantiation of frontier capitalism characterized by the privatization and enclosure of the commons, dispossession and displacement, boom-and-bust cycles, and the maldistribution of profits.[16] And, because extraction disproportionately takes place in communities marginalized along the lines of race, class, or ethnicity, such communities are often relegated to an afterthought, subject to a heightened risk of environmental degradation and economic volatility related to underenforced environmental regulations, a lack of institutional oversight, and volatile energy markets.[17]

Extractive fictions portray communities located adjacent to extraction sites as sacrifice zones, or geographical regions designated as expendable in the name of what government and industry stakeholders consider the greater good, often articulated in terms of economic growth, modernization, or national security. In *The Tainted Desert*, Valerie Kuletz uses the foreboding phrase "geographies of sacrifice" to describe the disproportionate effects of Cold War–era nuclear testing, uranium mining, and hazardous waste on Indigenous communities. Such activities were justified by officials as necessary for nuclear deterrence and energy development at the height of the Cold War, but also demonstrated how "racism, militarism, and economic imperialism have combined to marginalize a people and a land that many within government or industry, consciously or not, regard as expendable."[18] In Appalachia, communities and ecosystems equally bear the burden of sink status, saddled with the entangled externalities of fossil fuel extraction. For industry and government officials, this represents a necessary and acceptable cost of doing business, and cultural attachments to extraction generate widespread social license to continue such activities.

By approaching energy from a bottom-up, culturally situated examination of raw-materials extraction and its implications for ecologies and communities, I hope to advance existing conversations on the cultural significance of energy. In naming the genre *extractive fictions*, I borrow from Amitav Ghosh's notion of petrofiction, which he famously coined in his 1992 review of Saudi writer Abdul Rahman Munif's *Cities of Salt* (1984), an underrecognized novel that fictionalizes an early twentieth-century clash between U.S. oil prospectors and a Bedouin oasis community and the emergence of the modern Arab petrostate. In the review Ghosh laments what he views as a dearth of petrofiction, or literature dedicated to exploring the Oil Encounter—the collision of Euro-Western geopolitical interests, petroleum-driven capitalism, and local communities impacted by extractive processes.[19] Ghosh's essay has in part inspired the formation of the energy humanities, an emergent subfield of the environmental humanities that seeks to delineate humans' "being-in-relation" to energy and the extent to which energy, especially oil, has become utterly critical to the functioning of capitalist modernity.[20] Like petrofiction, extractive fictions represent a critical means of delineating energy's embeddedness within the cultural imagination of modernity, specifically *at the point of extraction*. However, such texts do not merely render visible the degradations and depredations inherent to extractive capitalism; they also problematize the very meaning of extraction as a cultural practice. They engage in a sort of politics of introspection, questioning the long-standing centrality of energy development to regional or national identity politics and the conflation of resource reserves with collective wealth and a so-called greater-good. Thus, the notion of extractive fiction is also suggestive of a textual landscape from which meaning can be withdrawn or "extracted," so to speak—in this case, the notion of extraction is culpable for historical patterns of social inequity and environmental injustice. Extractive fictions render visible the crumbling epistemological foundations that have historically undergirded the unchecked and often violent accumulationist tendencies of extractive capitalism. While extractive fictions do not guarantee the emergence of a transformative politics, they make space for alternative, restorative engagements between humans and nonhuman nature.

### Extraction Culture in *Strange as This Weather Has Been*

Ann Pancake's *Strange as This Weather Has Been* (hereafter *Strange*) is largely known for its nuanced exploration of the cultural politics and ecological impacts of mountaintop removal (MTR) coal mining in the Appalachian Mountains of southern West Virginia. Drawing on interviews with survivors of MTR-related social and environmental issues, the novel follows an impoverished family of six living in a landscape best described as "Vesuvian."[21] The novel has garnered recognition for its deployment of southern Gothic conventions to signify "the haunting vestiges of humans' aggressive pursuit of wealth" through extraction.[22] Pancake's protagonists contend with dynamite blasts forceful enough to crack the foundations of residents' homes, dwindling and polluted mountain streams, forest dead zones, and the constant threat of catastrophic flooding. The novel begins in the wake of just such an event—the May flood—in which a wave of coal slurry has torn through the community of Yellowroot Hollow, threatening the lives of fast-food worker Lace See; her husband, an out-of-work coal miner named Jimmy Make; and their four children, Bant, Corey, Dane, and Tommy. Though the flood spares human lives, it drastically alters the physical and psychic topographies of the community, washing away lawns and homes and exacerbating widespread economic and ecological anxieties. Much of the novel's plot revolves around an ongoing debate between Lace and Jimmy. Lace refuses to leave and becomes involved in anti-MTR activism, while Jimmy urges her to move the family to pursue a livable future elsewhere.

MTR coal mining began gradually replacing subsurface mining operations in Appalachia in the 1990s after an amendment to the Clean Air Act lowered nationwide emissions standards. The method was developed as an economically viable means to extract cleaner-burning, low-sulfur coal abundant in southern West Virginia. Ironically, the local environmental costs have been drastic, as MTR has been blamed for the "decapitation" of a once lush, hospitable mountain region. The MTR process involves the literal removal of mountaintops to access hard-to-reach coal seams. Forests are clear-cut, topsoil is stripped, and underlying earth and rock are blasted intensively to remove overburden, which is then placed into a fill, an area used for waste disposal. Coal seams are then plundered using a dragline, a piece of machinery that can approach twenty stories in height.[23] The impacts of this process are wide-ranging: in addition to rampant violations of the Clean Water Act through illegal dumping, one of the most pointed effects of MTR has been erosion and water contamination. Digging, blasting, and the construction of temporary infrastructure such as access roads and drainage ditches turn large loads of sediment and chemical waste into watersheds, elevating stream pH to dangerous levels. Fills, typically situated atop streams at the head of mountain hollows, stifle water dispersal, alter seasonal water cycles, and increase the possibility of flooding and the release of coal slurry, a toxic cocktail of chemical waste and sediments typically stored behind earthen impoundment dams.[24]

The ecological impacts of MTR in West Virginia parallel patterns of economic marginalization that have been unfolding for decades. In the early to mid-twentieth century, especially during the Coal Boom era of the 1930s through the 1950s, coal towns prospered and grew rapidly to accommodate workers lured to the region to answer growing labor demands.[25] For a time, coal mining was framed as an essentially patriotic endeavor, essential to the success of the nation. Woodrow Wilson even exempted coal workers from the draft during World War I, citing coal as critical to the war effort.[26] Beginning in the mid-1950s, however, mechanization began to drive down labor demands, spurring worker flight. Combined with coal companies' anti-unionization efforts and increased dependence on out-of-state, non-union contract labor, unemployment levels in coal country have been rising steadily, turning previously prosperous communities into ghost towns.[27] MTR represents a continuation of this trajectory: it requires only a third of the workers to extract the same amount of coal from subsurface mines.[28] According to 2010 figures, coal mining employment levels have declined, in large part due to MTR, by more than 50 percent since 1975.[29] Moreover, by promoting a false jobs-versus-environment dichotomy to promote its business model, the coal industry has perpetuated what has been described as a form of "internal colonialism" in which wealthy urban centers reap disproportionate benefits from coal extraction, and rural "resource colonies" bear the burden of environmental degradation and unstable employment prospects. Many communities have become economically dependent on coal and are therefore less likely to oppose unregulated or irresponsible extraction and waste dumping activities.[30] Rich in resources but impoverished, Appalachia arguably bears a "resource curse," a central feature of extractive capitalism in which resource-rich regions of the world nonetheless fail to reap social benefits expected to arise from a burgeoning economy and are instead plagued by poverty, conflict, and environmental degradation.[31]

The novel's dual interest in rendering visible the impacts of MTR on humans and nonhumans is apparent in its cover art, which bears a photo of Appalachian artist Jeff Chapman-Crane's mixed-media sculpture *The Agony of Gaia*. Composed of both natural and artificial materials like clay and Styrofoam, the sculpture was designed to raise awareness and narrativize the impacts of MTR. The sculpture features the figure of a woman, signifying Gaia, Greek goddess of the earth, lying in the fetal position, hands covering her weeping face. Her bare flesh forms the features of a partially strip-mined mountain; her arms and neck, still covered with trees, give way to a lower body devoid of vegetation, scarred with roads and crawling with draglines and bulldozers. Engraved at the base of the sculpture is a poem written by Chapman-Crane decrying the violence of MTR, represented in the sculpture as a simultaneous affront to landscapes and human bodies, ecosystems, and communities. As Chapman-Crane has explained in interviews, he deliberately chose the image of Gaia, a figure external to Judeo-Christian traditions, as a necessary metaphor to "to invoke the creative and critical thinking needed to break the historical connection between Appalachians and the coal industry."[32]

*Strange*'s aesthetics of MTR-related environmental dystopia lend credence to the idea that, as literary critic Heather Houser suggests, the novel ultimately "conceives of activism as a process of making visible."[33] According to Houser, Lace exposes the social and ecological impacts of MTR through "environmental engagement"—by walking the forests, documenting damage, and circulating photographic evidence and letters within the community.[34] But the novel's activist propensities arguably extend beyond a documentary function. By framing coal as antithetical to a greater good, Pancake writes against what sociologist Rebecca Scott has called a culture of extraction, which has long pervaded the coalfields of Appalachia. In a place where the extractive economy has become synonymous with prosperity and central to regional cultural identity, Scott writes, coal "can either be told as an exemplar of an American story of progress and technological development or as a story of social injustice and conflict."[35] The former, often viewed as symbolic of American exceptionalism, was a key part of President Trump's economic nationalist rhetoric in which he promised to end the so-called war on coal waged by federal regulatory overreach on poor rural coal communities. Yet this established regional affinity for extraction is complicated by longstanding cultural stereotypes of Appalachia as a region predominately populated by "hillbillies, white trash, and other poor whites," an assumption reified and reinforced in national and regional cultural representations that reproduce tropes of social backwardness and moral abjection. Such (mis)representations have served to stigmatize Appalachians on "quasi-racializing terms," as deviating from the idealized figure of the productive, patriotic (white) American citizen.[36] As Scott notes, such "epistemologies of disgust and social distance help create the conditions of possibility for some of the most dangerous environmental exploitation in the United States and the designation of Appalachia as a sacrifice zone."[37] In other words, the combination of local cultural pride associated with coal's historical status as an important national commodity and the simultaneous stigmatization of Appalachia as culturally and socially inferior, and therefore expendable, contributes to ongoing environmental and economic injustices associated with extraction.

Water, in *Strange*, signifies both ecological degradation and the erosion of the region's intense ties to the coal industry. Polluted streams and ponds are ubiquitous, contributing to the novel's deployment of what Lawrence Buell famously called toxic discourse, a mode of writing pervaded by a "fear of the poisoned world."[38] The most textured descriptions of toxicity occur in sections of the novel that follow Lace's mechanically inclined son Corey, for whom exploring nearby streams littered with industrial debris is "like walking the aisle of a Walmart."[39] By likening a romp in a polluted stream to a gleeful journey through a low-end retail store, Pancake emphasizes a central paradox of extraction culture: coal's simultaneous fetishization by, and exploitation of, the working poor. Throughout the novel, Corey and his younger brother Tommy move about this grotesque "playground" in search of metal scrap, splashing about in the toxicity of a "pigshit-colored creek" and ponds with "water opaque as mustard and colored like the inside of a sick baby's diaper."[40] In a moment of dramatic irony, the region's perceived expendability is affirmed during a literal scene of sacrifice in which Corey crashes a stolen four-wheeler into a chemical-laden catchment pond and drowns.[41]

Other characters also experience the horror of degraded landscapes through past trauma associated with industrial disaster. Avery Taylor, a man in his mid-twenties, repeatedly reflects on his childhood experience as a survivor of the real-life Buffalo Creek flood that took place in Logan County, West Virginia, in February 1972. When an impoundment dam collapsed during a period of heavy rain, 130 million gallons of coal slurry gushed through Buffalo Creek hollow, at times reaching heights of 30 feet. The flood devastated sixteen coal towns, killing more than 125 people and displacing more than 4,000.[42] In the novel, Avery recalls being washed miles downstream and waking up to take stock of his surroundings after regaining consciousness on an unfamiliar hillside: "The waters have peeled the railroad right off the ground, scattered ties everywhere, then coiled up the rails into lassoes. Water did that, [he] thinks."[43] His mother Mrs. Taylor is also preoccupied with water, her constant reminisces about Buffalo Creek ending with a refrain that another "wall of black water" will return on Judgement Day.[44] Her flood-related trauma transverses generations, too. After listening to Mrs. Taylor's sermons warning of an impending, watery apocalypse, Lace's emotionally sensitive twelve-year-old son Dane (who cooks and cleans for Mrs. Taylor) begins to "feel the weight. The water hovering overhead."[45]

Lace and Bant exhibit the novel's most pointed anti-MTR rhetoric, but their opposition to coal emerges less from daily encounters with toxic topographies or disaster-related trauma than from a productive tension between their sense of closeness with rural Appalachia and socially conditioned difficulties ascribing its degradation to coal extraction. As such, they cannot be described as conventional environmentalists. Lace comes from a coal family, and as she witnesses her father dying from black lung disease contracted from decades in the mines, she struggles to square her place-based identity with the dangers of coal extraction. Her father's lungs are "being buried by it, by coal," but to Lace coal "is earth, which is this place.... We eat off it, dig in it, doctor from it, work under it ... we grow up swaddled in it."[46] Likewise, when Bant sees photographic evidence of MTR's impacts on nearby mountains, she is incredulous, describing the images as taboo items, "like looking at pictures of naked people. Like looking at pictures of dead bodies."[47] She is also conflicted when her boyfriend, an older, out-of-state contract miner, urges her to accept things the way they are: "If you-all wanna stay in here, you want your brothers to have jobs, your husband, you better just get used to this here."[48] On the other hand, both Lace and Bant harbor a deep affinity for their mountainous surroundings based on their time spent foraging—an activity necessitated by their poverty—and fostering a kinship with what Bant calls "the deep of here."[49] After the May flood, reverence gives way to anxiety; the novel's protagonists frequently remark about the "threat of rain" or impending precipitation, a narrative tic that betrays a growing awareness of their residence in a sacrificial landscape.[50] When Lace visits friends in a nearby community ravaged by floods and dynamite blasts, she describes it as a "beautiful painting that had been ripped in two."[51] When Bant discovers a second impoundment dam above the family's home, she imagines the next flood: "Our house would be the first to go."[52] In a momentary bid to numb the pain of loss, she tells herself "*I don't care.*"[53] Here, alienation becomes anguish, as Bant experiences intense feelings of ecological grief, a condition that has gained increasing recognition against the backdrop of the accelerating climate crisis to describe "the grief felt in response to experienced or anticipated ecological losses, including the loss of species, ecosystems and meaningful landscapes due to acute or chronic environmental change."[54]

As Scott notes, a significant aspect of Appalachian identity arises from a deep sense of indigeneity, or what she describes as "other ways of relating to the land" that conflict with the cultural role of extraction.[55] Though problematic for obvious reasons, the descriptor "indigenous" has often been used metonymically to refer to the supposed primitivism of early European settlers in Appalachia who have traditionally lived "close to the land" through subsistence lifestyles.[56] While this construction simultaneously enacts an erasure of Native culture in the area and further marginalizes rural Appalachian communities, some anti-MTR activists nevertheless make claims to indigeneity as the environmental ethos driving their yearning for a pre-extraction past.[57] Lace and Bant's activism emerges from this dynamic and as a result both fit the more "nontraditional" profile of anti-MTR activists as white women and first-time activists from coal families who espouse community values, who have no broad environmentalist agenda beyond remediating local environmental and public health issues, and who have come to these insights through their own life experiences, and are thus firsthand witnesses to the impacts of MTR.[58] In the novel's closing lines, Bant resolves to "tell Lace what [she's] found"[59]—a second impoundment dam, a renewed threat of flooding—and, in doing so, she overcomes feelings of both skepticism and grief and announces her commitment to fighting MTR. Through this activist turn, the novel does important epistemological work, fostering the conditions of possibility for a reconnection with, and resurrection of, a sacrificed landscape. In doing so, it envisions an important first step toward imagining a post-extraction Appalachia.

### Fracking and Post-Coal Culture in Pennsylvania

There is a growing consensus that fracking poses significant environmental risks. Groundwater contamination is a primary concern; numerous studies have confirmed elevated levels of methane in aquifers and residential wells abutting drill sites,[60] and industry watchdogs have become increasingly concerned about dangers posed by leaky, poorly regulated wastewater injection wells.[61] In Oklahoma, fracking has been blamed for a five- to tenfold increase in seismic events.[62] Yet the fracking process and its ecological impacts occur largely out of sight. During the drilling process, a water-chemical solution is injected deep underground at high-pressures to free up pockets of natural gas, and while 80 percent of fracking fluids return to the surface in the form of "produced water," most of it is piped into tanks, trucked away, and pumped back into wastewater wells deep underground.[63] Visual indicators of the actual act of drilling are difficult to detect beyond enigmatic drill-site infrastructure dotting the pastures and backyards of gas country. Contamination tends to unfold slowly and unspectacularly, detectable only through anecdote or rigorous scientific studies that take time to complete. In short, while gas extraction represents a particularly strong marker for the emergence of new sacrifice zones, its ecological effects fall short of the visual spectacle of MTR, epitomizing Rob Nixon's conception of slow violence, in which ecological degradation "is neither spectacular nor instantaneous, but rather incremental and accretive."[64]

The slow and concealed violence of fracking also inhabits the exploitative practices of oil and gas companies seeking to leverage impoverished rural communities—often reeling from the slow implosion of coal markets—into permitting drilling in pastures, backyards, and public spaces. Research has shown that gas wells are typically more concentrated in low-income rural communities that lack the institutional support or political capital to engage with oil and gas companies as equals.[65] Residents also face a slew of obstacles when seeking information and industry accountability, including the legally protected reticence of gas companies to disclose chemicals used during the drilling process.[66] In one study, researchers interviewed over thirty farmers in rural Pennsylvania who had leased land for gas extraction and found that landowners were largely denied insight into or participation in drilling and extraction processes. When environmental concerns arose, most lessees were unable to gain information about drilling processes and chemical usage.[67] Some contended with corporate bullying tactics, too; in one instance, a lessee reported that when they organized a meeting at a local church to discuss concerns with gas company representatives, company officials arrived with armed guards.[68] Moreover, pro-gas public relations campaigns often manipulate public opinion by associating fracking with patriotism and regional pride and citing methodologically questionable and rhetorically deceptive scientific studies that insist hydraulic fracturing is safe and economically viable.[69] This propensity for disinformation is broadly reflective of an industry that has long thrived on deception, even at the legislative level. When the Energy Policy Act was passed in 2005, for example, it included the infamous "Halliburton loophole," a provision buried deep within the bill's language to exempt hydraulic fracturing operations from key provisions of the Safe Drinking Water Act. Included at the behest of then-vice president Dick Cheney, former CEO of drilling supplier Halliburton, the provision amounts to a single, inauspicious paragraph in the vast 550-page bill.[70] This development is particularly harrowing for residents of Appalachian gas country, many of whom depend on private wells. Moreover, the loophole seemingly undercuts industry claims as to the safety of fracking; if it were truly safe, no exemption would be necessary.

If the modus operandi of the natural gas industry is willful and deliberate obfuscation, then *Shale Play: Poems and Photographs from the Fracking Fields*—a 2019 collection of poems and photographs by poet Julia Spicher Kasdorf and photographer Steven Rubin—works to demystify the natural gas industry in central and western Pennsylvania. Drawing on conversations and interviews with rural residents, *Shale Play* evokes modernist poet Muriel Rukeyser's *The Book of the Dead*, a sequence of poems she wrote in 1938 in response to the Hawk's Nest Tunnel disaster in Gauley Bridge, West Virginia, seven years prior. After 764 mostly Black migrant workers were killed due to exposure to silica dust while working on a hydropower project for Union Carbide, Rukeyser visited Gauley Bridge and later authored the poems based on congressional testimony, media reports, and scientific and medical documents.[71] The work of Kasdorf and Rubin aggregates testimony in a similar fashion, drawing on conversations and interviews with people in diners and at public meetings as well as research from transcripts and miscellaneous industry and legal documents. Rubin's photographs punctuate Kasdorf's poetry, which she describes as "strained beneath its documentary freight," in much the same way the photographs of Nancy Naumburg, who accompanied Rukeyser to Gauley Bridge, enhance Rukeyser's testimonial verses in the 2018 reissue of *The Book of the Dead* from West Virginia University Press.[72]

Rubin's photos focus largely on infrastructure. In the book's foreword, writer Barbara Hurd alerts readers to the fact that more than 20 percent of Rubin's photographs are of roads, a testament to the exploitation of rural infrastructure by gas companies and a reminder that "to alter roads in a rural county is to alter its residents' orientation to place."[73] Many of his photographs also consider water. One image depicts a narrow road clogged with water trucks, a caption in the appendix reminding readers of the many millions of gallons of water needed to frack a well and the impacts of heavy truck traffic on local infrastructure and carbon emissions.[74] The relegation of photo captions to the appendix, in fact, can be read as a comment on the representational difficulties of fracking more generally. Only after consulting the appendix do we learn that one image, which appears to show raindrops making impressions on the surface of a puddle or pond, actually depicts methane bubbles breaking the surface of a family's spring near a drill site in Fayette County.[75] Such dissonance seems intentional: Kasdorf's long-form poems function as captions, with explanatory blurbs relegated to the back of the volume. The abovementioned photograph is situated adjacent to the closing lines of Kasdorf's poem "A Mother Near the West Virginia Line Considers Public Health." The poem is written through the voice of a mother whose land has been leased out from under her for drilling and who worries as crayfish turn up dead in a nearby stream and her sons develop unexplained stomach pains and nosebleeds. "We didn't have internet before this," explains the poem's narrator, "but you have to follow the permits / because the industry tells you nothing . . . Let them think I'm too dumb to back down. My son / won't play on any T-ball team with industry logos on their shirts."[76] The tension between speaking out against exploitative industry practices and social ostracization is also evident in a poem entitled "What This Picture Can't Tell You." Juxtaposed with a Rubin photograph of protestors holding picket signs in a parking lot, the poem describes a scene in which a man hides his face behind his sign as cars drive by.[77]

Kasdorf's poem "F Word" captures the disconnect between the violence of well drilling and water injection and the semantics of deceptive industry public relation campaigns, which seek to highlight the process as safe and transparent. The opening lines, which are prefaced by a side note stating, "*The industry spelling of fracking is actually fracing,*" read:

> Without the *k*, it looks less violent:
> *Water pressure creates fractures that allow*
>
> *the oil and gas to escape*—as if they were
> trapped—*under tight regulatory control.*

100   Post-Extraction Futurisms

The tension between a view of fracking as ecologically violent or financially emancipatory persists throughout the poem. The phrases in italics, representing language plucked from an industry pamphlet or website, are subverted by cynically critical unitalicized phrases. The phrase "*water pressure creates*" suggests the generative nature of water (chemicals unmentioned) as it liberates natural gas (and revenue). But the remainder of the poem undermines this industry-friendly narrative, equating the forceful injection of water, in a bid to free pent-up fossil-fuel deposits, to rape. "*Frack her til she blows*, says the T-shirt stretched / over a roughneck's belly at the Williamsport Wegman's," conflating sexual and terrestrial violence against a feminized landscape. Two stanzas later, the verb "Frack" affirms such disturbing connotations: "*Are you going to say what the word suggests / a student timidly asks, to women, I mean?*" The violence of fracking and unwanted sexual penetration can be traced to the hard "K," which effectively masks the violence of water weaponized for extractive processes. By the poem's closing lines, the hostility of water is suppressed, giving way to surface ruminations on a "fracket"—an old jacket worn to fraternity parties "that won't matter if it gets stolen / or left behind on flagstone patio, splattered / with someone else's vomit." As terrestrial violator, water lurks unseen as a sexual predator might slink about a college party, a corollary to gas-rich landscapes, abundant with "deposits" to be fracked by force. "F Word" ultimately comments on the tension between hyper-masculine tendencies toward terrestrial and sexual violence and a process whereby these tendencies and their aftermaths are disavowed or obscured.[78]

Kasdorf's poem explicitly raises questions about consent and malintent that bubble beneath the surface of Jennifer Haigh's 2015 novel *Heat and Light*. Like *Strange as This Weather Has Been*, Haigh's novel unfolds in an economically depressed pocket of Appalachia. The events of the novel largely take place in fictional Bakerton, Pennsylvania, a declining coal town that serves as the setting for Haigh's previous novel *Baker Towers* (2005) and her short story collection *News from Heaven* (2013), both of which explore the convulsions and contradictions of extraction culture in the twenty-first century. *Heat and Light* is a character-driven exploration of class and poverty in rural America against the backdrop of the gas boom of the early 2000s, which for many communities has represented a potential path to restored prosperity in the wake of coal's decline. Unlike the 2012 film *Promised Land*, which frames the gas industry as monolithically craven, *Heat and Light* humanizes interactions between Bakerton's economically vulnerable inhabitants, oil and gas representatives, and environmental activists. To the extent to which the novel can be said to have a plot, it unfolds in a series of intricately threaded narrative vignettes that attend to the daily struggles of and interactions amongst an expansive cast of stakeholders in the region's extractive economy, including Bobby Frame, a dogged energy company sales representative; the Devlin family, deeply in debt and eager to sign a gas lease; Mack and Rena, organic dairy farmers skeptical of newly arrived gas companies; and Herc, a roughneck drill rig manager from Texas. While Pancake's novel highlights environmental degradation, *Heat and Light*'s class themes overshadow its ecological messages.[79]

*Heat and Light* differs significantly from more well-known engagements with fracking, such as Josh Fox's documentary *Gasland*.[80] Fox, who won a directorial Emmy for the film and was nominated for an Academy Award for best documentary, embarks on a sleuth-like journey to uncover fracking's impact on local water supplies, going house-to-house from his home in western Pennsylvania to the gas fields of Texas, Oklahoma, and Colorado. As a banjo-playing, self-proclaimed "natural gas detective," he does less to document the cultural politics of natural gas than to raise awareness of its public health risks and the obstacles encountered by citizens seeking to hold oil and gas companies accountable.[81] *Gasland* earned Fox widespread praise for bringing fracking "into the nation's living rooms" and contributed to the perception of natural gas extraction as a spectacularly pollutive enterprise.[82] From the famous flammable water scene—in which residents of Weld County, Colorado, light methane-contaminated tap water on fire—to jars of yellowed, turpentine-scented well water and exploding backyard gas wells, Fox leverages his medium to render visible the ecological stakes of fracking.[83]

Haigh is certainly aware of environmental concerns surrounding fracking and has acknowledged the influence of intense antifracking opposition movements in Pennsylvania on her writing process.[84] However, *Heat and Light*, as the first serious literary response to the cultural politics of fracking, offers an account of what could arguably be described as a post-coal culture of extraction in which key elements of coal-era extraction culture—the mythos of energy development as a path to progress and grandiose claims as to Appalachia's centrality to narratives of American exceptionalism—persist even in the face of coal's decline.[85] Rather than rendering visible extraction's ecological impacts, as Pancake does, Haigh narrativizes the collision between poor rural communities and an industry that leverages poverty to gain access to fossil fuels. The novel is pervaded by a historical subtext that emphasizes Pennsylvania's originary status in the U.S. energy economy and an unnamed narrator that emphasizes, in the novel's opening pages, that "more than most places, Pennsylvania is what lies beneath."[86] The phrase "what lies beneath" is multivalent: Bakerton is not merely defined by a resource-rich topography and the perpetual presence of extraction sites but also by the suspected degradation of local water supplies, a gas industry that thrives on misinformation and deception, and an internal battle being waged by residents and neighbors over the post-coal future of Appalachia.

For example, Rich and Shelby Devlin eagerly sell drilling rights on their property so that Rich can quit his low-paying prison guard position and revive his 40-acre family farm. For them, the presence of gas on their property amounts to what door-to-door gas "salesman" Bobby Frame calls *"buried treasure"*—a path out of paycheck-to-paycheck poverty.[87] However, after their water begins to take on a strong chemical odor, they have little recourse beyond buying bottled water from Walmart. Attempts to confirm fracking-related contamination are largely stifled by a confusing bureaucracy of corporate offices and private contractors. When Rich questions a drill crew in his backyard, they deny responsibility and disassociate themselves from the Devlins' original contract with the gas company. "You'll have to take that up with Dark Elephant," Rich is told. "We're Stream Solutions. We're subcontractors."[88] Results from a water test administered by the Pennsylvania Department of Environmental Protection prove inconclusive, too. The test confirms the presence of methane in their water supply, but the state tells Rich that it "appears to be related to background conditions" not gas drilling. The raw lab report is no help to the poorly educated Rich, whose "eyes slide over the columns of figures, values for methane, ethane, SMCLs. He has no idea what he's looking at."[89] Unable to obtain answers from corporate and government stakeholders, Rich and Shelby can do little other than "*be vigilant*," the lone advice provided by state authorities.[90]

*Heat and Light* never quite affirms Rich's suspicions, nor does it offer hard evidence of fracking's broader impacts on Bakerton's water supply. Such ecological equivocating can arguably be viewed as a metaphor for the industry writ large. It speaks to undisclosed practices, disavowed aftermaths, deceptive public relations, inscrutable institutional hierarchies, and the absence of corporate responsibility. Rich's bewildering experience, from the giddy anticipation of a financial windfall to the inability to find someone to take responsibility for his contaminated well, reveals a critical disconnect between the optimistic semantics of industry marketing and the ever-present possibility of environmental catastrophe. Rather than approaching fracking through the spectacle of contamination, as Pancake does in *Strange*, Haigh's novel is pervaded by speculation and suspicion. When organic dairy farmers Mack and Rena refuse to sign a gas lease to preserve the integrity of their business, for example, the gas company is legally prohibited from drilling beneath neighboring properties. As a result, the women are pressured and intimidated by neighbors eager to gain a financial windfall; as one frustrated neighbor tells Mack, "Once you start taking money out of my pocket, I got to say something."[91] Later, the women lose an account with a farm-to-table restaurant in Pittsburgh whose owner tells Rena that "our customers read the newspaper. They know what's going on in your part of the world."[92] The restaurant owner is less environmentally savvy than attentive, her fear of tainted water affirmed by the region's television and billboard advertisements for the services of personal injuries attorney Paul Zacharias who, in his quest to obtain "FrackountabilityTM," implores the public: "Does your tap water have a foul odor? Is it cloudy or greasy looking? How's your health?"[93]

Ultimately, *Shale Play* and *Heat and Light* confront the irrepresentability of hydraulic fracturing and its aftermaths by calling attention to the ways in which the natural gas industry disrupts the social fabric of rural Appalachia, saddling communities with the burden of proof in the face of environmental risk and forcing them to choose between financial rewards and a sacrificed landscape or economic marginalization. While Pancake's *Strange* diagnoses the visible symptoms of MTR through the spectacle of decapitated mountains, washed-out hollows, and toxic streams, Haigh's novel, Kasdorf's poetry, and Rubin's photographs underscore new realities in post-coal America. Those who suspect their water has been spoiled by gas drilling must navigate a labyrinth of institutions, from state environmental departments to private subcontractors, corporate liaisons, and even the American healthcare system. As Hurd speculates in the foreword to *Shale Play*, perhaps listening to the stories of frack-weary rural Pennsylvanians will sway policymakers.[94] And while *Heat and Light*'s seeming lack of resolution could arguably be ascribed to representational difficulties inherent to crafting a coherent fracking narrative, a process physically and institutionally shrouded in uncertainty, for the novel to proselytize about the ecological risks of fracking would be to undermine its central point. Debates surrounding fracking are as much about environmental impacts as they are a battle for the soul of Appalachia in the twenty-first century, the future of which may or may not be defined by new and novel instantiations of an extraction culture that has pervaded the region for more than a century. If, as Haigh insists, Pennsylvania is "what lies beneath," then struggles surrounding fracking likewise unfold beneath the surface—between neighbors, friends, business owners, and community leaders, in kitchens and backyards, on front porches, and in city council meetings.

## Post-Extraction Futurism and Reclamation Art

Extractive fictions render visible long-standing patterns of social and ecological violence associated with extraction culture in Appalachia. By exposing the epistemological limits of extractive capitalism, they make space for the articulation of a just transition beyond the destructive path-dependence of the modern energy economy. Two such visions stand out: AMD & Art Park in Vintondale, Pennsylvania, and artist-activist John Sabraw's toxic art initiatives in southeastern Ohio. Both projects exhibit an aesthetics of what I term *post-extraction futurism*, wherein extraction is repurposed as a critical method to envision livable, equitable futures. If extraction can be understood as an act of removal resulting in an array of externalities or "remainders," then post-extraction futurism harnesses extractive processes to heal ecosystems and communities. For AMD &

Art Park and Sabraw's toxic art initiative, healing involves the physical removal of coal-related toxins from ecosystems and, through memorial art, prompting communities to connect a pollutive past to visions of a healthy, habitable Appalachia. The notion of post-extraction futurism connects with the existing impetus within energy studies to explore the social and political changes necessary for a post–fossil fuel energy transition. As the Petrocultures Research Group at the University of Alberta explains in *After Oil*, an equitable energy transition is impossible without "changing how we *think, imagine, see,* and *hear*"—a task best met by engaging with literary texts, visual art, performance, and scholarship.[95] Extractive fictions work to enact change by interrogating the values and belief systems driving extractive modes of accumulation and making space for alternatives. Post-extraction futurism renders such change tactile and tangible.

The AMD & Art Park in Vintondale has been described by founder T. Allan Comp as "art that works" in part because of an innovative water filtration system that removes AMD—groundwater tainted by sulfuric acid and iron oxides—from nearby Blacklick Creek, which has been inundated by leftover toxins from the Vinton Colliery Site since its closure in the 1950s.[96] Completed in 2005 through the collaborative efforts of Comp, environmental artist Stacy Levy, landscape architect Julie Bargmann, and hydrologist Robert Deason, the park emerged from a previously unused tract on the town's western edge. The filtration system itself is a work of art. Water is cleansed using passive water treatment methods: Contaminated creek water is rerouted into a pond lined with limestone, which naturally filters dissolved iron from water, and is then discharged downhill into other ponds where it is treated further (see fig. 7). A thousand trees were strategically planted beside the ponds so that in the fall, the changing leaves of the many different tree species would mimic the changing color of water, as it is progressively cleansed during its journey downhill (see fig. 8). Levy, part of the park's core design team, describes the filtration system as "doing while telling" by giving a visual indication of the water filtration process in real time as the autumn trees "vivify the process from acid to basic."[97] The 35-acre park also functions as a walkable, multiuse community space featuring multiple art exhibits, including a wetlands section with a pathway through colliery ruins; the

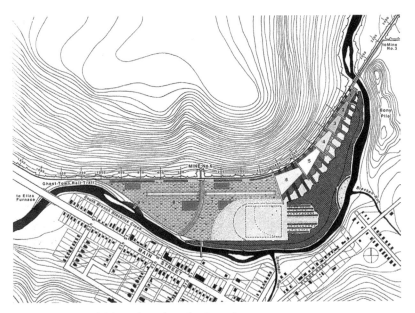

7. AMD & Art Park blueprint. Photo by Stacy Levy.

8. AMD & Art Park holding pond. Photo by Stacy Levy.

Miner's Memorial, a polished black stone framed by a reconstructed timber mine portal and etched with images of early twentieth-century miners; a recreation area; and a large tile mosaic map bordered by historical photographs of the mine site.[98] According to Comp, the park is designed to "symbolize the success of local residents in healing these waters and this whole site, not only by finishing a job unknowingly abandoned by past generations, but also by developing a new community asset for their families and their families' futures."[99]

Artist-activist John Sabraw and environmental engineer Guy Riefler, both professors at Ohio University, have taken a similarly innovative approach to confront the legacies of Appalachia's extractive economy. Riefler's research focuses on the chemical and biological dimensions of water pollution, including AMD, which often transforms streams into gaudy hues of orange, yellow, and red. When he discovered AMD was chemically similar to commercial paint, he began working with his students to develop a method for filtering iron oxides from contaminated stream water, converting it into pigments, and returning clean water to streambeds. While refining the process, he began collaborating with Sabraw, a pigment specialist who has long used natural materials in his own artwork. Sabraw has since refined and incorporated the bold, wide-ranging pigments into his paintings, resulting in collections like "Chroma" (see fig. 9), which has been featured in galleries across the United States and garnered substantial media coverage as toxic art. In his artist's statement, Sabraw explains that the goal of his work is to understand the "underground excoriations" that are coal mines and the ways in which they affect human-nonhuman relations.[100] In 2018 Sabraw and Riefler teamed-up with a hydrologist to design and build a pilot treatment and processing facility on the banks of Sunday Creek in the small town of Corning, Ohio. The goal is to prove scalability of the process and, through a partnership with commercial paint-maker Gamblin, sell pigments and reinvest the proceeds in local stream cleanup efforts. The team crowdsourced over $30,000 and solicited input from residents to construct an art wall around the facility featuring AMD paints.[101] The community, with which the team has worked on a one-on-one basis, was receptive to the project. Residents were excited at the prospect of a clean-running creek where many people fished and swam before it

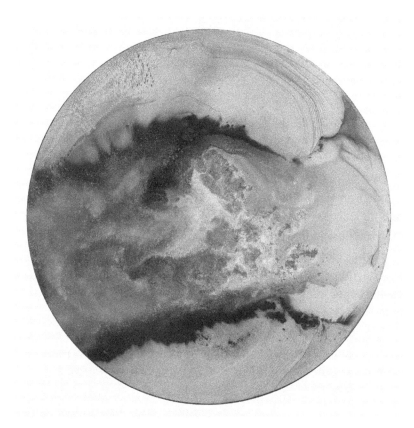

9. *Chroma S4 Chimaera* by John Sabraw, 2017.

was contaminated by acid mine runoff. Working in conjunction with his students, Sabraw hopes the wall will "tell the story about how the pollution got here," explain the water treatment process, make a case for the necessity of the plant, and highlight the history of Corning, once a thriving coal town that has been declining since the mid-1950s.[102]

By acknowledging coal's historic centrality to regional cultural identity, both AMD &Art Park and Sabraw's toxic art initiative function as zones of transition between a pollutive industrial past and restorative visions for the future. Each engages in a form of material storytelling, joining the Pueblo Grande Archaeological Park in Phoenix (see chapter 1) to prompt viewers to imagine just, sustainable futures by reconsidering our relationships to the past.[103] By combining memorial aesthetics with science-based environmental reclamation processes, AMD & Art

Park and Sabraw's water filtration plant could arguably be viewed as ecological "counter monuments" in the spirit of historian James Young's famous characterization of Holocaust memorials in Germany as "brazen, painfully self-conscious memorial spaces conceived to challenge the very premises of their being."[104] The traditional monument—a Nazi-favored propagandistic medium—has historically functioned as a "state-sponsored memory of a national past," meant to entrench national narratives and uphold collective values. By contrast, the counter monument serves a subversive purpose, both in form and meaning, celebrating "its own physical impermanence . . . and the contingency of all meaning and memory."[105] Likewise, if coal can be understood as symbolic of a quintessentially U.S. narrative of progress, with extraction culture its epistemological embodiment, AMD & Art Park and Sabraw's art subvert that narrative, memorializing extraction not as emblematic of some bygone era of "progress," but as an impermanent, replaceable practice the pollutive effects of which can be extracted, so to speak, from landscapes and communities impacted by and beholden to the fossil fuel economy.

Highlighting the region's extractive heritage is critical to environmental reclamation efforts in a region that has a reputation for being skeptical of outside environmental groups who profess altruistic intentions, where energy extraction remains central to place-based identity, and where communities often display an "appallingly passive acceptance of environmental conditions."[106] To overcome these challenges, the AMD & Art Park team took pains to consider the complex cultural and historical forces shaping the region. "AMD is more than just a water problem," insists Comp. "It is deeply emblematic of the economic and environmental abandonment throughout Appalachian Coal Country."[107] While scientific approaches to reclamation can be materially effective, Comp argues, approaching degraded environments as cultural artifacts enables a more community-based approach to reclamation.[108] The siting of AMD & Art Park reflects these ambitions: Vintondale has long been defined by coal, both in its heyday as a company town controlled by Vinton Coal Company and its decline after the last underground mine closed in 1950, sparking an exodus and plunging the town into decades of slow economic decline.[109] By acknowledging local history and working with the community to remediate its worst effects, the project became an opportunity for civic healing that mobilizes citizens to prioritize healthy environments and communities over economic development.[110] Likewise, Sabraw's treatment plant and art wall works to connect southeastern Ohio's extractive past to a more livable future. He explains its anticipated role as a structure that "educates and celebrates" its location in the town of Corning. Though some locals were initially skeptical of the project, by involving the community, Sabraw hopes to emphasize that the wall "isn't a tombstone for their town, but ... something that they might look forward to."[111]

While levels of economic prosperity generated by the mid-century coal boom are unlikely to return to the region, extractive fictions and the post-extraction futurist aesthetics of Comp's AMD & Art Park and Sabraw's toxic art initiative can be viewed as representative of a broader movement committed to advancing radically inclusive visions of a habitable, thriving post-extraction Appalachia. This includes the editorial staff at the *Appalachian Voice*, a bimonthly newspaper that covers environmental and cultural news throughout the region; the Appalshop media arts collective and education center in Whitesburg, Kentucky, which supports community-generated film, radio, music, and performance art that explores environmental, economic, and cultural issues throughout Appalachia;[112] and the editors of Queer Appalachia and the *Electric Dirt* zine, which shares stories of "queers in nature" and, as they explain, takes pride in "foraging for pieces of ourselves within the intersections of coal mines and class, race and religion, food justice and colonialism."[113] These culturally reflexive, community-driven efforts to redefine Appalachia beyond its historical ties to the national energy economy each offer models for equitable post-extraction futures throughout the region. While extractive fictions challenge the epistemological foundations of extractive capitalism by rendering visible its socioecological externalities, post-extraction futurisms connect a long history of ecological degradation and social marginalization to a reclaimed future unfolding in real-time. By striving to change the ways communities think, imagine, see, and hear about extraction, each offer hope and a roadmap for equitable transitions into a post-extraction future.

# 4 /

## On the Wrong Side of the Levee

*Sea Level Rise Narratives in the Decade of the Green New Deal*

When the Intergovernmental Panel on Climate Change (IPCC) issued the special report *Global Warming of 1.5° C* in October 2018, it generated numerous headlines about its claim that there remain just twelve years to reduce global carbon emissions and avoid climate catastrophe.[1] Among the many risks associated with a failure to limit the average global temperature increase to 1.5° C, the report projected catastrophic sea level rise of up to 2.5 feet by 2100. Potential impacts include significant deterioration of the Greenland ice sheet, the inundation of low-lying islands and coastal regions, increased severity of coastal storm surge flooding, the salination of coastal groundwater, and the displacement of tens of millions of people.[2] As one of three special reports prepared by the IPCC as part of the sixth assessment cycle, the report on warming preceded the *Special Report on the Ocean and Cryosphere in a Changing Climate*, released in September 2019. The numbers presented in that report are even starker: the Greenland ice sheet and the Antarctic ice sheet have been losing mass rapidly for several years, driving global mean sea level rise to unprecedented levels over the last century, and extreme sea level rise events are projected to occur increasingly frequently—up to once per year—by 2050. The report also notes that nearly 700 million people reside in low-lying coastal zones. Due to projected increases in storm intensity and frequency, coupled with rising sea levels and other impacts, yearly damages from coastal flooding are expected to double or even triple by 2100 in population-dense coastal regions. Adaptation to these threats, the report concludes, requires not just intergovernmental coordination, data sharing, and climate literacy, but also "addressing social vulnerability and equity" through capacity building, institutional support, and participatory governance.[3]

During the same time period the IPCC reports were released, climate justice platforms in the United States rapidly coalesced around proposals for a Green New Deal (GND). In November 2018 a new class of policy makers was elected to the U.S. House of Representatives, including Democrat Alexandria Ocasio-Cortez of New York's Fourteenth District who quickly collaborated with climate advocacy groups like the Sunrise Movement on a loose proposal for a GND, an ambitious plan to decarbonize the economy and address rising inequality by investing in clean energy jobs and green infrastructure. Initially outlined in an eleven-page Google doc, the GND policy platform is deliberately modeled after President Franklin Delano Roosevelt's 1930s New Deal, a package of economic policy reforms, jobs programs, and public works projects that helped pull the United States out of the Great Depression. Over the course of the winter, interest in the GND skyrocketed.[4] In January 2019 over six-hundred environmental organizations sent a letter to Congress urging the adoption of a GND, and a poll conducted by the Yale School for Climate Change Communication showed remarkable bipartisan support for the plan before it was politicized in conservative media circles.[5] On February 7, 2019, Rep. Ocasio-Cortez, Massachusetts senator Ed Markey, and sixty-seven cosponsors introduced House Resolution 109 for a GND.[6] The proposal cites the 2018 IPCC special report *Global Warming of 1.5° C* in the very first sentence as the primary impetus for urgent, equitable climate action. Over the course of the 2019–2020 Democratic presidential primary, the majority of candidates expressed support for the GND in some form.[7] The GND has since become central to climate justice platforms both in the United States and abroad, with advocates declaring this the "Decade of the Green New Deal."[8]

Speculative sea level rise narratives, such as Kim Stanley Robinson's novel *New York 2140* and Benh Zeitlin's film *Beasts of the Southern Wild*, function as important heuristics by which to measure the extent to which GND-style policies are truly equitable.[9] By considering vastly different sea level rise scenarios, each prompts readers and viewers to imagine the possibilities and vulnerabilities of a GND in an age of widening inequality and intensifying political polarization. This chapter's focus on sea level rise narratives is a response to the fact that inundated coasts have become a primary marker for the progression of the climate crisis and attendant human displacement associated with extreme weather events. Communities with limited social, economic, or political capital are disproportionately impacted by flooding from intensifying storms and frequently excluded from official mitigation efforts. The uneven distribution of risk can be ascribed to "racial coastal formation"—historically uneven and racialized processes of coastal development and environmental adaptation policies.[10] Such processes were laid bare in the aftermath of Hurricane Katrina in 2005, when predominately Black neighborhoods in New Orleans were devastated by flooding in part due to the city's failure to construct and maintain effective levee systems in majority-Black neighborhoods enjoyed by wealthier, whiter segments of the city. Not unlike the Flint water crisis, events of Katrina can be tied to the privatization of public services and the broader neoliberalization of the state.[11] This dynamic is not unique to Katrina: in 2012 Hurricane Sandy disproportionately flooded minority communities and disabled the mass transit systems on which New York City's low-income residents depend, while in 2017 Hurricane Harvey inundated Houston, where devastation could be "measured not only in feet of floodwater but also by the vulnerability of its victims," many of whom were low-income Latinx and Black residents.[12] Meanwhile, Indigenous Biloxi-Chitimacha-Choctaw peoples in Terrebonne Parish, Louisiana, have been labeled "the first American climate refugees" as their land tumbles into the sea after decades of dredging and levee construction have decimated protective mangroves.[13]

Much of this book has considered how large-scale water systems are both the products of and the vehicles for social ideologies that render low-income communities and communities of color expendable within market logics. In this chapter, I am concerned with the maldistribution of financial and political capital as expressed through coastal development and environmental management efforts designed to protect, first and foremost, the interests of the neoliberal regime. The extent to which GND policy can drive a just water transition in coastal communities depends in large part on who controls the narrative around climate policy. Robinson's *New York 2140*, for example, is set in near future New York City submerged by floodwaters after a series large scale melting events at the poles of the planet. The novel imagines a GND-style economic and political revolution, challenging what Rob Nixon refers to as the "watery metaphors" of neoliberalism: pro-market mantras like the "the trickle-down effect," "global flows," and the notion that "a rising tide lifts all boats." But *New York 2140* also remains inattentive to the racialized dimensions of climate risk, advancing a GND scenario that largely ignores how coastal and urban climate policy have failed to meet the needs of low-income communities and communities of color. Zeitlin's *Beasts of the Southern Wild*, on the other hand, explores what it is like to live on the "wrong side of the levee," where uneven patterns of coastal development and environmental planning have prioritized the interests of capital at the expense of Black and Indigenous communities.[14] Taken together, the novel and film offer a stark reminder that a truly reparative, antiracist, decolonial GND is likely not possible without a commitment to place-based, community-driven policy responsive to histories of violence and exclusion.

If enacted as envisioned in House Resolution 109, a GND could have a tremendous impact on peoples most vulnerable to catastrophic sea level rise. The GND is, foremost, an ostensible proposal for a society-wide just transition. While it explicitly aims "to achieve net-zero greenhouse gas emissions through a fair and Just Transition for all communities and workers," the plan itself reaches far beyond social safety net programs for fossil fuel workers. One of the GND's five stated goals is "to promote justice and equity by stopping current, preventing future, and repairing historic oppression of Indigenous peoples, communities of color, migrant communities, deindustrialized communities, depopulated rural communities, the poor, low-income workers, women, the elderly, the unhoused, people with disabilities, and youth." It is easy to focus on the meat of the GND's ambitious policy goals, such as meeting energy demands through 100 percent clean and renewable sources; investment in clean manufacturing jobs, sustainable agriculture, and family farms; commitment to ecosystem restoration; and bread-and-butter progressive policy goals like expanding access to healthcare and education. But key to the GND's potential is its commitment to just transition principles based on reparative and restorative justice and emphasis on participatory approaches to decision making at the community level. The resolution urges "transparent and inclusive consultation, collaboration, and partnership with frontline and vulnerable communities, labor unions, worker cooperatives, civil society groups, academia, and businesses," and, moreover, contains a specific provision for honoring Indigenous sovereignty.[15] The GND has also inspired related policy proposals, most notably Massachusetts senator Elizabeth Warren's Blue New Deal, an ocean-focused climate plan released during her presidential campaign. The Blue New Deal emphasizes a holistic approach to support disaster preparation in coastal communities, such as leveraging federal and local emergency management agencies to design better escape routes and evacuation plans and prohibiting the construction of public housing in flood zones. The plan also supports directing federal funds to aid coastal Indigenous communities to restore wetlands and culturally significant sites.[16]

The GND should be considered an *ostensible* proposal for a just transition, however, because it is at present an "exercise in messaging rather than policymaking."[17] At the time of writing this book it exists only in the form of a nonbinding House resolution, and it is unlikely a sweeping package of reforms like the GND will be passed into law at the federal level anytime soon. More likely, GND-style policy will emerge at the local and state level at best. GND discourse presents an exciting narrative of possibility in the climate movement. But it remains to be seen who the protagonists will be. Put another way, while the GND offers a promising framework for radically equitable climate action, it also remains an empty vessel, vulnerable to co-optation by those who insist on market-based climate solutions and view social and economic equity as afterthoughts. After all, talk of GND-style policy dates at least to the mid-1990s and has been envisioned variously as a global climate plan contingent on leadership in the Global North; a plan primarily focused on energy rather than socioeconomic policy; and a plan focused on market-based principles of innovation, competition, and economic growth. In short, there exists a very real risk that the GND, as a policy platform, is infiltrated by what Adrian Parr has called the "Trojan Horse of neoliberal restructuring" that has often animated climate action by subsuming it under the principles of competition and individual choice.[18] Narrative, then, will play a critical role in the development and implementation of GND policy.

## New Narratives for a Green New Deal

In April 2019 the *Intercept* published a seven-and-a-half-minute film entitled *A Message from the Future with Alexandria Ocasio-Cortez* in which Rep. Ocasio-Cortez narrates a speculative story about how things might look if the United States manages to pass GND-style legislation. Her story follows a young woman of color named Ileana who, after graduating college, joins the AmeriCorps Climate Program and works alongside displaced oil workers to restore coastal wetlands in Louisiana by dismantling fossil fuel infrastructures and planting mangroves. All of them receive the same pay and benefits, and they are aided by Indigenous peoples who share traditional knowledge about land reclamation. Ileana eventually takes advantage of other climate-related jobs programs, including a brief stint in the solar industry, before deciding to become a teacher supported by a universal childcare initiative that Ocasio-Cortez describes as "valuable, low-carbon work." To be sure, things are not entirely rosy in this imagined scenario; the world has been battered by wildfires, droughts, and hurricanes, and Miami has been permanently submerged beneath rising seas. But the GND has prepared society to respond effectively. Social, political, and economic systems appear resilient. Because of GND-style reforms like universal healthcare and support for meaningful work, society is "not only modern and wealthy, but dignified and humane." Eventually, Ileana runs for and wins Ocasio-Cortez's former congressional seat and takes office in 2028. At the film's conclusion, Ocasio-Cortez insists that such a vision is attainable. The first step, she insists, is "just closing our eyes and imagining it." In a nod to the GND's commitment to racial equity, the film's illustrations almost exclusively depict people of color as elected officials, climate advocates, workers, teachers, and citizens.[19] In an essay accompanying the video, Naomi Klein explains that the film was inspired by climate writer Kate Aronoff. In a 2017 article in the *Intercept*, Aronoff presents a fictional future world navigated by a character named Gina in the year 2043, twenty-two years after federal GND legislation passed. Her world is one of zero-carbon transportation, abundant locally sourced food, widespread unionization and federal jobs programs in climate friendly sectors, and robust support for public arts programs. This is a world made possible by the promise of a GND.[20]

However, such optimistic scenarios are not necessarily a foregone conclusion if, indeed, a GND comes to fruition. The risk of an empty vessel GND, existing as it does only as a nonbinding House resolution lacking the specificity of a comprehensive bill, is that it could become implemented in ways that betray its existing commitments to restorative and reparative justice. This danger presents itself in two ways. First, GND proponents frequently evoke FDR's Depression-era New Deal as a model for the type of mass, government-assisted job creation and industry regulation necessary to simultaneously address economic inequality and the global climate crisis. But as Raj Patel and Jim Goodman rightly point out, "just as during the New Deal, we live in a time of incipient fascism, racism, and class divide. The Green New Deal can learn from its antecedent's successes and failures."[21] For example, New Deal-era federal housing policy carried out through the Federal Housing Administration—ostensibly designed to improve access to housing—ushered in the practice of redlining, a primary vehicle for racial segregation.[22] Discriminatory lending practices have continued into the present despite the passing of the 1968 Fair Housing Act. This can be viewed as an example of what George Lipsitz calls the possessive investment in whiteness, wherein the impacts of institutional racism are borne out in public policy.[23] Countless instances of environmental racism, such as the siting of toxic waste dumps and industrial infrastructure adjacent to politically and economically disempowered minority neighborhoods, can be traced to New Deal-era housing policy.[24] Another problematic legacy of the New Deal can be traced to the Indian Reorganization Act of 1934, also known as the Indian New Deal, which was intended to strengthen tribal sovereignty and reverse assimilationist policies of the past by supporting tribal self-government. However, the act required tribal governments to adopt frameworks modeled after the U.S. Constitution and, as Kyle Whyte explains, to reorganize into "year-long, voter-elected councils designed to facilitate extractive industries in Indigenous territories."[25] As a result, what was viewed by advocates like Bureau of Indian Affairs head John Collier as an effort to support tribal sovereignty ultimately undermined tribal collective continuance, which is based on sets of shifting and dynamic relationships and governance structures closely tied to natural cycles and traditions of reciprocity and interdependence (see chapter 1). GND advocates must remain cognizant of, and seek to avoid, the original New Deal's possessive investment in whiteness.

Second, while New Deal–era policy was driven by heavy government spending and increased regulation, the pre-2018 history of the GND suggests an overall lack of consensus over pathways to implementation. Outside climate justice circles, proposed routes to a GND range from eco-socialism, to proenvironmental Keynesian fiscal policy, to a reliance on market mechanisms. As a result, the GND runs the risk of co-optation by those who prioritize a "green" version of the economic status quo over commitments to reparative justice. On the one hand, some of the fiercest advocates for a GND argue for left populist, proworker, antiracist, and decolonial policies—the spirit of which animates much of House Resolution 109—and frame the debate over a GND as a choice "between eco-socialism and eco-apartheid."[27] On the other hand, the closest legislative precedent for GND-style policy is evident in the green energy initiatives built into President Barack Obama's American Recovery and Reinvestment Act of 2009, known broadly as the stimulus. As a predecessor to the GND, the law was passed on the heels of the Great Recession and invested $90 billion into clean energy, including $25 billion for renewables.[27] Explicit calls for a GND precede 2009. Environmental journalist Mark Hertsgaard outlined his vision for a "Global Green Deal" in a 1999 article in the *Nation* in which he called on the United States to draw on FDR's New Deal policies to lead a global shift toward clean energy.[28] Thomas Friedman coined the phrase itself in a 2007 *New York Times* column, in which he outlined a detailed plan for top-down, "green" economic reform such as massive federal investments in renewable energy and the elimination of fossil fuel subsidies. Like Hertsgaard, Friedman specifically insists on the concept's roots in the original New Deal.[29] However, Friedman's vision focuses explicitly on the strategic reorientation of existing economic systems around low-carbon energy regimes to ensure their continued survival in the age of the global climate crisis. Friedman's soaring rhetoric of "innovation," "industry," and "security" stands out as the type of giddy neoliberal vernacular typically reserved to describe newly discovered frontiers of profitability. Since 2018 others have advanced more explicit arguments in favor of what could be described as a neoliberal GND as the most politically expedient way to address climate change.[30]

The adoption of neoliberal climate policy under a GND moniker that prioritizes private investment as a path to climate action runs the risk of policy design that, like the original New Deal, entrenches social inequities. After all, claims about the emancipatory potential of privatization, deregulation, and unfettered free-market exchange to solve the climate crisis are incommensurable with the widening chasm between the world's wealthiest and poorest inhabitants.[31] Systemic inequality has emerged as a key marker for human exposure to climate risk, the vulnerability of communities tethered to relative access to financial and political capital necessary for long-term climate resilience, such as flood mitigation infrastructures to protect against sea level rise and affordable, climate-resilient housing.[32] More broadly, there is growing consensus about capitalism's outsize role as a driver of anthropogenic global warming, from eco-Marxist analyses of political economy and environmental degradation and the rise of fossil fuel regimes as an efficient means to subordinate labor to efforts to map the contours of the Capitalocene as an alternative accounting of the global climate crisis.[33] There are, to put it lightly, many reasons to be skeptical about whether "capitalism can crack climate change."[34] Questions have also arisen about the extent to which market-based solutions exacerbate rather than ameliorate existing inequalities along the lines of race, class, gender, and ethnicity.[35] As Adrian Parr has shown, climate action often reflects the imperatives of a "more virulent strain of capital accumulation" in which "the collective nature of the [climate] crisis is restructured and privatized, then put to work for the production and circulation of capital at the expense of the majority of the world living in abject poverty."[36] Ostensible solutions like carbon-trading have largely served as a profit-making instrument of finance capital with little impact on emissions reductions.[37] Furthermore, such responses disincentivize efforts to improve living conditions for frontline and fenceline communities.[38] Likewise, so-called green consumerism has been rightly recognized as an effort to place the burden for climate action on individual choice, therefore reinscribing the neoliberal fetishization of the individual over the collective.[39]

The possibility of a watered-down GND, stripped of key commitments to racial and reparative justice, poses significant risks to communities facing inundation from rising seas. The continuation of racial coastal formation, a concept coined by R. Dean Hardy, Richard Milligan, and Nik Heynen to refer to colorblind climate adaptation planning that inadequately responds to histories of racial exclusion, is cause for concern. Racial coastal formation evokes Michael Omi and Howard Winant's concept of racial formation theory, which holds that race is irreducible to ethnicity, nationality, or cultural difference but rather is shaped by social, economic, and political factors. Racial formation theory provides a theoretical accounting for systemic racism; the notion of racial coastal formation spatializes what was originally an argument about social relations.[40] Racial coastal formation is evident in landscapes physically altered through slave labor and uneven labor and property relations that have persisted into the present and impact climate adaptation planning and capacity. Hardy, Milligan, and Heynen draw on ethnographic research on Sapelo Island in coastal Georgia, where the lineage of plantation-era slave labor continues to shape the social and environmental contours of the community of Hog Hammock, ultimately arguing that equitable sea level rise adaptation planning requires awareness of the legacies of racial coastal formation—that is, the avoidance of colorblind climate policies in favor of explicitly antiracist, participatory efforts to bolster community resilience.[41] As the sea level rise scenarios below reveal, new narratives for a GND must reckon with the legacies of racial coastal formation to imagine a truly antiracist, decolonial just transition.

### *New York 2140* and the Racial Capitalocene

Kim Stanley Robinson has called his 2017 novel *New York 2140* a "comedy of coping," representative of his efforts to dispense with the pessimism of apocalyptic climate change narratives, neo-Malthusian tales of survival, and post-collapse conflict over limited resources.[42] The novel imagines a future New York City that has overcome a century of catastrophic, climate-related coastal flooding resulting from two multiyear events, known officially as the First and Second Pulses, that have submerged the coastal United States under sea waters 50 feet higher than their 2017 levels. The resultant humanitarian crises can be measured, according to a pseudo narrator character named the Citizen, in "katrinas."[43] But the city has proven remarkably resilient. Though it has relinquished its status as the world's premier financial and cultural center to landlocked metropoles like Denver, it remains a major player in the global capitalist economy. Advances in construction and engineering technology have enabled the city's oldest buildings—including the former MetLife building, where most of the novel's characters reside—to be retrofitted with waterproofing materials and transformed into sprawling, self-sufficient housing cooperatives with rooftop gardens, indoor farms, and the psychic perks of biophilic design. The flooded intertidal zones are lined with thriving aquaculture farms. Former streets are now bustling, and boat-filled canals become walkable or skate-able when iced-over in the winter. The newly located financial district uptown has bloomed into a cluster of superscrapers connected by walkable skybridges. Affectionately dubbed "SuperVenice" by its inhabitants, Robinson's New York City has largely overcome the Anthropocide and the Hydrocatastrophe and is now thriving thanks to the Georevolution, a period of geoengineering breakthroughs and human cooperation that has rendered the city livable in a climate changed world.[45]

At first glance, Robinson's future New York appears to exist in what Holly Buck has called a "charming Anthropocene" in which species-level human agency is viewed not as destructive but capable of collectively establishing a renewed ethics of care and connection through geoengineering.[45] As the novel unfolds, however, it becomes clear that Robinson is less invested in happy tales of human resilience in the Anthropocene than human inequality in what Jason W. Moore has called the Capitalocene, or "the historical era shaped by relations privileging the endless accumulation of capital."[46] According to the Citizen, the effects of flooding in the city have largely unfolded along class lines: It "had been bad for people—most of them," but the richest 1 percent, in possession of 80 percent of the world's wealth, had simply left the coastlines, abandoning those with less financial mobility to "cope with their new Rust Belt status."[47] During subsequent, deep recessions, big banks were bailed out by the federal government which, in turn, became financially weakened, increasingly tethered to the fates of their debtors, compelled to enact a series of austerity measures, and unable to fund public flood relief or urban reclamation projects. As a result, New York's entrenched social inequities have worsened: downtown, a new class of "desperate scavengers and squatters and fisherpeople and . . . water rats" have settled into the city's cramped, precarious intertidal zones.[49] Uptown, oligarchs and plutocrats experience the pinnacle of climate privilege, inhabiting superscrapers with "one giant apartment per floor."[49]

A sprawling critique of capitalism through the prism of climate change, *New York 2140* is Capitalocene fiction. An alternative to the Anthropocene origin story, the Capitalocene troubles dominant Anthropocene narratives that overdetermine the agency of a collective, undifferentiated *anthropos* while failing to account for how uneven relations of power and production have driven planetwide, ecosystemic breakdown and continue to shape the uneven distribution of climate risk.[50] The Capitalocene narrative holds that current ecological crises can be traced to the long sixteenth century (1451–1648), the *longue durée* periodization favored by world-systems theorists as a time of epochal revolution in which the processes that would eventually become known as capitalism came to represent a "fundamentally new law of environment-making."[51] The Capitalocene functions as the primary unit of periodization of Moore's world-ecology paradigm in which capitalism, power, production, and nature are coproduced.[52] Within the framework of world-ecology, capitalism does not actually abide by its assumed organizing logic whereby humans, in pursuit of capitalist accumulation, unilaterally alter or reorganize a passive, malleable more-than-human nature.[53] Instead, "humans make environments, and environments make humans—and human organizations."[54] Each periodically reconfigures the other in dialectical unity. *New York 2140*'s narrative structure uniquely lends itself to a world-ecological analysis by interweaving accounts of the city's environmental, economic, and cultural histories in the longue durée. This history primarily unfolds in the Citizen's sections of the novel, in which they detail how the bight of New York was formed when the Hudson River, "one dripline coming off the world-topping ice cap of the Ice Age," was met by the Atlantic after "the great ice monster melted ten thousand years ago"; the city's architectural history, including the proliferations of skyscrapers beginning with the late nineteenth century construction of the MetLife tower in Madison Square; the city's economic and ecological histories, described as "dark pools" both of money associated with the finance world and of aquatic ecosystems in the New York Harbor; and the events of the First and Second Pulses.[55] In doing so, Robinson's New York emerges as series of shifting, pulsing, contingent topographies, infinitely malleable within the dialectic of capitalism and nature, human and more-than-human forms of environment making.

But the Capitalocene is not merely an alternative way of framing human-environment interactions as coproduced. Rather, within the framework of world-ecology, the forces of capital rely on the availability of "seven cheaps"—nature, money, work, care, food, energy, and life.[56] The exhaustion of the seven cheaps correlates with the exhaustion or diminishment of the others, thus necessitating the search for new frontiers of profitability.[57] The process of ensuring cheap nature—generally, easily exploitable raw materials—is contingent on cheap, expendable lives. Within the Capitalocene, the primary mechanisms for this process—systematic othering of African and Indigenous peoples through colonialism and the slave trade—were buttressed by social ideologies of scientific racism, the European civilizing mission, and the rise of nationalism.[58] The Plantationocene, a second proposed alternative to the Anthropocene, crucially centers the material and discursive legacies of plantation economies, the "racialized violence, land alienation, and species loss" that remain the focus of fields like Black, Caribbean, Indigenous, and Afrodiasporic studies.[59] Different epochal designations serve different analytical aims, but the promise of the Capitalocene narrative is that it offers an opportunity to conceive of environmental change within the longue durée of white supremacist settler colonialism that persists into the present. Françoise Vergès calls this the "racial Capitalocene" and insists, channeling Laura Pulido (see chapter 2), that the environmental justice movement would do well to incorporate critiques of racial capitalism to respond to the climate crisis more effectively.[60]

To some degree, *New York 2140* is attuned to this dynamic, imagining a submerged world replete with newly exploitable frontiers of profitability, most notably in the realms of finance, real estate, and "green" capitalism. Early in the novel, we learn that efforts to initiate the "regentrification" of the city are well underway; well-heeled private equity and real estate firms, with the acquiescence of city government, have been offering outlandish sums for intertidal properties and housing cooperatives and attempting to coerce building owners and co-op executive boards to sell in order to flip the buildings for profit.[61] Moreover, as Roberto Ortiz has argued, the novel is a "literary reflection on the consequences of climate change via the structuring of finance."[62] This is primarily achieved through the character of Franklin Garr, a hedge fund manager at WaterPrice, who gets rich working in the field of "coastal futures" by speculating on the continued viability of real estate development in the city's precarious intertidal zones.[63] His success depends on a self-developed algorithm and correlating index, the Intertidal Property Pricing Index, that incorporates a variety of factors to monitor the financial health of intertidal zones, including housing prices, sea level projections, advances in construction technology, and estimated rates of depreciation based on environmental conditions.[64] His stated goal is to profit from overinvestment in "submarine mortgages"—a clear play on the 2008 subprime mortgage crisis—by anticipating a bubble and shorting the market.[65] Climate change, Franklin reflects, has been "good for capitalism."[66] By profiting from similar regulatory vacuums of neoliberal capitalism that contributed to the 2008 crisis, Franklin is participating in a finance industry governed by extractive logics, which Saskia Sassen describes as "similar to mining, albeit dressed in much finer clothes."[67] It is against this dynamic that the novel's eventual class revolution unfolds, resulting in the passing of a number of GND-style policies at the federal level including financial regulations, labor protections, environmental laws, and free public education.

However, the novel's GND scenario is ultimately diminished by an endemic inattention to the historically produced racial contours of climate inequality. It commits what Kathryn Yusoff describes as the primary sin of dominant Anthropocene narratives, "a failure to do the work to properly identify its *own* histories of colonial earth-writing, to name the masters of broken earths, to redress the legacy of racialized subjects that geology leaves in its wake."[68] Paradoxically, the novel calls attention to extractive logic of neoliberal capitalism without attending to its racialized instantiations: the slave trade, colonial extractivism, and ongoing, systemic racism—the underpinnings of racial capitalism.[69] For example, Robinson's blithe use of katrinas as the metric by which readers are asked to measure the severity of the novel's fictional climate catastrophe masks the intersections of racial inequality and climate vulnerability as a material discursive process rooted in histories of segregation and urban neglect in New Orleans. While Hurricane Katrina *has* become something of a benchmark by which the severity of climate-related coastal flooding events is determined, the storm's defining feature was the way in which it laid bare the contours of systemic racism in a supposedly post-racial U.S.[71] Yet *New York 2140* fails to engage with these histories. As far as readers can tell, the impacts of the so-called Hydrocatastrophe have been distributed solely along class lines. Perhaps more significantly, despite Robinson's clear familiarity with progressive climate politics, the novel's imagined revolution features no perspectives from people of color—save for the somewhat minor character of Inspector Gen, a Black NYPD detective—despite the central role of BIPOC activism and leadership in the U.S. climate justice movement. While *New York 2140* envisions the type of large-scale social and economic reforms central to the GND, it stands in marked contrast with Ocasio-Cortez's fictional *Message from the Future* film, in which people of color play a central role in societal transformation. We are invited to imagine an epochal break from the Capitalocene, but not the *racial* Capitalocene.

To be sure, much of Robinson's revolutionary vision does sync with the GND's focus on redistributive justice as a vehicle for equitable climate action. In *New York 2140*'s future-present, the neoliberal world order of 2017 has prevailed. The novel opens in a waterproofed, underwater shipping container where Ralph and Jeff Muttchopf, two computer savvy financial analysts known as quants, are being held captive by a shadowy entity after a failed attempt to hack the U.S. tax code by siphoning a small percentage of capital gains income into federal coffers to democratize wealth. As Jeff explains, "I pikettied the U.S. tax code," invoking Thomas Piketty, a French economist who has written extensively on extreme inequality.[71] In *Capital in the 21st Century*, Piketty argues that when the rate of return on capital—dividends, profits, interest, and rents—outpaces economic growth, or the total sum value of goods and services, wealth becomes concentrated and privatized amongst an ever-shrinking group of investors. Piketty draws on a vast amalgamation of data on wealth distribution in the United States and Western Europe that had hitherto not been considered in conjunction in previous studies. Inequality, he suggests, is a natural outgrowth of capitalism. The egalitarian promise of market forces so long espoused by capitalism's most ardent proponents is, in fact, false, and what Piketty calls the "compression of inequality" in the twentieth century was anomalous because rates of return on capital investments were artificially depressed by systemic shocks like the Great Depression and World War II.[72] In effect, inequality has been on the rise in the United States and Europe since the advent of neoliberalism 1980s due to "political shifts ... especially in regard to taxation and finance."[73] In response, Piketty proposes a global tax on capital, a progressive tax on assets and wealth rather than income to achieve a more equitable distribution of wealth, particularly in the form of public spending on infrastructure, schools, and other publicly held assets.[74]

Robinson's early evocation of a global tax on wealth foreshadows the novel's primary focus on wealth inequality as a marker for climate vulnerability. The novel's cast of protagonists come to espouse an "eat the rich" positionality, including Charlotte, a Marxist-minded lawyer who represents climate migrants for the Householder's Union, and known by her friends as "Red Charlotte"; and Amelia Black, a television host and animal rights activist who narrates aerial nature shows from her world-travelling zeppelin. The narrative also follows the travails of Franklin, the hedge fund manager who ultimately develops a social conscience and uses his intertidal real estate market index to invest in affordable, climate resilient housing, and Stefan and Roberto, two adventurous orphan boys who mostly serve as comic relief. A key subplot in the novel unfolds around anxieties about green gentrification. Much of city is being overlain by what Adrian Parr calls "neoliberal landscapes" produced by a certain brand of green urbanism that reproduce rather than ameliorate structures of inequality.[75] Ostensibly intended as climate-friendly urban development initiatives, such efforts nevertheless risk being deployed in the service of capital—with private enterprises the primary beneficiaries of remedial measures often funded by taxpayers—and thus constitute a form of redistribution of public assets to private hands. As an example, Parr cites former Chicago mayor Richard Daley's efforts to promote a green Chicago through the development of mixed-income housing and public-school integration, the elimination of food deserts, the implementation of stricter energy-use standards, the establishment of green spaces, and the development of a Chicago Climate Action Plan. While these efforts yielded some impressive results, they failed to significantly ameliorate conditions in the city's poor and nonwhite neighborhoods, in many cases reinscribed existing social inequities, and primarily encouraged private investment under the guise of sustainability.[76]

In the novel, much of the city's climate resilient development initiatives have been built to protect the city's financial districts and middle- and upper-class housing infrastructures, all of which have relocated uptown. Meanwhile, all of Manhattan south of Chelsea has become part of the ruined and structurally precarious intertidal zone, where low rents correlate with the likelihood of buildings "melt[ing] into the drink."[77] While some areas are a "hotbed of theory and practice," inhabited by artist colonies and home to "free open universities, free trade schools, and free art schools," others are destitute.[78] As Franklin notes while conducting field research for future investment opportunities, "life there probably resembled earlier centuries of squalid tenement reality, moldier than ever, the occupants risking their lives by the hour. Same as ever, but wetter."[79] Desperate and destitute on the one hand, and bohemian and lively on the other, the intertidal zone is clearly modeled after formerly abandoned industrial sections of Brooklyn such as Williamsburg and Greenpoint that, due to low rent prices, emerged as arts districts and cultural centers in the 1980s and 1990s before undergoing rapid gentrification and urban greening initiatives designed primarily to benefit the affluent.[80]

*New York 2140* levies a pointed critique against neoliberal urban greening initiatives. For example, when longtime city resident Hexter recalls the fictional inundation of lower Manhattan during the Second Pulse, he describes the catastrophic breaching of Bjarke's Wall, which forced the city's financial center and its wealthiest residents to relocate uptown. Bjarke's Wall is a fictionalization of the real-world Dryline project, also known as the Big U, a proposed 10-mile-long berm intended to protect of Manhattan from sea level rise. Imagined in the spirit of the city's Highline park, the Dryline is one of six projects being federally bankrolled as part of the Rebuild by Design competition, the goal of which is to render the city more climate resilient in the wake of Hurricane Sandy in 2012.[81]

It represents one of several projects under the purview of wunderkind Danish architect Bjarke Ingels and his firm the Bjarke Ingels Group (BIG), which operates according the principle of "Hedonistic Sustainability," the notion that sustainable, climate-aware design can and should improve standards of living.[82] The Dryline is designed to embody this philosophy through a series of bridges, parks, and green space connecting the city's neighborhoods. However, the Dryline is mostly designed to prevent the submersion of Wall Street and high-value real estate in Lower and Midtown Manhattan. Analyses of flood scenarios reveal that storm surges repelled by the berm will be rerouted to lower-income areas like Red Hook in Brooklyn, Harlem, and other lower-lying areas north of Midtown.[83]

While the Dryline *has* been touted as a way of connecting lower-income, culturally diverse sectors to the city's financial and arts sectors vis-à-vis a massive greenbelt, plans to anchor major segments of the berm with high-value residential buildings undermines BIG's seemingly altruistic intentions. In one of these developments, BIG's VIA 57 West residential building in Midtown along the Hudson River, rent ranges from $3,500 per month for a studio to $13,500 per month for a three-bedroom, two-bathroom unit.[84] In this regard, the Dryline arguably contributes to the city's ongoing housing crisis and perpetuates entrenched patterns of inequality contributing to climate vulnerability. *New York 2140* anticipates this dystopian reality: Following a major hurricane and widespread flooding, thousands of city residents are displaced and forced into refugee camps in Central Park while high rent superscrapers in Midtown, redolent of VIA 57 West, remain largely empty. After the mayor refuses to open the units to storm refugees, fearing "capital flight," the people collectively revolt against police and private security firms hired to protect the assets of their affluent clients.[85] The angry mob, described as "white-eyed, open-mouthed ... a general movement, a human storm surge," appears poised to enact a spontaneous revolution. When police tell them to return home, they respond, "We *are* home!"[86]

But like Robinson's problematic use of katrinas, his description of protesting climate refugees is a tell. As "a general movement, a human storm surge," they more closely resemble what Marx called the *lumpenproletariat*, a disorganized mob of lower-class citizens, than the multiracial coalition of climate justice activists and advocates who support a GND based on reparative justice.[87] Instead, the novel's revolutionary class—Charlotte, Amelia, and Franklin—amount to a progressive but privileged class of white, middle-class political leftists that reside safely in the MetLife tower's upper floors, far removed from the submerged slums of the intertidal zone. The novel's eventual revolution, which pivots on progressive fiscal policy, is largely colorblind. As Charlotte, Amelia, and Franklin plot a general strike, Charlotte proclaims that the ultimate goal is the "euthanasia of the rentier," a phrase plucked from early twentieth-century economist John Maynard Keynes's foundational *General Theory of Employment, Interest, and Money*.[88] Keynes maintained that a limited amount of capital investment was necessary to achieve full employment and a fully functional economy, so that the rentier class—those who own and profit from debt—would be rendered obsolete. As a result, the "euthanasia of the rentier" would occur naturally and the "cumulative oppressive power of the capitalist to exploit the scarcity-value of capital" would disappear.[89] To facilitate this process, Amelia implores her millions of viewers during a live broadcast to stage a general financial strike and refuse to pay rents, mortgages, student loans, and other forms of private debt, precipitating a massive financial collapse. Charlotte runs for and is elected to represent the Twelfth District of New York in the image of a democratic socialist, Ocasio-Cortez-style progressive and persuades her ex-husband Larry Jackman, chair of the Federal Reserve, to nationalize the banks. The newly elected Congress of the year 2143 rapidly passes a Piketty Tax accompanied by new labor protections and environmental regulations. New tax revenue is used to fund free public education and guarantee employment.[90]

At this point, Robinson is clearly using his imagined GND-style scenario to relitigate the federal response to the 2008 financial crisis and the Bush administration's failure to hold big banks accountable for the predatory lending practices behind the subprime mortgage crisis. The novel's fictional antibailout Fed chair is named Larry, a clear parody of Larry Summers, former chief economist of the World Bank and director of the National Economic Council under President Obama. Long considered a neoliberal villain amongst the political left, Summers actually considered nationalizing banks in response to the 2008 financial collapse.[91] But this amounts to the novel's biggest missed opportunity.

*New York 2140* fails to adequately interrogate or imagine a just transition beyond the racialized roots of the subprime mortgage crisis. To review, due to rising housing prices and low interest rates in the early 2000s, homebuyers were able to secure home loans or take second mortgages significantly beyond their means. Banks, moreover, were willing to lend against what they viewed was a real estate market forever on the upswing. When the housing bubble burst due to decreasing home prices in 2007, borrowers began to default on their homes, lenders began filing for bankruptcy, and market chaos ensued.[92] In the aftermath of the crisis, studies revealed that nonwhite borrowers were disproportionate recipients of high-interest, high-risk mortgages, leading to higher rates of foreclosures than white borrowers. Lax regulation and the spatial legacies of segregation, which can be traced to the height of the redlining era, were primary enabling factors.[93] One major consequence has been the widening of the racial wealth gap; disproportionate number of Black households are still struggling to recover from the Great Recession.[94] This can be viewed as a contributing factor to climate risk.

Despite *New York 2140*'s imagined solution to a fictional submarine mortgage crisis, it pays no mind to these dynamics. Instead, the novel depends on the whims of a reformed hedge fund manager who finally decides to pull the levers of an extractive financial industry and leverage market mechanisms for what he views as a greater good. As the novel closes, Franklin decides to finance the design and construction of affordable, sustainable housing, drawing his deep knowledge of recent advances in housing construction technology to concoct an idea for floating intertidal housing developments modeled after eelgrass, a type of long sea grass rooted to the ocean floor that sways in motion with tidal flows. At first glance, Franklin's transformation into a "social justice warrior," a title he derisively assigned to Charlotte earlier in the novel, appears significant.[96] The novel's conclusion, a hopeful vision for the potential of wealth redistribution and technical innovation as a path to climate equity, reflects Robinson's views expressed elsewhere on the value of geoengineering. In a 2018 interview, Robinson cautions against outright dismissal of geoengineering: "As a leftist, I think there is a bad tendency amongst some leftists to conflate science with capitalism. They are not the same. I am against capitalism, I am for science.... We need to choose to put science, technology, engineering, and good medicine to good human and biospheric work, rather than let it be bought to serve profit for the most wealthy."[96] However, his framing—"good human and biospheric work"—parallels *New York 2140*'s general inattention to racial justice, reinscribing a generalized, deracialized *anthropos*. Therefore, while the novel engages in a tantalizing thought exercise, prompting readers to imagine the possibilities of an incipient GND, it ultimately settles on a largely colorblind, eco-socialist adjacent climate revolution. Missing are the more radical demands articulated by U.S. climate justice groups like the Climate Justice Alliance, which outlines a vision for an explicitly antiracist, decolonial just transition based on the radical redistribution of wealth and political power. As such, it functions as an important heuristic by which climate justice advocates can measure proposed GND-style policy proposals going forward.

### The "Wrong Side of the Levee" in *Beasts of the Southern Wild*

If Robinson's *New York 2140* outlines the contours of a colorblind GND in a drowned world, then Zeitlin's film *Beasts of the Southern Wild* offers a useful complement through its exploration of the impacts of sea level rise on Black and (by proxy) Indigenous communities in the climate sacrifice zones of Louisiana's Mississippi River Delta. The film unfolds from the perspective of the precocious Hushpuppy, a young Black girl living with her alcoholic father Wink in the Bathtub, a poor multiracial community located on the fictional Isle de Charles on the outer banks of the delta. Superficially, the Bathtub is presented as a symbol of freedom from the external imposition of order, the site of frequent, alcohol-fueled celebrations and little parental oversight of children. It quickly becomes clear, however, that the community is a casualty of the politics of abandonment by the state. Throughout the film, Hushpuppy contrasts the Bathtub with richer, safer communities "up in the dry world," insulated from rising seas, coastal subsidence, and storm surge flooding. The perceived division between worlds is rendered tangible by the presence of a large concrete levee that protects a sprawling petrochemical facility and the city beyond. When a hurricane strikes, the structure diverts floodwaters into the Bathtub, submerging the community. In what can arguably be viewed as the film's defining scene, Wink and his companions attach a dynamite-laden carcass of an alligator gar fish to the levee and blow it up, draining the Bathtub and allowing residents to briefly return to salvage their community.

Critics have read the film as an allegory for events surrounding Hurricane Katrina's disproportionate submergence of mostly Black neighborhoods in New Orleans like the Lower Ninth Ward.[97] Heavy flooding in the Lower Ninth Ward was due in part to its location adjacent to the Industrial Canal, a 1920s-era artificial waterway used as a shipping route connecting Lake Pontchartrain to the Mississippi River. The canal has contributed to severe coastal erosion in the river delta, dissolving natural flood barriers that once protected coastal communities. When Katrina made landfall in 2005, an 18-foot storm surge barreled up the canal and overtook crumbling, long-neglected levees adjacent to the Lower Ninth Ward, effectively destroying the neighborhood and killing dozens of residents.[98] The neighborhood has since become emblematic of the ways in which the neoliberalization of the state has exacerbated the racialized politics of abandonment and climate vulnerability.[99] Christopher Lloyd rightly points out that *Beasts* provides insight into the ways in which Black bodies were "seen as throwaway" and "discardable" by the state and the media in the wake of Katrina.[100] Likewise, literary and film critic Alexa Weik von Mossner sees the Bathtub as residing "on the 'wrong side' of the Louisiana levees" and views the film's lone levee as demarcating "boundaries that are both geographical and socioeconomic in nature."[101] I would add that the boundaries also demarcate racial divides. While others have noted the film's use of magical realism to connect local experiences of climate change and community dissolution to a larger global reality, here I am interested in the political symbolism of the levee, the necessity of its destruction, and the dangers of colorblind climate policy.[102] The film is not merely an example of speculative climate fiction, but speculative climate *justice* fiction, prompting viewers to consider what it means to reside on the wrong side of the levee in a city that owes its existence to keeping floodwaters at bay and shifting deltaic landscapes under control.

Two parallel readings of *Beasts* lead to two distinct but overlapping conclusions. First, if the film is to be viewed as a straightforward allegory of the racialized aftermaths of Hurricane Katrina, then the "wrong" side of the levee can be understood as poor, majority-Black coastal communities that have been abandoned by the state and rendered disposable by the machinations of capital. In this case, the levee is indicative of Louisiana's racial coastal formation, serving as a monument to the inbuilt inequities of neoliberal governance. In New Orleans, this is made manifest by an intricate network of flood control and levee systems that have been erected and maintained primarily to safeguard the city's economic interests, especially the shipping and oil industries, at the expense of residential neighborhoods, especially those that are poor and Black.[103] Hushpuppy, Wink, and other residents of the Bathtub can be viewed as representative of a post-Katrina Black precariat contending with the exclusionary tendencies of neoliberal environmental governance.[104] Second, *Beasts* can also be read as a comment on climate change as part of the longer, cyclical history of settler colonialism.[105] Like the large dams explored in chapter 1 of this book, the levee represents an infrastructural legacy of racially exclusionary settler land management policies of the nineteenth and twentieth centuries. In fact, Zeitlin's chief geographical inspiration for *Beasts* was the Isle Jean de Charles, a low-lying sliver of land in Terrebonne Parrish in the Mississippi River Delta and the principal homeland of the Biloxi-Chitimacha-Choctaw peoples.[106] Between 1932 and 2015, over 1,800 square miles of coastline in the Gulf has melted into the ocean; over the last sixty years, the Isle de Jean Charles has shrunk by more than 90 percent, leading residents to be informally designated the first climate refugees in the United States.[107]

In the first reading of *Beasts*, the levee serves as a metaphor for the racialization of climate risk—an issue, I contend, that any GND must address. The levee establishes a clear demarcation between racialized affluence and precarity, the latter punctuated by the film's use of a slum aesthetic, or what Mike Davis has called a slum ecology, characterized by "overcrowding, poor or informal housing, inadequate access to safe water and sanitation, and insecurity of tenure."[108] A defining feature of slums, and a major determinant of human vulnerability to environmental change, is shaky infrastructure—including ad hoc living quarters, pieced together with scrap materials, and rarely adhering to city building codes—that are extremely susceptible to damage or destruction from fire, flooding, earthquakes, or spontaneous collapse. Sequestered from wealthier quarters of cities, slums also serve as the epicenters of public health crises.[109] As Anna Hartnell has shown, *Beasts* levies a critique of New Orleans's long-repressed relationship with water and general environmental volatility emerging from a complex relationship between urban planning and economic prosperity, which since the nineteenth century has been contingent on taming and redirecting the meandering waters of the Mississippi River. Drawing on Zygmunt Bauman's notion of liquid modernity, Hartnell argues that the city exists in a permanent state of "liquid precarity," simultaneously under siege from physical floodwaters while preoccupied with unevenly distributed and short-term profits that are related to the relative liquidity of capital investments.[110] This dynamic is evident in the city's many navigation canals that were carved through and around the city in the mid-twentieth century to provide additional shipping routes connected to the Gulf of Mexico. While economically beneficial, these efforts also provided new routes for floodwaters to inundate the city's interior, threatening the city's less infrastructurally sound low-income and nonwhite neighborhoods.[111]

While the Bathtub's rural setting distinguishes it from traditional notions of the slum as an urban space, the settlement is nevertheless an improvised, ill-defined municipality in which residents are exposed to a similar degree of environmental precarity as slums located in the megacities of the Global South. The opening scenes in *Beasts* reveal Hushpuppy and Wink living in leaky, improvised, living quarters composed of rotting wood and rusted metal and glassless windowpanes, propped unevenly above-ground in anticipation of floodwaters and filled with free-ranging livestock and nonworking, rusted appliances. At one point, Wink pulls a whole raw chicken from the inside of a broken cooler filled with melted ice and sets it to cook on a makeshift cooking surface. Later, he ferries Hushpuppy around the bayou in a fishing boat composed of an old truck bed tethered to large plastic barrels and mounted with a weathered outboard motor. At one point, they gaze from their boat at the levee as the sun sets, the skyline defined by a large petrochemical processing facility and, presumably, a wealthy metropole beyond. As Hushpuppy explains, "Daddy says up above the levee, on the dry side, they're afraid of the water. They built the wall that cuts us off. They think we all going to drown down here. But we ain't going nowhere." When the hurricane eventually strikes, the levee diverts floodwaters into the Bathtub, submerging the community and saturating the landscape with saltwater, killing much of the flora and fauna. When Wink eventually destroys the levee, it represents an act of resistance against racially exclusionary urban planning efforts and an assertion of community sovereignty. Bathtub residents are then free to return to their community and reclaim the wreckage of their homes.

At this point, it should be acknowledged that Zeitlin, who is white, has been accused by critics of sentimentalizing Black poverty.[112] The late cultural critic bell hooks eviscerated the film for taking what she views as an uncritical stance on race and the strategic use of fantasy tropes to create an unrealistic world in which "black and white poor folks live together in utopian harmony."[113] These are valid criticisms, but I would add the caveat that the film nevertheless materializes a racial Capitalocene in ways rarely seen in cultural representations of climate change. If the Bathtub is an allegorical representation of New Orleans, then the city's abandonment through a tragically slow and inadequate federal response to Katrina can be ascribed to the city's racialization as Black. Just as the Flint water crisis is emblematic of the color of water, Katrina-era New Orleans is emblematic of what Michael Eric Dyson has called the "color of disaster."[114] This dynamic can be detected not merely through patterns of floodwater distribution but also in recovery efforts that neglected or ignored the needs of the city's Black residents. Following the levee's demolition, Bathtub residents are forcibly evacuated from the rubble of their homes to an emergency shelter. The shelter space is portrayed as a sterile, whitewashed environment, its neatly partitioned hospital rooms overcrowded with displaced peoples, its highly processed cafeteria food inedible. Bathtub residents are effectively imprisoned, though as Hushpuppy explains, "it didn't look like a prison. It looked more like a fish tank with no water. They say we are here for our own good."

The authoritarian paternalism of the shelter refers to the neoliberalization of post-Katrina relief and rebuilding efforts. While widespread criticisms of the inadequate federal response to Katrina tend to focus on unpreparedness, lack of institutional coordination, and failures in leadership, the disaster's aftermaths can also be understood as a function of the privatization of emergency management infrastructure. This dynamic is visible in the trend toward the neoliberalization of public services, specifically an over-reliance on private contractors who, in the wake of Katrina, "aggravated the pains of displacement" by providing inadequate housing for displaced peoples.[115] One prominent example of this dynamic is actor Brad Pitt's Make It Right (MIR) Foundation that, while well-meaning, risked imposing neoliberal landscapes on the city's poorer, majority Black enclaves. MIR was conceived as a plan to rebuild the Lower Ninth Ward through the construction of 150 environmentally sustainable single-family homes featuring rainwater recycling systems and solar panels.[116] As Cedric Johnson writes, MIR was rooted in "bourgeois notions of homeownership and private real estate development," wherein "norms and expectations regarding nuclear family cohabitation, self-reliance, and neighborhood life are constituted by bourgeois, individualist assumptions rather than collective values."[117] Rather than focusing on the construction and maintenance of equitable, comprehensive flood control infrastructures, MIR-built homes featured 10-foot concrete pillars and rooftop escape hatches as a contingency against future storm surges. Johnson refers to this approach as "neoliberal urbanism," a concept akin to Parr's neoliberal landscapes paradigm, wherein so-called green development ultimately serves the broader interests of capital.[118]

*Beasts* does not allegorize the post-Katrina politics of urban reclamation New Orleans. However, when Bathtub residents escape the shelter in the fashion of a heroic prison break, sneaking about in hospital gowns and doctor disguises, they effectively stage a protest against the embedded neoliberalism of post-disaster recovery efforts. In the film's defiant final scene, Hushpuppy leads a determined group of Bathtub residents along a storm-damaged highway, surrounded by encroaching tidewaters. To a triumphant-sounding score, punctuated by harmonizing brass and symbols clashing, a little girl holds a black funeral flag aloft in honor of Wink, who has just died from a congenital disease. This scene can be viewed as symbolizing an anarchist resolve and desire for autonomy in the face of ecological catastrophe. Hushpuppy's defiance—"We ain't going nowhere"—exemplifies the "edgy freedom" of the Bathtub, whose inhabitants remain in the face of rising sea waters and an uncertain future.[119] Despite this defiant insistence on community sovereignty, however, the film hardly imagines a just transition. As several critics have acknowledged, the film's strong libertarian themes position its ideological commitments directly opposite neoliberalism on the same coin of individualism.[120] It is, rather, suggestive of the ways in which communities abandoned by the state and facing climate catastrophe have limited recourse beyond defending their rights to self-determination on a rapidly eroding coastline.

On the other hand, if the film is viewed as commentary on climate-related Indigenous dispossession, the levee emerges as a legacy of settler colonialism as expressed through the exclusionary dimensions of neoliberal governance. The levee should be understood as representative of early- and mid-twentieth-century efforts to render the Mississippi River Delta navigable for cargo ships and oil tankers through the construction of dikes, levees, and canals, resulting the literal erosion of tribal lands into the ocean as sea levels continue to rise. The Isle de Jean Charles, a thin strip of land in Terrebonne Parish south of New Orleans and the chief geographical inspiration for *Beasts*, has been heavily affected by the coast's shifting topography due to climate change; its residents, the Biloxi-Chitimacha-Choctaw, face imminent displacement.[121] Driven to the region during Indian Removal in the 1830s, the tribe has long maintained a thriving community through trapping, fishing, and netting shellfish.[122] As the island continues to erode, however, the tribal community has dwindled.[123] The causes are many: the collective impact of upstream levees and dikes, dredging, and oil extraction and refinery infrastructure have contributed to widespread soil erosion, coastal subsidence, and extensive saltwater intrusion on the Louisiana coast, and the disappearance of wetlands, which long served as natural storm barriers, have rendered human populations increasingly vulnerable to hurricanes and storm-surge flooding. Chemical runoff from commercial agriculture has also negatively affected fisheries on which the community depends, a problem exacerbated by the BP *Deepwater Horizon* oil spill in 2010. Both have contributed to the emergence of hypoxic dead zones, significantly impacting local fishing economies.[124]

Brianna Burke has written insightfully on *Beasts* as a reflection on "community, exploitation, and extinction" in the era of global climate change.[125] The film contains a parallel narrative that follows aurochs, a species of wild cattle that were hunted to extinction in the seventeenth century in Europe, Asia, and North Africa.[126] For much of the film, multitusked, pig-like aurochs haunt Hushpuppy, at first in her imagination as she envisions them emerging from melting ice and reinhabiting the world, and later in their physical arrival at Wink's deathbed. Many read these scenes as an effort to connect local and global experiences of climate change.[127] Considered alongside the extinction-level loss of traditional lifeways facing the Biloxi-Chitimacha-Choctaw, the film connects planet-level species loss to cultural loss facing Indigenous peoples due to climate change. Cultural loss, here, is connected to a "loss of emplacement."[128] Early in the film, Hushpuppy expresses a deep affinity for the island's living beings, proclaiming that "all the time, everywhere, everything's hearts are beatin' and squirtin' and talkin' to each other in ways I can't understand." Here, explains Burke, Hushpuppy articulates a cosmopolitical stance, an articulation of a cosmos predicated on living in "close interdependence with local ecosystems" like that espoused by Indigenous peoples such as the Biloxi-Chitimacha-Choctaw.[129] In other words, Hushpuppy's loss of emplacement, punctuated by auroch scenes meant to evoke climate change and the threat of mass extinction, mirrors that faced by the Biloxi-Chitimacha-Choctaw.

In this view, it becomes impossible to designate a "wrong" side of the levee, for such an exercise suggests that successfully addressing environmental precarity is as simple as evacuating or drawing on political capital to advocate for public spending on socially equitable flood mitigation infrastructure. Burke, writing of Zeitlin's creative process, argues the same: "To view a place as 'doomed,' to imagine that a community can simply pick up and leave (With what money? And to where?) betrays a specific imperialist construction of the cosmos where nature is separate from culture and thus separate from self."[130] Not only is such capital nonexistent for the Biloxi-Chitimacha-Choctaw, the notion of a right and wrong side of the structure makes little difference given that the *raison d'etre* for the structure's existence is to further the interests of white supremacist settler colonialism. The detonation of the levee, then, can also be viewed as a proactive effort to restore bayou ecosystems and recuperate Indigenous lifeways. Throughout, *Beasts* features multiple expressions of collective continuance: community gatherings in the

Bathtub frequently take place around piles of freshly caught shellfish, and Wink takes pains to teach Hushpuppy to fish so that she can care for herself when he's gone. Wink even insists that "we've got the prettiest place on earth," a sentiment at direct odds with the film's slum aesthetic, suggesting that what some view as poverty can also be interpreted as aesthetics of loss in the face of climate catastrophe. By subsisting on domesticated chickens and navigating the bayou in a leaky, improvised fishing boat, Hushpuppy and Wink are not merely cash-poor but on the verge of losing an entire lifeway, which the film poignantly renders visible in a scene in which Wink pilots his boat through a flooded landscape, mournfully retrieving the bodies of drowned birds and mammals.

According to state officials, the Isle de Jean Charles will likely be submerged by 2050. Though the state of Louisiana is pushing forward with 50-year master plan for the coast to restore barrier islands and ecosystems and build additional levees and diversions to protect against flooding and erosion, there are no plans to include the Isle because it does not fit within so-called required cost-benefit analyses.[131] The community has also been excluded from the Morganza to the Gulf of Mexico Hurricane Protection Project, a planned 72-mile levee system, for the same reason.[132] While the Federal Department of Housing and Urban Development awarded the isle $48 million grant to relocate inland in early 2016, tribal members have been resistant to the idea of leaving their homes. They understandably distrust the federal government, and the prospect of relocation to more populous areas inland,—where participation in the market economy will take the place of subsistence lifeways—has led some tribal members to compare relocation to imprisonment.[133] As one resident explains, "I've lived my whole life here, and I'm going to die here. . . . We always find a way."[134] In this context, the film's shelter scenes do not merely reflect the imposition of "order" by the neoliberal state, they also gesture to an institutional legacy of the settler-colonial project begun nearly two centuries ago. In one disturbing scene during her shelter stay, Hushpuppy stands solemnly while being berated by a white aid worker. She is wearing a clean, ironed blue dress, her previously unkempt hair—symbolic of the Bathtub's freedom and autonomy—pulled into a formal up-do. As Burke writes, the scene is eerily redolent of the "countless before-and-after photographs from the Indian boarding school era" and, as such, "invokes the long history of indigenous forced removal and assimilation, compulsory absorption into a capitalist wage economy, and the attempt to erase indigenous cosmologies."[135] Presently, more than thirty families plan to relocate to a resettlement site called the New Isle 40 miles north.[136] According to the community's website, resettlement will offer them the best chance to "reunite [their] displaced tribal members and rekindle [their] traditional lifeways."[137] However, the process has been slow. Residents were first able to view their future homes in April 2021, five years after the initial resettlement plan was first announced in 2016.[138] *Beasts* seemingly anticipates this failure in governance: Hushpuppy, Wink, and their fellow Bathtub residents, as marginalized peoples within an emergent climate apartheid, have no choice but to dismantle the levee and resist state-sponsored resettlement initiatives in a reassertion of cultural sovereignty.

### Grassroots over Grasstops

While *New York 2140* imagines a political-economic revolution redolent of the GND in a future New York City submerged by rising seas, its vision for a just transition falls short by failing to consider the racialized dimensions of urban development and environmental governance policies in the past and present. *Beasts of the Southern Wild*, as a speculative sea level rise narrative, calls attention to racial coastal formations that have rendered Black and Indigenous communities on the "wrong" side of the levee most vulnerable to submergence and displacement. Read together, both the novel and film function as important heuristics by which GND advocates can measure the relative adequacy of climate policy proposals to support restorative and reparative justice in coastal zones on the frontlines of a warming climate. More importantly, they serve as stark reminders of a key provision in House Resolution 109, that a "Green New Deal must be developed through transparent and inclusive consultation, collaboration, and partnership with frontline and vulnerable communities, labor unions, worker cooperatives, civil society groups, academia, and businesses."[139] While consultation of frontline communities and organizations of color is important (and certainly would have shored up some of *New York 2140*'s narrative blind spots), collaboration and partnership are even more critical to ensure a just transition.

It is important to note that proponents of the GND like Ocasio-Cortez have faced criticism since the initial rollout of the GND. Weeks after the initial proposal was posted online, the Climate Justice Alliance released a statement of support with a major caveat: Grassroots environmental justice groups had been excluded from the proposal-drafting process. The letter included at least eighteen signatories, including Black- and Indigenous-led grassroots community organizations. "The proposal for a Green New Deal was made public at the grasstops level," they wrote, cautioning that the "process for achieving any new deal cannot be conducted in the same old way, in which power, privilege, and money trump communities' needs, well-being, and democratic rights." The statement acknowledges the proposal's strengths, including attention to systemic racism and inequality, but outlines the alliance's priorities for a GND, including recognition of Indigenous rights, an emphasis on redress and reparations, and the prioritization of community-level input. It emphasizes that "jobs and resources generated for and from the GND should be directed first to frontline, climate impacted communities, including tribes and tribal communities" and that climate adaptation processes and policies "should be guided by the communities themselves, since they are in the best position to assess local needs and priorities."[140] To their credit, the GND's primary torchbearers have been responsive to such criticism. Shortly after the letter was posted, Ocasio-Cortez met with representatives from the alliance to discuss the inclusion of just transition principles into what eventually became House Resolution 109.[141] Such amenability to community-level input is a good sign for the potential of a transparent, democratic GND.

In 2019 Ocasio-Cortez announced a promotional GND art series featuring retro-style poster prints inspired by works produced by the Federal Art Project (FAP), a New Deal program under the purview of the Works Progress Administration that employed 5,300 artists to support the arts between 1935 and 1943. Collectively, these artworks told a story of possible post-Depression futures and helped lift the country out of the Depression psychically.[142] The GND posters, replete with gaspipe font, earthy pastel coloring, and stenciled graphics, were designed by New York marketing firm Tandem and artist Gavin Snider to resemble the FAP's most iconic posters, which touted the beauty of national parks and monuments in the United States.[143] The first two prints in the GND series featured scenes from the Bronx: One poster depicts Pelham Bay with the Bronx Victory Memorial set against a backdrop featuring high-speed rail and public green spaces, while the other shows a vibrant green Flushing Meadows Corona Park populated with the silhouettes of recreating people and likewise set against a high-speed rail system (see fig. 10). The posters engage in speculative storytelling, imagining utopic futures redolent of a surface reading of *New York 2140*.[144] More posters have been since been released for sale on Ocasio-Cortez's website, including one arguably problematic depiction of the Public Garden in Boston featuring the large statue of George Washington on horseback against the backdrop of a city skyline that includes wind turbines, high speed rail, and vast green space (see fig. 11). While it may seem like a minor issue, the depiction of a white settler riding confidently west seems incongruent with a policy proposal that purports to advocate for the redress of past injustices against Black and Indigenous communities. In an era when reckoning a national past steeped in racism and genocide means reenvisioning the place of monuments and memorials in public spaces, such a poster represents a narrative setback for GND advocates, imagining a future in which structures of oppression persist even amidst positive climate action.

There clearly remain a bevy of political, economic, discursive, and narrative obstacles to enacting a GND that is truly antiracist and decolonial and that prioritizes redress and reparations for past injustices against low-income communities and communities of color. It is important to imagine scenarios such as that outlined by Ocasio-Cortez in her *Message from the Future* film featuring a young woman of color taking on a leadership role in a utopic future shaped by progressive climate policy. But it is also important to imagine cautionary GND scenarios that emphasize the dangers of failing to engage meaningfully with frontline and fenceline communities. Narrative and storytelling play an important role in signaling the seriousness of GND advocates in staying true to their professed commitments. The seas are rising, and there is little time to waste.

10. Green New Deal poster: Flushing Meadows Corona Park, Queens, New York. Art by Gavin Snider and Tandem Design.

11. Green New Deal poster: The Public Garden, Boston, Massachusetts. Art by Dayi Tofu and Tandem Design, 2019.

# Conclusion

*Imagining a Community-Driven
Just Transition in Wyoming*

If it has not become clear by now, water justice struggles are about more than just water. This has been a subtext throughout this book, in which I have sought to show accelerating water crises in the United States emerge from social ideologies, and attendant economic systems, that presume the expendability of Indigenous peoples, low-income peoples, and people of color. While each chapter could be read as a separate case study, the common thread that connects them is evidence of a refusal in frontline and fenceline communities to accept the narratives that justify exclusion, erasure, and devalued life that have long animated large-scale water systems. Against the settler colonial rhetoric of erasure that continues to propel hydropolitics and drought planning in the western United States, Indigenous writers and artists present alternative narratives of collective continuance that resist settler myths of native disappearance, victimhood, and unsophisticated natural resource governance. Against a racialized politics of abandonment and the neoliberalization of public services—against racial capitalism—performance, fashion, and street art are helping Flint, Michigan, imagine freedom dreams of a strong, thriving, resilient community. Against a deep-seated cultural attachment to fossil fuel extraction, writers, poets, photographers, and landscape architects are working with communities to imagine a post-extractive Appalachia. Such alternative epistemologies offer renewed possibilities of coalitional solidarity amongst geographically and culturally distant communities based on shared struggles and hopes. Moreover, storytelling through literary fiction, film, music, photography, museum exhibits, public murals, fashion, and landscape reclamation art serve an important role as modes of expression by which communities can litigate the roots of injustice and imagine and plan for equitable futures. To paraphrase Julie Sze, in environmental and social struggles, culture matters.[1]

While this book has highlighted the work of artists and activists, it is important to recognize that they are not necessarily the authoritative arbiters of their respective communities' values and hopes. I would like to close this book as it opened: by thinking through the concept of a just transition as a theory of social change. More specifically, I would like to focus on my current state of Wyoming to consider the importance of community-driven, place-based storytelling in a unique political landscape during a time of upheaval. Much of this book was completed during my time as a scholar in residence at the University of Wyoming from 2019 to 2021, during which the state began experiencing an expected but accelerated epochal shift of its own. In Wyoming, as in most places, climate challenges are expressed through water. Decreased mountain snowpack and diminished stream flows continue to affect fisheries, drought conditions have forced ranchers to seek supplemental feed for their livestock, and the threat of wildfires is ever present.[2] But the state faces additional challenges given its long-term dependence on a fossil fuel industry that appears to be in permanent decline. Wyoming is the nation's largest net exporter of energy and produces fifteen times the energy it uses.[3] In 2019 over half of the state's revenue was derived from coal, oil, and gas severance taxes—fees paid by industry to remove minerals from the ground.[4] These funds provide residents with nearly eight times the value in social services that they pay in taxes.[5] At the time of writing, however, the state is facing a bevy of challenges in the energy sector that began even before the COVID-19 pandemic. A protracted, secular downturn in coal production has led to a number of coal company bankruptcies and layoffs, punctuated by the industry-rattling bankruptcy of coal giant Blackjewel in July 2019, resulting in two abrupt mine closures and hundreds of layoffs in coal-rich Campbell County.[6] Coal-fired power plants, employing large swaths of the population of small rural towns, face similar existential crises as regional utilities incorporate renewables as a larger share of their power generation portfolios. A slowdown in oil production related to the oil market crash in March 2020 has exacerbated a dismal near-term financial outlook. In late 2020 the state forecasted a decline in severance tax revenue exceeding 50 percent.[7] The state has initiated severe budget cuts in areas like higher education, K–12 education, and healthcare. There have been inklings about a coming politics of abandonment redolent of Flint—in November 2020 Governor Mark Gordon suggested to the legislature's Join Appropriations Committee that it might be necessary to abandon some of the state's smallest towns due to the cost of upkeep for roads and sewers.[8] While workers and communities have weathered cyclical downturns in the past, many now face the possibility of a permanent contraction, rising unemployment, increased youth out-migration, and sharp decline in quality of life.

Given these challenges, it seems difficult to imagine a just transition in Wyoming. At present, difficulties abound. Many challenges are economic and technical in nature, including questions about how or whether to diversify the economy, find higher value opportunities for coal beyond electricity generation, or pursue unproven technologies like carbon capture and storage or advanced nuclear. But the key sticking points are cultural and political. In a case study of the Powder River Basin (Campbell County) following the jarring Blackjewel mine closures in 2019, J. Mijin Cha interviewed industry, government, and community stakeholders and found little appetite for a statewide energy transition, even compared to Appalachia. Heavy partisanship and cultural identification with extraction, supported by some of the same manipulative industry tactics as in Appalachia (see chapter 3), drove intense skepticism over just transition policies and influenced perceptions that the coal industry is more resilient than it is. Residents expressed hostility toward the notion of government intervention to support a transition despite coal's continuing decline, reflecting the state's longstanding, professed aversion to federal assistance.[9] Such perceptions feed into Wyoming's enduring mythos of rugged individualism that ignores a long history of federal and state assistance for agriculture, ranching, and mineral extraction, which have nevertheless failed to reap long-term benefits and have locked the state into a cyclical, boom-and-bust economy.[10] An "energy colony," Wyoming exports both energy and wealth, remaining dependent on a fossil fuel industry eager to avoid taxation.[11] The result of this dependence, despite the antitransition bravado of industry and government stakeholders, has been an endemically fragile state economy accustomed to long downturns and brief bursts of prosperity when markets are favorable.

On the one hand, resistance to change is understandable. Wyoming coal workers, who produce 40 percent of the nation's coal, have long taken pride in their role in providing electricity for much of the United States.[12] To many Wyoming residents, the energy transition represents not only a threat to the enduring mythos of the state, but also to their very livelihoods and identities. On the other hand, the perpetuation of the narrative that Wyoming is self-sufficient, rich in mineral wealth, and imminently destined for prolonged prosperity defies reality. As Samuel Western wrote in his controversial revisionist history of the state, *Pushed Off the Mountain, Sold Down the River* (2002), "Wyoming has stood where Ireland remained for centuries: a poor, friendly, hardworking state that exports everything, especially talent."[13] Indeed, younger populations, facing few local job opportunities beyond an unreliable mineral sector, tend to leave the state in droves during downturns.[14] In times of slow or no growth in the fossil fuel sector, the state has often sought to reassert itself as "open for business," where low taxes and minimal regulations represent an ideal setting for business development. Such rhetorical repositioning has seldom borne results. In 1985, after years of declining oil and coal prices and an exodus of nearly twenty thousand people from the state over a four-year period, legislators invested $100,000 in the Wyoming Futures Project, which entailed public meetings to discuss diversifying the state's economy and creating new opportunities for Wyomingites. Despite the establishment of an economic development fund and other programs, the state soon turned its attention back to fossil energy and natural resources.[15] And thus the cycle has continued: in 2012 Wyoming was fourth in the nation in population growth during a decades-long coal boom, but by 2017 it was dead last as coal prices plummeted in competition with natural gas.[16]

Unfortunately, political inertia and blind partisanship have stripped state leadership of the will to take a proactive stance to ensure resilience against a prolonged downturn. At the legislative level, discussions about what comes next in Wyoming have largely been limited to considering ways to maintain the status quo. In the western United States, Wyoming stands largely alone in its continued commitment to coal despite regional trends toward renewable power generation and increasingly evident impacts of climate change.[17] As a result, there remain ongoing efforts to keep coal viable through artificial and unconventional means. In February 2020, for example, Oregon-based PacifiCorp released an Integrated Resource Plan detailing plans to replace multiple coal-fired power plants in southern Wyoming with wind and solar, threatening jobs and livelihoods for workers in communities like Kemmerer and Rock Springs. During a raucous public comment session, workers and community members accused PacifiCorp of "political correctness" and of catering to "radicals" in states controlled by Democratic governors and legislatures. Implying climate denial, some said that the necessity of renewables to stem carbon emissions in the face of climate change was just a suggestion from "pointy-headed liberals."[18] Since then, political pressure has mounted on the Wyoming Public Service Commission, whose primary function is to protect ratepayers, prevent plant closures, and commission a study challenging the economic viability of the utility's plans.[19] Moreover, despite concerns over scalability and economic viability, carbon capture and storage technology has been revered as a silver bullet for Wyoming's coal industry, with tens of millions in Department of Energy funds awarded to projects in the state.[20] While further investments in wind would likely offset job and revenue losses in the fossil fuel sector, opposition has also emerged in unexpected places, such as those who worry about the impacts of renewables on local environments and the outdoor recreation and tourism industry.[21]

How, then, can we imagine a just transition in Wyoming? If we turn to narrative, storytelling, and the arts—the subject of this book—we are immediately reminded of the *Carbon Sink* controversy. In 2010 renowned British land artist Chris Drury was commissioned, using anonymously donated funds, to create an outdoor exhibit at the University of Wyoming. His eventual project, *Carbon Sink*, commented on the intersection of fossil fuel extraction and burning and climate change. The installation used burnt logs from trees killed by pine bark beetles, a phenomenon driven by increasingly warm winters in the western United States. Drury arranged the logs in a large vortex interspersed with chunks of sub-bituminous coal like that found in the Powder River Basin. Looking in from the outside, the center of the vortex appeared as a blackened void. The clear critique of fossil fuel extraction as a driver of the climate crisis was installed next to Old Main on the university's campus in Laramie.

Statewide outrage ensued. Elected officials viewed it as an attack, on behalf of the university, against both the fossil fuel industry and the thousands of workers statewide it employs. Some viewed the sculpture as hypocritical given the university's reliance on state funding from coal, oil, and gas severance taxes. Threats to reduce the school's budget ensued, and angry representatives from the energy sector deluged the university with phone calls. The university's School of Energy Resources sought to pacify the industry by condemning the sculpture and reassuring donors of their loyalty to the industry.[22] The administration threw Drury under the bus, disavowing prior knowledge of the project. Escalating threats against funding over the sculpture garnered national attention, viewed by many as an effort to censor art and free speech. The university eventually acquiesced to pressure and removed the sculpture, and legislators took steps to ensure future proposals for artistic installations on campus must be reviewed and approved by the governor.[23]

In a state where many express, in my experience, something ranging from skepticism to outrage in response to any mention of a "transition," this episode might be viewed as having a chilling effect on future efforts to leverage the arts to advocate for social change. On the other hand, it is not difficult to understand why *Carbon Sink* elicited such outrage, even beyond its pointed critique of the fossil fuel industry. It makes a political statement—one I happen to agree with—without proposing an alternative path forward or reaching out to communities that stand to lose out economically from the widespread decarbonization of the U.S economy. This shortcoming, of course, does not excuse the actions of university officials or state legislators. But from a formal and aesthetic standpoint, the limits of *Carbon Sink*'s political critique stem from its failure to apprehend the centrality of energy extraction to the state's cultural and political imaginary and material economic realities. Moreover, reactions from university officials, state legislators, and the fossil fuel industry do not represent a consensus of opinion in the state. Despite the partisan tinge evident in the opposition to renewables expansion, the reality is more complex. In all, 60 percent of Wyomingites believe climate change is happening.[24] A recent study conducted by researchers at the University of Wyoming's School of Energy Resources found that residents grant broader social license to the development of renewable energy than previously assumed. In a survey of five hundred randomly selected residents, 66 percent of respondents supported wind development, 69 percent supported solar development, and many signaled an openness to nuclear energy. The survey also asked respondents about what they value most about Wyoming on a ranked scale of fourteen choices. Top values included aesthetics and scenery, biodiversity, recreation opportunities, economic opportunities, and a sense of community.[25] Such findings tell an alternative story about how Wyomingites view the many possible futures of the state and represent an opportunity to engage with diverse stakeholders to imagine a community-driven just transition.

There presently exist a handful of initiatives working to support ongoing conversations about transition in a more holistic way, focusing broadly on social resilience rather than narrowly on energy, that either are being led by or foreground the perspectives of citizen storytellers. During my first semester at the university, I partnered with fellow newcomer Dr. Corrie Knapp, a human ecologist who had just joined the faculty from out of state, to design a project entitled Imagining a Future Wyoming: Youth Narratives in a Time of Transition. The project involved partnering with high school teachers in communities impacted by the energy transition, especially coal's market downturn, to hold a series of scenario-planning workshops and conducting narrative research with high school seniors to explore how they "story" their places in their communities and the state. Project outcomes included discussing with students the importance of cultural narratives in their lives and the issues that they care about, and the project was expected to culminate in a statewide writing contest urging high school students to express their visions for a future Wyoming in nonfiction essays, fiction, and poetry. Twelve winners would have their work published in a digital anthology that would be distributed statewide, including to every member of the state legislature and the governor's office. The overall goal was to provide a platform for Wyoming youth, who we view as a largely ignored constituency, to have a say in the future direction of the state. However, our grant proposal with the Wyoming Humanities Council was rejected; despite enthusiasm from the judges, we had failed to secure adequate community buy-in during the frantic first few months of our tenure at the University of Wyoming. This episode was instructive. We learned quickly that community engagement in the state, often described by residents as a "small town with long streets," requires real relationship-building that we, as newcomers from out of state, had not yet had time to cultivate. In the ensuing months, we refined the project, committed time and resources to community outreach and, despite the COVID-19 pandemic, garnered interest in the project.

In September 2021 I collaborated with colleague Emilene Ostlind to relaunch the initiative as Imagining Wyoming's Future: A Youth Vision for 2030, a statewide multimedia contest asking youth to express their hopes for Wyoming by the year 2030 (see fig. 12). The contest was managed in the Ruckelshaus Institute for Environment and Natural Resources at the University of Wyoming with the generous support of the Wyoming Humanities Council, Wyoming Afterschool Alliance, and other community organizations, and we secured a diverse panel of judges from across the state. By the contest's deadline in November 2021, we had received over sixty submissions from nearly every county in the state. Entries included music, poetry, short fiction, nonfiction essays, documentary film, and visual art. In January 2022, after three rounds of review, judges selected three winners and seven runners up. The work of finalists and winners was published in an anthology and sent to state lawmakers, and we hope to make the contest an annual event. Compared to our earlier, failed bid to secure funding for the project, Imagining Wyoming's Future responds more directly to the fact that youth remain an underrepresented constituency and untapped source of political power in the state. In the classroom, I frequently hear from students that they love Wyoming but are disillusioned by political leadership and feel the state is headed in the wrong direction. Many, frustrated by the state's conservative stances on social and political issues and seeing few career opportunities beyond healthcare, education, and extractive industries, plan to leave after graduation.[26] At the same time, vocal young constituents have also flexed their political power to advocate for transition in recent years. For example, after months of opposition to the Rail Tie Wind Project near Laramie in Albany County due to homeowner concerns about wind turbines obstructing the views from their homes, county commissioner Sue Ibarra cast the deciding vote in favor of the project due specifically to youth advocacy for renewable energy. Young

12. Flyer for Imagining Wyoming's Future: A Youth Vision for 2030 Contest, 2021. Design by Emilene Ostlind.

climate organizers succeeded in telling a compelling story about the need for urgent climate action in Wyoming.[27]

We have not been alone in our efforts to pursue alternative narratives that imagine a transition beyond Wyoming's one-track reliance on extractive capital. Despite declining financial support for local news both nationally and in Wyoming, the state is home to a handful of terrific, dogged journalists. One of them is Dustin Bleizeffer, a former coal miner and oilfield mechanic turned journalist. Formerly the editor-in-chief at *WyoFile*, the state's primary independent news source, Bleizeffer now freelances with a focus on the politics of energy statewide. Recently, he collaborated with Mason Adams, a journalist who covers energy issues in Appalachia, on a reporting series entitled Transition in Coal Country. The project, funded by a grant awarded by the Just Transition Fund to the *Energy News Network* and *WyoFile*, takes a comparative approach to explore long-term challenges facing coal towns in Wyoming and Appalachia and to consider how geographically disparate communities can learn from one another and chart a path toward a sustainable, equitable future. Feature stories have covered issues such as regional political inertia, economic diversification and renewable energy, tax policy, healthcare and social welfare policies, and other issues associated with the coal transition. Through their reporting, which runs locally, Bleizeffer and Adams offer a humanizing narrative of what is likely to be a protracted, painful transition away from coal in Wyoming and Appalachia.[28]

Finally, at the University of Wyoming, I teach Environmental Justice in Literature and Culture, a class themed around imagining a just transition. The course goal is to prompt students to explore generative visions for equitable futures beyond simply documenting various instances of injustice. Because many of my students are from Wyoming, the class offers a critical opportunity to discuss various theories of social change and to consider how storytelling, narrative, and the arts can complement advocacy and policy to help communities imagine desirable futures. Along with units on Indigenous environmental activism, Latinx environmentalisms, and environmental racism, the class features a unit on energy justice that takes a comparative approach to exploring socio-ecological issues related to coal, oil, and gas extraction in Wyoming and Appalachia. The class also features a semester-long just transition project in which students are asked to express their own visions for a just transition through speculative scholarship or creative projects, a format that permits students a wide degree of latitude to explore issues of personal importance. Final projects have included a cookbook and community resource guide for food insecure students at the University of Wyoming; a podcast-style audio essay exploring the link between fossil fuel extraction, man camps, and missing and murdered Indigenous women; a plan for expanding community gardening initiatives in Detroit; and a persuasive essay imploring Wyomingites to reimagine their conception of the American dream to better prepare for the impending energy transition. By the end of the semester, students are better able to understand how narrative and storytelling function as important mechanisms to strengthen social resilience, and my hope is that such lessons prepare them and their communities in Wyoming to grapple with energy and climate challenges for years to come.

Though this book approaches the concept of a just transition through the lens of water insecurity in the United States, it is ultimately a theory of social change that can be adapted to consider potential pathways to sustainable, equitable futures more broadly. Most importantly, it should be clear that just transition frameworks must include more than provisions and policies for strengthened environmental regulations, remuneration, job training, economic diversification, and other sociotechnical fixes. Environmental injustice is inextricably linked to the extractive logics and corresponding social ideologies of a capitalist system that relies on the differentiation of human value. A just transition has the potential, by contrast, to support community-led, explicitly antiracist, decolonial approaches to environmental governance based on redress, reparations, and ongoing, meaningful engagement with historically marginalized stakeholders. To forge prosperous, equitable futures, it is critical that we deeply engage with other ways of knowing, submerged perspectives, and silenced constituencies. Indigenous collective continuance, the Black radical imagination, post-extraction futures, the emancipatory potential of the Green New Deal—each embody the imaginative possibilities of a just transition. The story of water in the United States is one of systemic disruption and social injustice. But new narratives are critical to imagining and working toward just, sustainable futures.

# Notes

## Introduction

1. Courtney Wheaton, "1st Annual Water Is Life Expo Kicks Off This Friday," *NBC 25 News*, March 24, 2017, https://nbc25news.com/news/nbc25-today/1st-annual-water-is-life-expo-kicks-off-this-friday; and Darren Thompson, "Water Is Life Expo," *Powwows.com*, March 13, 2017, https://www.powwows.com/water-life-expo/.
2. Mays, *Hip Hop Beats*, 110–12.
3. Kyle T. Mays, "From Flint to Standing Rock: The Aligned Struggles of Black and Indigenous People," *Fieldsights*, Society for Cultural Anthropology, December 22, 2016, https://culanth.org/fieldsights/from-flint-to-standing-rock-the-aligned-struggles-of-black-and-indigenous-people.
4. Petrella, "Standing Rock." The literature on global water justice is vast. See, e.g., Shiva, *Water Wars*; Barlow and Clarke, *Blue Gold*; and Harris et al., "Water Justice."
5. Dig Deep and U.S. Water Alliance, "Closing the Water Access Gap."
6. Brad Udall, Douglas Kenney, and John Fleck, "Opinion: Western States Buy Time with a 7-Year Colorado River Drought Plan, But Face a Hotter, Drier Future," *Colorado Sun*, July 16, 2019, https://coloradosun.com/2019/07/16/colorado-river-drought-plan-temporary-fix/.
7. Jose A. Del Real, "How Racism Ripples through Rural California's Pipes," *New York Times*, November 29, 2019, https://www.nytimes.com/2019/11/29/us/water-racism-california.html.
8. Nidhi Subbaraman, "Poison in the Pipes," *Buzzfeed News*, November 4, 2019, https://www.buzzfeednews.com/article/nidhisubbaraman/new-orleans-lead-water-hidden-report; Emma G. Fitzsimmons, "In Echo of Lead Water Crisis, Newark Offers Bottled Water," *New York Times*, August 11, 2019, https://www.nytimes.com/2019/08/11/nyregion/newark-water-lead.html?module=inline.
9. Kristi Pullen Fedinick, "What's in Your Water?: An Updated Analysis," *Natural Resources Defense Council Expert Blog*, September 14, 2018, https://www.nrdc.org/experts/kristi-pullen-fedinick/whats-your-water-updated-analysis.

10. Benny Becker, "Clean Water Wanted: Contaminated Wells and the Legacy of Fossil Fuel Extraction," *100 Days in Appalachia*, March 4, 2020, https://www.100daysinappalachia.com/2020/03/clean-water-wanted-contaminated-wells-and-the-legacy-of-fossil-fuel-extraction/.
11. Thomas Frank, "Flooding Disproportionately Harms Black Neighborhoods," *Scientific American*, June 2, 2020, https://www.scientificamerican.com/article/flooding-disproportionately-harms-black-neighborhoods/. After Hurricane Harvey hit Houston in 2017, nearly 70 percent of the city's nonwhite residents affected by severe flooding were left homeless, compared to just 38 percent of white residents (Fitzpatrick and Spialek, *Hurricane Harvey's Aftermath*, 55).
12. Hardy, Milligan, and Heynen, "Racial Coastal Formation."
13. See, e.g., Dominic Boyer and Imre Szeman, "Breaking the Impasse: The Rise of the Energy Humanities," *University Affairs*, February 12, 2014, https://www.universityaffairs.ca/opinion/in-my-opinion/the-rise-of-energy-humanities/; Szeman and Boyer, "Introduction"; and Dimianti and Bellamy, "Editors Introduction."
14. Harding and Margulis, "Water Gaia," 41.
15. See, e.g., Haddeland et al., "Global Water Resources"; Rodell et al., "Emerging Trends in Global Freshwater Availability"; van Loon et al., "Drought in the Anthropocene" and "Drought in a Human Modified World"; and Vörösmarty et al., "Global Threats to Human Water Security and River Biodiversity."
16. Deckard, "Water Shocks," 2–5.
17. Sassen, *Global City*, 3–4; Dawson, *Extreme Cities* 3.
18. Melamed, "Racial Capitalism."
19. EXTRACTION, "Decolonial Visual Cultures."
20. The term *sacrifice zone* here is inspired by the use of the term *sacrifice area* in a 1974 National Academy of Sciences report entitled *Rehabilitation of Western Coal Lands*, which explored the long-term impacts of surface coal mining in the western United States. In her book *The Tainted Desert*, Valerie Kuletz uses the term *geographies of sacrifice* when mapping the nuclear landscapes of the U.S. Southwest, where the horrors of environmental contamination and radiation-related illness have ravaged Indigenous communities. Kuletz explores how such actions were justified as part of a so-called greater good in support of energy independence, national security, and scientific research during the height of the Cold War. As Ward Churchill has pointed out, while the sacrifice area designation has remained unofficial in policy and industry circles, it is disproportionately composed of Indigenous lands, including the Four Corners and Black Hills regions (Kuletz, *Tainted Desert*, 38).

21. Patel and Moore, *History of the World*, 22; Nixon, *Slow Violence*, 150–74.
22. Patel and Moore, *History of the World*, 37.
23. For an overview of widening global inequality, see Piketty, *Capital in the Twenty-First Century*. For an overview of the environmentalism of the poor, see Martin-Alier, *Environmentalism of the Poor*.
24. Robinson, *Black Marxism*, 2.
25. See, e.g., Robinson, *Black Marxism*, 9–28; Melamed, "Racial Capitalism" and *Represent and Destroy*; Wang, *Carceral Capitalism*; Pulido, "Flint" and "Geographies of Ethnicity and Race II"; Vergès, "Racial Capitalocene."
26. According to Preston, because racial capitalism "centers race as an organizing principle of the economic order," it can be viewed as integral to extractive economies wherein "race is absolutely present, determining the value of bodies and of the land itself" (Preston, "Racial Extractivism," 355). Writing of extractive capitalism in Canada, Preston coins the term *racial extractivism*, a paradigm that "positions race and colonialism as central to extractivist projects under neoliberalism" and traces a direct line to settler colonialism.
27. Pulido, "Flint"; Wang, *Carceral Capitalism*, 72–74.
28. Estes, *Our History Is the Future*, 28; Whyte, "Dakota Access Pipeline."
29. See Adamson, Evans, and Stein, "Introduction"; Adamson, *American Indian Literature*; and Sze, "From Environmental Justice Literature" and *Environmental Justice in a Moment of Danger*.
30. Sze, *Environmental Justice in a Moment of Danger*, 76.
31. Di Chiro, "Seaweed, 'Soul'-ar Panels, and Other Entanglements," 70–72.
32. Isis Simpson-Mersha, "Flint Activists and Leaders Demand Flint to Be 'Made Whole' Following $600m Water Settlement," *MLive*, August 21, 2020, https://www.mlive.com/news/flint/2020/08/flint-activists-and-leaders-demand-flint-to-be-made-whole-following-600m-water-settlement.html.
33. Bill Chappell, "Michigan Agrees to Pay $600 Million to Flint Residents over Water Debacle," *NPR*, August 20, 2020, https://www.npr.org/2020/08/20/904258763/michigan-will-pay-600-million-to-flint-residents-over-water-debacle.
34. Patel and Moore, *History of the World*, 209.
35. Sze, *Environmental Justice in a Moment of Danger*, 78–79. As Sze notes, restorative environmental justice draws from principles of restorative justice, a concept in the criminal justice system that focuses on repairing harms caused by crime rather than merely punitive measures. For more on restorative justice, see Latimer, Dowden, and Muise, "Effectiveness of Restorative Justice Practices."
36. See McCauley and Heffron, "Just Transition."

37. Mazzocchi, "Superfund for Workers," 40.
38. Leopold, *Man Who Hated Work and Loved Labor*. See, also, Commoner, *Making Peace with the Planet*, and Mazzocchi, "An Answer to the Jobs-Environment Conflict?"
39. Trumka, "We'll Either Have a Just Transition or No Transition at All."
40. Adamson, "Campaign for a Just Transition"
41. Purdy, "Long Environmental Justice Movement."
42. Henry, Bazilian, and Markuson, "Just Transitions."
43. Climate Justice Alliance, "Green New Deal."
44. Climate Justice Alliance, "Green New Deal."
45. Indigenous Environmental Network, *Indigenous Principles of a Just Transition*.
46. U.S. Congress, House, *Duty of the Government to create a Green New Deal*.
47. Warren Democrats, "We Need a Blue New Deal."
48. Mazzocchi, "Answer to the Jobs-Environment Conflict?"
49. See, e.g., Klein, *This Changes Everything*.
50. Holm et al., "Humanities for the Environment."
51. For concise genealogies of the environmental humanities, see Adamson, "Humanities" and "Introduction: Integrating New Knowledge." For an overview of ecocritical literary studies, see Buell, *Future of Environmental Criticism*; and Garrard, ed., *Oxford Handbook of Ecocriticism*. For research on museum studies and the environmental humanities, see Newell, Robin, and Wehner, *Curating the Future*. For work on film studies and the environmental humanities, see Rust, Monani, and Cubitt, *Ecocinema Theory and Practice*; and Ziser, "Ecomedia."
52. See, e.g., Iovino and Opperman, "Introduction"; DeLoughrey, Didur, and Carrigan, "Introduction"; Di Chiro, "Environmental Justice and the Anthropocene Meme"; Malm and Hornborg, "Geology of Mankind?"; Moore, *Capitalism in the Web of Life*; and Rob Nixon, "The Great Acceleration and the Great Divergence: Vulnerability in the Anthropocene," *Profession*, March 2014, https://profession.mla.hcommons.org/2014/03/19/the-great-acceleration-and-the-great-divergence-vulnerability-in-the-anthropocene/.
53. Wenzel, "Turning over a New Leaf," 165.
54. Adamson and Ruffin, "Introduction," 7.
55. Adamson, *American Indian Literature*, 129.
56. Sze, "From Environmental Justice Literature," 166.
57. Nixon, *Slow Violence*, 3.
58. Richard Perez-Peña, "College Classes Use Arts to Brace for Climate Change," *New York Times*, April 1, 2014, https://www.nytimes.com/2014

/04/01/education/using-the-arts-to-teach-how-to-prepare-for-climate-crisis.html.
59. Schneider-Mayerson, von Mossner, and Maiecki, "Empirical Ecocriticism."
60. Schneider-Mayerson, "Influence of Climate Fiction" and "'Just as in the Book'?"
61. Jarva, "Introduction to Narrative for Futures Studies," 5–6.
62. This book does not seek to make a meaningful intervention in climate adaptation research, scenario planning, or narrative research methods. I am a practitioner of interdisciplinary environmental humanities research, and such an intervention is beyond my expertise. I would be remiss, however, not to acknowledge that scenario-planning both originated in the corporate sector and was in fact popularized by Royal Dutch Shell as it planned for contingencies during the 1970s oil crash (Angela Wilkinson and Roland Kupers, "Living in the Futures." *Harvard Business Review*, May 2013, https://hbr.org/2013/05/living-in-the-futures). It is my hope that *Hydronarratives* will highlight the potential of scenario *imagining*, through narrative and storytelling, as a catalyst for a just transition.
63. Star et al., "Supporting Adaptation Decisions through Scenario Planning," 88–91.
64. Wiseman et al., *Scenarios for Climate Adaptation*.
65. Amer, Daim, and Jetter, "Review of Scenario Planning," 23.
66. Jarva, "Introduction to Narrative for Futures Studies"; Amer, Daim, and Jetter, "Review of Scenario Planning," 25; Inayatullah, "Six Pillars."
67. Paschen and Ison, "Narrative Research in Climate Change Adaptation," 1084.
68. See Jarva, "Introduction to Narrative for Futures Studies"; and Paschen and Ison, "Narrative Research in Climate Change Adaptation."
69. Paschen and Ison, "Narrative Research in Climate Change Adaptation," 1086.
70. Paschen and Ison, "Narrative Research in Climate Change Adaptation," 1087–88.
71. Szeman and the Petrocultures Research Group, *After Oil*, 41.
72. Szeman and Boyer, "Introduction."
73. See, e.g., Amitav Ghosh, "Petrofiction: The Oil Encounter and the Novel," *New Republic*, March 2, 1992, 29–34; LeMenager, *Living Oil*; and Macdonald, "'Monstrous Transformer.'"
74. Wilson, Carlson, and Szeman, *Petrocultures*, 14. For examples of research on petrocultures, also see Szeman and Dimianti, *Energy Culture*, and Barrett and Worden, *Oil Culture*.

75. See, e.g., Hecht, *Being Nuclear*; Jones, *Routes of Power*; and Mitchell, *Carbon Democracy*.
76. Jones, "Petromyopia."
77. von Mossner, "Cinematic Landscapes in *Beasts of the Southern Wild*," 64
78. Boast, *Hydrofictions*, 6.
79. Boast, *Hydrofictions*, 21.
80. Deckard, "Water Shocks," 109.
81. Deckard, "Water Shocks," 111.
82. Gómez-Barris, *Extractive Zone*, 5.
83. Pulido, "Flint," 11.
84. Coral Davenport, "E.P.A. Moves to Rescind Contested Water Pollution Regulation," *New York Times*, June 27, 2017, https://www.nytimes.com/2017/06/27/climate/epa-rescind-water-pollution-regulation.html; Julie Eilperin and Brady Dennis, "EPA Eases Rules on How Coal Ash Waste is Stored Across U.S.," *Washington Post*, July 17, 2018, https://www.washingtonpost.com/national/health-science/epa-eases-rules-on-how-coal-ash-waste-is-stored-across-the-us/2018/07/17/740e4b9a-89d3-11e8-85ae-511bc1146b0b_story.html.
85. Benny Becker, "Clean Water Wanted: Contaminated Wells and the Legacy of Fossil Fuel Extraction," *100 Days in Appalachia*, March 4, 2020, https://www.100daysinappalachia.com/2020/03/clean-water-wanted-contaminated-wells-and-the-legacy-of-fossil-fuel-extraction/.
86. Ghosh, "Petrofiction: The Oil Encounter and the Novel," *New Republic*, March 2, 1992, 29–34.
87. Rob Nixon, "Great Acceleration and the Great Divergence: Vulnerability in the Anthropocene," *Profession*, March 2014, https://profession.mla.hcommons.org/2014/03/19/the-great-acceleration-and-the-great-divergence-vulnerability-in-the-anthropocene/.

## 1. Decolonizing Drought

1. Elena Saavedra Buckley, "One Tribal Nation Could Decide the Fate of Arizona's Drought Plan," *High Country News*, January 28, 2019, https://www.hcn.org/articles/colorado-river-one-tribal-nation-could-decide-the-fate-of-Arizonas-drought-plan; Howard Fischer, "GRIC Pulls Back on Drought Plan," *Pinal Central*, February 14, 2019, https://www.pinalcentral.com/breaking/gric-pulls-back-on-drought-plan/article_ed205069-6f59-5496-ac5b-5c7e58caaf1f.html; Ian James, "Gila River Indian Community Moves Ahead with Colorado River Drought Plan after Clash with Lawmaker," *Arizona Republic*, February 23, 2019, https://www.azcentral.com/story/news/local/arizona-environment/2019/02/23/gila-river-indian-community

-moves-ahead-colorado-river-deal/2962350002/. The Akimel O'odham are often referred to as their Hispanicized name, the Pima, but here I will use the noncolonial designation.

2. The Winters Doctrine emerged from the 1908 Supreme Court Case *Winters v. United States* and granted tribes exclusive rights to "all water sources which arise upon, border, traverse, or underlie a reservation" (qtd. in Sheridan, *Arizona*, 371). The bill was designed to weaken these rights by nullifying the state's "use it or lose it policy," which dictates that landowners may forfeit rights if allocations go unused for five years. Non-Indigenous farmers, many of whom grow water-intensive crops like cotton and alfalfa, have argued that they are entitled to waters of the Gila even if they are not always able to put them to productive use and argued the GRIC was using those waters illegally. See Buckley, "One Tribal Nation"; Meg Wilcox, "As Water Sources Dry Up, Arizona Farmers Feel the Heat of Climate Change," *Civil Eats*, September 18, 2019, https://civileats.com/2019/09/18/as-water-sources-dry-up-arizona-farmers-feel-the-heat-of-climate-change/; and Ian James, "Showdown over Water Bill Averted, Clearing Way for Arizona to Finish Colorado River Deal," *Arizona Republic*, February 13, 2019, https://www.azcentral.com/story/news/local/arizona-environment/2019/02/19/arizona-water-dispute-heats-up-threatening-derail-drought-plan/2910994002/.

3. "Use it or lose it" laws were upheld in Arizona by the Ninth Circuit Court of Appeals in 2018, sparking outcry from farmers in Pinal County (Buckley, "One Tribal Nation").

4. Christopher Conover, "Bill That Nearly Scuttled Drought Plan Shelved," *Arizona Public Media News*, February 20, 2019, https://news.azpm.org/p/news-splash/2019/2/20/146566-bill-that-nearly-scuttled-drought-plan-shelved/.

5. The reservation was federally recognized as the Gila River Indian Community in 1939.

6. As historian David DeJong explains, "The federal government created a crisis on the Gila River and then proposed a self-serving solution" to take possession of Indigenous lands (*Stealing the Gila*, 79).

7. For an overview of settler theft of Gila River waters and the intergenerational effects on GRIC, see DeJong, *Stealing the Gila*.

8. See Brown, "When Our Water Returns" for an overview of public health and food injustice issues in the GRIC.

9. Pima-Maricopa Irrigation Project, *History of the Gila River Water Settlement Act of 2004*. See also Bark and Jacobs, "Indian Water Rights Settlements."

10. Buckley, "One Tribal Nation."

11. Lillian Donahue, "Tribes' Role in Drought Contingency Plan Marks Turning Point for Inclusion," *Elemental: Covering Sustainability*, April 17, 2019, https://elementalreports.com/water/2019/04/17/tribes-role-in-drought-contingency-plan-marks-turning-point-for-inclusion/.
12. U.S. Bureau of Reclamation, "Colorado River Basin Ten Tribes Partnership Tribal Water Study."
13. Brett Walton, "With Water Leasing Vote, Colorado River Indian Tribes Will Seek Consequential Legal Change," WaterNews, *Circle of Blue*, January 30, 2019, https://www.circleofblue.org/2019/world/with-water-leasing-vote-colorado-river-indian-tribes-will-seek-consequential-legal-change/.
14. Water Education Foundation, "Colorado River."
15. Daniel Kraker, "New Water Czars," *High Country News*, March 15, 2004, https://www.hcn.org/issues/270/14616.
16. Wolfe, "Settler Colonialism," 388.
17. Whyte, "Dakota Access Pipeline," 159.
18. Estes, *Our History Is the Future*, 28.
19. A growing range of indicators confirm the drought's unique severity. For scientific studies, see Belmecheri et al., "Mid-Century Evaluation"; Cook, Ault, and Smerdon, "Unprecedented 21st Century Drought"; Griffin and Anchukaitis, "How Unusual Is the 2012–2014 California Drought?"; and Mann and Gleick, "Climate Change and California Drought." For in-depth reporting on the drought, see Robinson Meyer, "The Southwest May Be Deep into a Climate-Changed Mega-Drought," *Atlantic*, December 18, 2018, https://www.theatlantic.com/science/archive/2018/12/us-southwest-already-mega-drought/578248/.
20. Whyte, "Settler Colonialism," 131.
21. Whyte, "Settler Colonialism," 128.
22. Whyte, "Settler Colonialism," 129.
23. Whyte, "Settler Colonialism," 132.
24. Whyte, "Settler Colonialism," 136.
25. Vizenor, *Manifest Manners*, vii.
26. Whyte, "Settler Colonialism," 130.
27. Powell, *Report on the Lands*, 3.
28. For an overview of Powell's report and its initial reception, see Reisner, *Cadillac Desert*, 15–51.
29. Reisner, *Cadillac Desert*, 125.
30. For an overview of the historical factors behind the 1922 compact, see Hundley, *Water in the West*.
31. Summitt, *Contested Waters*, 43.
32. Summitt, *Contested Waters*, 114.

33. For an overview of the connections between human activity such as groundwater pumping, dam building, and reservoir storage on and drought and climate change, see AghaKouchak, "Water and Climate"; Deemer et al., "Greenhouse Gas Emissions"; and van Loon et al., "Drought in a Human-Modified World" and "Drought in the Anthropocene."
34. As Stephanie LeMenager notes in *Manifest and Other Destinies*, Powell's report "employs the words 'redeem' and 'redemption' so often that it begins to sound like a bizarre captivity narrative, with western lands hostage in their own aridity and the United States betting its legitimacy upon its ability to deliver the West from unfortunate weather" (23).
35. Powell, "From Savagery to Barbarism," 184-5. For an excellent overview of Powell's complicity in advancing the settler colonial project in the western U.S., see Carl Thompson, "John Wesley Powell's Settler-Colonial Vision for the West," *Edge Effects*, January 30, 2020, https://edgeeffects.net/john-wesley-powell/.
36. Nash, *Wilderness and the American Mind*, 23-43.
37. Reisner, *Cadillac Desert*, 5.
38. Reisner, *Cadillac Desert*, 114.
39. U.S. Bureau of Reclamation, "About Us."
40. Estes, *Our History Is the Future*, 148-49.
41. For an overview of the how federal land and water policies worked in tandem to displace Indigenous peoples from their lands, see Estes, *Our History Is the Future* 133-67; and Tyrell, *Crisis of the Wasteful Nation*, 99-125.
42. Estes, *Our History Is the Future*, 134.
43. Estes, *Our History Is the Future*, 134.
44. Estes, *Our History Is the Future*, 134-135.
45. Tyrell, *Crisis of the Wasteful Nation*, 108.
46. Preston, "Racial Extractivism," 358.
47. Griffith, "Hoover Damn," 31.
48. Griffith, "Hoover Damn," 32.
49. Qtd. in Griffith, "Hoover Damn," 32.
50. Griffith, "Hoover Damn," 34.
51. Reisner, *Cadillac Desert*, 12.
52. Sabo et al., "Reclaiming Freshwater Sustainability in Cadillac Desert."
53. Reisner, *Cadillac Desert*, 111.
54. Reisner, *Cadillac Desert*, 187-90.
55. Reisner, *Cadillac Desert*, 255.
56. Reisner, *Cadillac Desert*, 261.
57. As others have argued, the book's status as the authoritative guidebook for western water is curious given that it was published in 1986 and its most

recent printing, revised and updated, was in 1993. Reisner never wrote a follow-up and died in 2000, and no one else has written an update to his history in the new millennium. See Arnie Cooper, "Greening the Desert? Not so Fast!" *Pacific Standard.*, June 14, 2017, https://psmag.com/environment/greening-the-desert-not-so-fast-30957. To be sure, more recent histories of water in the West, typically less comprehensive in geographical and temporal scope, more adequately account for Indigenous experiences of water insecurity resulting from large water infrastructure projects and Federal land use policies. See, e.g., Summitt, *Contested Waters*.

58. Mark Hertsgaard, "If You Only Read One Book about the Water Crisis: *Cadillac Desert*," *Daily Beast*, July 11, 2015, https://www.thedailybeast.com/if-you-only-read-one-book-about-the-water-crisis-cadillac-desert.

59. Allison K. Hill, "10 Books about Drought: A Reading List for Parched Southern Californians," *Los Angeles Daily News*, September 16, 2015, https://www.dailynews.com/2015/09/16/10-books-about-drought-a-reading-list-for-parched-southern-californians/.

60. Bacigalupi, *Water Knife*, 181.

61. Bacigalupi, *Water Knife*, 262.

62. See, e.g., Michael Friberg, "Picturing the Drought," *ProPublica*, July 7, 2015, https://projects.propublica.org/killing-the-colorado/story/michael-friberg-colorado-water-photo-essay; and Alan Taylor, "Dramatic Photos of California's Historic Drought," *Atlantic*, September 3, 2014, https://www.theatlantic.com/photo/2014/09/dramatic-photos-of-californias-historic-drought/100804/.

63. Burtynsky, Davis, and Lord, *Water*.

64. Baichwal and Burtynsky, *Watermark*.

65. For an overview of the 1944 U.S.-Mexico water-sharing agreement, ecological issues related to dams upstream from the border, and ongoing disputes over water sharing agreements, see Summitt, *Contested Waters*, 169–95.

66. Muehlmann, *Where the River Ends*, 3–11.

67. Whyte, "Our Ancestors' Dystopia Now," 207.

68. Silko, *Gardens*, 204.

69. Silko, *Gardens*, 212.

70. Julia Lurie, "Here's What I Saw in a California Town without Running Water," *Mother Jones*, September 7, 2015, https://www.motherjones.com/environment/2015/09/drought-no-running-water-east-porterville/.

71. Jeff Daniels, "California's Four-Year Drought Starts 'Water Truck' Boom," *CNBC*, April 8, 2015, https://www.nbcnews.com/storyline/california-drought/californias-four-year-drought-starts-water-truck-boom-n338016.

72. Michael Klare, "The Future of Oil Is Here—and It Doesn't Look Pretty," *Nation*, March 1, 2016, https://www.thenation.com/article/archive/the-future-of-oil-is-here-and-it-doesnt-look-pretty/.
73. For an overview of the ways in which poorly executed federal reclamation efforts affected tribal communities relocated to the CRIT Reservation, see Caylor, "A Promise Long Deferred."
74. U.S. National Park Service, "California: Parker Dam."
75. For an overview of the environmental impacts of damming, diverting, and storing Colorado River water, see Summitt, *Contested Waters*, 61–86.
76. Adamson, "Medicine Food," 218.
77. Ryan, "Nineteenth-Century Garden," 119.
78. Adamson, "Medicine Food," 218.
79. Hia-Ced Hemajkam, LLC, "Our History."
80. Sandfood remains culturally meaningful for Hia C-ed O'odham. See Nabhan's work cited in this chapter.
81. Nabhan, Hodgson, and Fellows, "Meager Living" 524. For an overview of traditional Hia C-ed O'odham lifeways prior to settler occupation see Nabhan, *Gathering the Desert* and "Ecology of Floodwater Farming."
82. Silko, *Gardens* 36.
83. Whyte, "Settler Colonialism," 127.
84. Whyte, "Settler Colonialism," 128.
85. Silko, *Gardens*, 218.
86. Silko, *Gardens*, 215.
87. Silko, *Gardens*, 337. Silko also fictionalizes Arizona's failed attempt, in the mid-1930s, to prevent the construction of Parker Dam because it was viewed as attempt by California to dip into less-populated Arizona's federally designated allocation of Colorado River water. After Arizona's governor, B.B. Moeur, sent the Arizona National Guard to occupy the dam site for seven months, the U.S. Supreme Court overruled Arizona's claims and allowed construction to proceed. For an overview of the Arizona-California "water wars," see Reisner, *Cadillac Desert*, 257–59.
88. Silko, *Gardens*, 211–12.
89. Silko, *Gardens*, 216.
90. Silko, *Gardens*, 431–52.
91. Qtd. in Dunar and McBride, *Building Hoover Dam*, 311
92. Griffith, "Hoover Damn," 31.
93. Griffith, "Hoover Damn," 37.
94. Griffith, "Hoover Damn," 204–5.
95. Silko, *Gardens*, 398–401.

96. Silko, *Gardens*, 476–77.
97. Ross, *Bird on Fire*, 15.
98. Ross, *Bird on Fire*, 41.
99. Arizona Department of Water Resources, *Phoenix Active Management Area*.
100. U.S. Climate Data, "Climate—Phoenix, Arizona."
101. Ross, *Bird on Fire*, 42.
102. Ross, *Bird on Fire*, 256 n34.
103. Ross, *Bird on Fire*, 21–30.
104. For an overview of Papago O'odham floodwater farming techniques, see Nabhan, "Ecology of Floodwater Farming."
105. Central Arizona Project, "Agua Fria."
106. Ross, *Bird on Fire*, 29.
107. Newell, Robin, and Wehner, *Curating the Future* 3.
108. Observations here are based on my visit to Pueblo Grande in March 2016.
109. Canal Convergence, "Su:dagi Haicu A:ga (Water's Story)."
110. Tasha Silverhorn, "O'odham Artists Win Water Public Art Challenge to Install Art Piece on Mill Avenue," *O'odham Action News*, December 6, 2018, https://oan.srpmic-nsn.gov/archives/2018/dec-06-2018/stories/story01.asp.
111. August, "Vision in the Desert," 114.
112. August, "Vision in the Desert," 120–21.
113. August, "Vision in the Desert," 130–31. For example, Hayden supported settler irrigation entrepreneurs such as William Ellsworth Smyth and George Maxwell and attended National Irrigation Congress meetings.
114. Cultural Coalition, "Portal to the Past"; Guerrero, "Zarco Guerrero Biography"; and Chelsea Hofmann, "You Can Now Run or Bike from I-17 to Tempe Town Lake With Improved Grand Canal," *Arizona Republic*, February 15, 2020, https://www.azcentral.com/story/news/local/phoenix/2020/02/15/renovated-grand-canal-complete-now-connects-phoenix-and-tempe/4738362002/.
115. Salt River Project, "A History of Canals in Arizona." See, also, August, "A Vision in the Desert."
116. For an overview of different hypotheses for the Hohokam's supposed disappearance, which ignore the fact that their descendants, the Tohono and Akimel O'odham, persist today. See Ross, *Bird on Fire*, 25–28.
117. Wright, *Beyond All Boundaries*.
118. Ross, *Bird on Fire*, 239.
119. Arizona State University, "ASU's Future $H_2O$."

120. John Sabo, "My Turn: 7 Ideas That Will Change How We Look at Water," *Arizona Republic*, March 22, 2016, https://www.azcentral.com/story/opinion/op-ed/2016/03/22/water-supply-arizona/82079120/.

## 2. Freedom Dreams for Flint

1. Emma Winowiecki, "Does Flint Have Clean Water? Yes, But It's Complicated." *Michigan Radio*, August 21, 2019, https://www.michiganradio.org/post/does-flint-have-clean-water-yes-it-s-complicated.
2. Nixon, *Slow Violence*.
3. Christopher F. Petrella, "Standing Rock, Flint, and the Color of Water," *Black Perspectives*, November 2, 2016, https://www.aaihs.org/standing-rock-flint-and-the-color-of-water/.
4. Bill Chappell, "Michigan Agrees to Pay $600 Million to Flint Residents over Water Debacle," NPR, August 20, 2020, https://www.npr.org/2020/08/20/904258763/michigan-will-pay-600-million-to-flint-residents-over-water-debacle.
5. Patel and Moore, *History of the World*, 207–12.
6. Climate Justice Alliance, "Green New Deal."
7. Movement for Black Lives, "Reparations."
8. Pulido, "Flint" and "Geographies of Race and Ethnicity II."
9. See, e.g., Associated Press, "A Timeline of the Water Crisis in Flint, Michigan," *AP News*, June 14, 2017, https://apnews.com/article/1176657a4b0d468c8f35ddbb07f12bec; CNN, "Flint Water Crisis Fast Facts," January 14, 2021, https://www.cnn.com/2016/03/04/us/flint-water-crisis-fast-facts/index.html; Jeremy C. F. Lin, Jean Rutter, and Haeyoun Park, "Events That Led to Flint's Water Crisis," *New York Times*, January 21, 2016, https://www.nytimes.com/interactive/2016/01/21/us/flint-lead-water-timeline.html; and Merrit Kennedy, "Lead-Laced Water in Flint: A Step-By-Step Look at the Makings of a Crisis," NPR, April 20, 2016, https://www.npr.org/sections/thetwo-way/2016/04/20/465545378/lead-laced-water-in-flint-a-step-by-step-look-at-the-makings-of-a-crisis.
10. See Highsmith, *Demolition Means Progress*; and Clark, *Poisoned City*.
11. Kelley, *Freedom Dreams*, 1–12.
12. Robinson, *Black Marxism*, 2.
13. Robinson, *Black Marxism*, 168.
14. Robinson, *Black Marxism*, 71–171. For a definitive overview of Robinson's work and its legacies in the present, see Johnson and Lubin, "Introduction."
15. Lipsitz, "What Is This Black?"
16. Melamed, "Racial Capitalism," 77. For recent critical approaches to racial capitalism, see Johnson and Lubin, *Futures of Black Radicalism*.

17. Lowe, *Intimacies of Four Continents*, 149–50.
18. Melamed, "Racial Capitalism," 77.
19. Melamed, *Represent and Destroy*.
20. Wang, *Carceral Capitalism*, 11–95.
21. Vergès, "Racial Capitalocene."
22. Pulido, "Geographies of Race and Ethnicity II," 526.
23. Pulido, "Geographies of Race and Ethnicity II," 527.
24. Pulido, "Geographies of Race and Ethnicity II," 529.
25. Pulido, "Geographies of Race and Ethnicity II," 524.
26. Pulido, "Flint," 4.
27. Pulido, "Flint," 2.
28. Pulido, "Flint," 1.
29. Wang, *Carceral Capitalism*, 72–74.
30. Pulido, "Flint," 530.
31. Lipsitz, "What Is This Black?"
32. Lipsitz, "What Is This Black?"
33. Johnson and Rubin, "Introduction," 18.
34. Johnson and Rubin, "Introduction," 21.
35. For an overview of Black radicalism in the contemporary moment, see Johnson and Lubin, *Futures of Black Radicalism*.
36. Kelley, *Freedom Dreams*, 6–7.
37. Kelley, *Freedom Dreams*, 10.
38. Kelley, *Freedom Dreams*, 114.
39. Kelley, *Freedom Dreams*, 118–34.
40. Climate Justice Alliance, "Green New Deal."
41. Quotations from the screenplay of Flint were derived from a recording of the play and a copy of the script, which is not publicly available, provided to me courtesy of José Casas. See Casas, *Flint* and "Flint by José Casas."
42. University of Michigan School of Music, Theatre & Dance, "'Flint:' A New Play by José Casas."
43. Michael H. Hodges, "Playwright Channels Anger into 'Flint,'" *Detroit News*, April 3, 2019, https://www.detroitnews.com/story/entertainment/2019/04/04/playwright-channels-anger-into-flint/3345094002/; and Julie Hinds, "U-M's 'Flint' Monologue Play Gives a Voice to the Pain, Truths of a City Betrayed," *Detroit Free Press*, April 3, 2019, https://www.freep.com/story/entertainment/arts/2019/04/03/flint-play-monologues-michigan-jose-casas/3334622002/.
44. John Monaghan, "A Story about Flint and Its Troubles Takes the Stage," *Detroit Free Press*, January 24, 2018, https://www.freep.com/story

/entertainment/arts/2018/01/24/flint-play-purple-rose-theatre-jeff-daniels/1056330001/.
45. David Smith, "'It Was Just Left to the People': Behind a Chilling Documentary on the Flint Water Crisis," *Guardian*, March 10, 2020, https://www.theguardian.com/film/2020/mar/09/flint-water-crisis-documentary-anthony-baxter.
46. Baglia and Foster, "Performing the 'Really' Real."
47. Martin, *Theatre of the Real*, 5.
48. Baglia and Foster, "Performing the 'Really' Real," 92.
49. Mienczakowski, "Theatre of Ethnography," 367.
50. Mienczakowski, "Theatre of Ethnography," 364.
51. See Delgado, "On Telling Stories in School."
52. See, e.g., Solarzano and Yosso, "Critical Race and LatCrit" and Croom and Marsh, *Envisioning Critical Race Praxis*.
53. See, e.g., Lawson, "Critical Race Theory as Praxis" and Stovall, "Forging Community in Race and Class."
54. Delgado, "Storytelling for Oppositionists and Others," 2413.
55. Delgado, "Storytelling for Oppositionists and Others," 2414-15.
56. Casas, *Flint*.
57. Casas, *Flint*.
58. Grossman and Slusky, "Impact of the Flint Water Crisis on Fertility."
59. Nestlé, "Facts and Figures."
60. Alice Yin, "Michigan to Close Flint's Free Bottled Water Sites," *Associated Press*, April 6, 2018, https://apnews.com/article/021ccddf1c8742f0a2524fb2bee6b21a.
61. "Flint Resumes Water Shutoffs for People Who Don't Pay Bills," *ABC12 News*, March 12, 2018, https://www.abc12.com/content/news/Flint-resumes-water-shutoffs-for-people-who-dont-pay-bills-476581683.html.
62. Trevor Bach, "As Flint Suffers and Nestlé Prospers, Many Are Asking: Who Owns the Rights to Michigan Water?" *Belt Magazine*, June 14, 2018, https://beltmag.com/flint-Nestlé-michigan-water-rights/; Jessica Glenza, "Nestlé Pays $200 a Year to Bottle Water Near Flint—Where Water Is Undrinkable," *Guardian*, September 29, 2017, https://www.theguardian.com/us-news/2017/sep/29/Nestlé-pays-200-a-year-to-bottle-water-near-flint-where-water-is-undrinkable.
63. Alexandra Shimo, "While Nestlé Extracts Millions of Litres from Their Land, Residents Have No Drinking Water," *Guardian*, October 4, 2018, https://www.theguardian.com/global/2018/oct/04/ontario-six-nations-Nestlé-running-water.

64. Jim Malewitz, "Flint Residents Welcome Nestlé Donations. But Its Ads? Not So Much," *Bridge Michigan*, January 30, 2019, https://www.bridgemi.com/michigan-environment-watch/flint-residents-welcome-Nestlé-donations-its-ads-not-so-much.
65. Bach, "As Flint Suffers"; Glenza, "Nestlé Pays $200 a Year."
66. "Nestlé on Criticism It's 'Exploiting' Flint: 'Water Is an Emotional Issue," *Deadline Detroit*, November 17, 2018, https://www.deadlinedetroit.com/articles/21039/Nestlé_on_criticism_it_s_exploiting_flint_water_is_an_emotional_issue.
67. Melamed, "Racial Capitalism," 77.
68. Casas, *Flint*.
69. Casas, *Flint*. For Mayor Weaver's response to Nestlé, see Jason Lorenz, "Flint Mayor Announces Acceptance of Nestlé Bottled Water Donation," *NBC 25 News*, May 10, 2018. https://nbc25news.com/news/local/flint-mayor-announces-acceptance-of-Nestlé-bottled-water-donation.
70. Jennifer Yachnin, "Flint Crisis: Fiasco Threatens Bid to Create Farms in Urban Wasteland," *E&E News*, February 1, 2016, https://www.eenews.net/stories/1060031582.
71. Kelley, *Freedom Dreams*, 132.
72. Casas, *Flint*.
73. Tracy Samilton, "Fear Prevents Some Undocumented Immigrants from Getting Water in Flint," *Michigan Radio*, January 27, 2016, https://www.michiganradio.org/post/fear-prevents-some-undocumented-immigrants-getting-water-flint.
74. Casas, *Flint*.
75. Queens Museum, "Flint Fit."
76. Brian Boucher, "Can an Art-Fashion Collaboration Really Help the People of Flint, Michigan? Artist Mel Chin Is Betting on It," *Artnet News*, November 7, 2017, https://news.artnet.com/art-world/mel-chin-tracey-reese-flint-fit-1132754; Queens Museum, "Flint Fit"; Jenna Igneri, "Tracy Reese Designed a Collection Using Plastic Bottles from Flint," *Nylon*, April 6, 2018, https://www.nylon.com/articles/tracy-reese-mel-chin-flint-fit-collection; Mekita Rivas, "Designer Tracy Reese Creates 'Flint Fit' Collection Using Plastic Water Bottles from Flint Water Crisis," *Teen Vogue*, April 6, 2018, https://www.teenvogue.com/story/designer-tracy-reese-flint-fit-plastic-bottles-flint-water-crisis.
77. Teresa Mathew, "Mel Chin's Look at Destruction and Hope," *Bloomberg*, April 11, 2018, https://www.bloomberg.com/news/articles/2018-04-11/mel-chin-s-new-show-at-the-queens-museum-is-truly-is-all-over-the-place.

78. Sebastien Malo, "Crisis Chic: Bottles Linked to Flint's Toxic Water Are Refashioned as Clothing Line," *Reuters*, April 6, 2018, https://de.reuters.com/article/us-usa-water-flint/crisis-chic-bottles-linked-to-flints-toxic-water-are-refashioned-as-clothing-line-idUSKCN1HD2FI.
79. Melamed, *Represent and Destroy*.
80. Flint Public Art Project, "Mission & Vision"; "Flint Public Art Project Brings Street Art to the City," *Inspiring City*, August 28, 2020, https://inspiringcity.com/2020/08/28/flint-public-art-project-brings-street-art-to-the-city/.
81. Peter Hinterman, "The Flint Public Art Project: 100 Murals by 2020," *My City Magazine*, August 1, 2019, http://www.mycitymag.com/the-flint-public-art-project-100-murals-by-2020/; Alexandria Brown, "Wave of New Murals Position Flint as One of the World's Top Destinations for Street Art," *Flintside*, August 7, 2019, https://www.flintside.com/features/waveofnewmuralspositionFlintasoneofworldstopdestinationsforstreetart.aspx.
82. Flint Public Art Project, "Free City."
83. "Flint Public Art Project Paints a Power Message Downtown," *ABC 12 News*, June 14, 2020, https://www.abc12.com/content/news/Flint-Public-Art-Project-paints-a-power-message-downtown-571255601.html.
84. Ron Fonger, "Flint Attorneys to Detail Proposed $641-Million Water Crisis Settlement," *MLive*, November 23, 2020, https://www.mlive.com/news/flint/2020/11/flint-attorneys-to-detail-proposed-641-million-water-crisis-settlement-in-virtual-briefing-monday-afternoon.html.

## 3. Post-Extraction Futurisms

1. Pancake, *Strange*, 101.
2. According the U.S. Energy Information Administration, West Virginia had 123 active coal mines as of 2016, or a rate of one mine per 195 square miles. For recent figures, see U.S. Energy Information Administration, *Annual Coal Report* 2020, 2–3.
3. For a gripping look at the social and topographic transformation of Appalachia through surface coal mining, see Jedediah Purdy, "The Violent Remaking of Appalachia," *Atlantic*, March 21, 2016. https://www.theatlantic.com/technology/archive/2016/03/the-violent-remaking-of-appalachia/474603/.
4. Benny Becker, "Clean Water Wanted: Contaminated Wells and the Legacy of Fossil Fuel Extraction." *100 Days in Appalachia*, March 4, 2020, https://www.100daysinappalachia.com/2020/03/clean-water-wanted-contaminated-wells-and-the-legacy-of-fossil-fuel-extraction/.

5. Brian Sewell, "Remembering Buffalo Creek," *Appalachian Voice*, February 21, 2012, https://appvoices.org/2012/02/21/remembering-buffalo-creek/.
6. Moore, *Capitalism in the Web of Life*, 68.
7. Deckard, "Ghost Mountains and Stone Maidens" and "Trains, Stones, and Energetics"; Niblett, "World Economy, World-Ecology, World Literature" and "Oil on Sugar."
8. LeMenager, *Living Oil*, 12–13.
9. For examples of such work, see Apter, *Pan-African Nation*; LeMenager, *Living Oil*, 125–133; Wenzel, "Petro-Magic Realism"; Nixon, *Slow Violence*, 68–127; Caminero-Santangelo, "Witnessing the Nature of Violence."
10. Helpful overviews of resource curse dynamics include Klare, *Resource Wars*; Humphreys, Sachs, and Stiglitz, *Escaping the Resource Curse*; and Ross, *Oil Curse*.
11. For a useful overview of the region's energy history, see Black, "Legacy of Extraction."
12. The Just Transition Fund is one such organization that pools and distributes philanthropic resources to foster an equitable economic transition in coal communities. See https://www.justtransitionfund.org/overview.
13. Appalachian Voices, "New Economy for Appalachia."
14. Just Transition Fund, "Building Jobs and Opportunity for the Mountain State."
15. EXTRACTION, "Decolonial Visual Cultures."
16. Watts, "Oil Frontiers," 190; Tsing, *Friction*, 31–32.
17. For an overview of environmental injustice associated with energy development, see Hess and Ribiero, "Energy and Environmental Justice," 153–58.
18. Kuletz, *Tainted Desert*, 6.
19. Amitav Ghosh, "Petrofiction: The Oil Encounter and the Novel," *New Republic*, March 2, 1992, 29–34.
20. Szeman and Boyer, "Introduction," 4.
21. Jack Pendarvis, "Buried Alive," *New York Times*, October 14, 2007, https://www.nytimes.com/2007/10/14/books/review/Pendarvis-t.html.
22. Robertson, "Gothic Appalachia," 110.
23. Burns, *Bringing Down the Mountain*, 5–7.
24. Burns, *Bringing Down the Mountain*, 118–140.
25. Scott, *Removing Mountains*, 140.
26. Scott, *Removing Mountains*, 139.
27. Burns, *Bringing Down the Mountain*, 19–32.
28. Burns, *Bringing Down the Mountain*, 4.
29. Scott, *Removing Mountains*, 4.
30. Scanlan, "Environmental Justice in Appalachia," 21–26.

31. Petras and Veltmeyer, *Extractive Imperialism in the Americas*, 11 n5.
32. Witt, *Religion and Resistance*, 163.
33. Houser, "Knowledge Work," 108.
34. Houser, "Knowledge Work," 108–9
35. Scott, *Removing Mountains*, 28.
36. Scott, *Removing Mountains*, 33–4.
37. Scott, *Removing Mountains*, 63.
38. Buell, "Toxic Discourse," 639.
39. Pancake, *Strange*, 25.
40. Pancake, *Strange*, 213.
41. Pancake, *Strange*, 343.
42. Stern, *Buffalo Creek Disaster*, ix.
43. Pancake, *Strange*, 224.
44. Pancake, *Strange*, 75.
45. Pancake, *Strange*, 76.
46. Pancake, *Strange*, 151.
47. Pancake, *Strange*, 58.
48. Pancake, *Strange*, 315.
49. Pancake, *Strange*, 36.
50. Pancake, *Strange*, 100; 108; 109; 160; 244.
51. Pancake, *Strange*, 272.
52. Pancake, *Strange*, 354.
53. Pancake, *Strange*, 355.
54. Cunsolo and Ellis, "Ecological Grief," 275.
55. Scott, *Removing Mountains*, 10.
56. Scott, *Removing Mountains*, 227–28 n5.
57. Scott, *Removing Mountains*, 212–13.
58. Barry, *Standing Our Ground*, 84–113.
59. Pancake, *Strange*, 357.
60. Jackson et al., "Increased Stray Gas Abundance"; Osborn et al., "Methane Contamination."
61. For an overview of fracking-related freshwater contamination and regulatory shortcomings in the United States, see Abraham Lustgarten, "Injection Wells: The Poison Beneath Us," *ProPublica*, June 21, 2012, https://www.propublica.org/article/injection-wells-the-poison-beneath-us.
62. Walsh and Zoback, "Oklahoma's Recent Earthquakes."
63. Jackson et al., "Increased Stray Gas Abundance," 3; Prud'homme, *Hydrofracking*, 85–89.
64. Nixon, *Slow Violence*, 2.
65. Ogneva-Himmelberger and Huang, "Spatial Distribution."

66. Prud'homme, *Hydrofracking*, 65; Colborn et al., "Natural Gas Operations."
67. Malin and DeMaster, "Devil's Bargain," 283.
68. Malin and DeMaster, "Devil's Bargain," 285.
69. Matz and Renfrew, "Selling Fracking."
70. U.S. Congress, Energy Policy Act of 2005, Section 322.
71. Cherniack, *Hawk's Nest Incident*, 104-5.
72. Kasdorf and Rubin, *Shale Play*, xxiii. West Virginia University Press's 2018 reissue of Rukeyser's work is the first to include Naumburg's photographs alongside Ruckeyser's poetry.
73. Kasdorf and Rubin, *Shale Play*, xxii.
74. Kasdorf and Rubin, *Shale Play*, 106.
75. Kasdorf and Rubin, *Shale Play*, 19, 107.
76. Kasdorf and Rubin, *Shale Play*, 16-18.
77. Kasdorf and Rubin, *Shale Play*, 90-91.
78. Kasdorf and Rubin, *Shale Play*, 12.
79. In an interview, Haigh emphasized that the novel is about "the soul of a place and how [it] is impacted by the choices we make, economic choices." Jennifer Haigh, interview by Lynn Neary. "'Heat & Light' Digs for the Soul of Coal Country," *All Things Considered*, NPR, May 4, 2016.
80. Jennifer Haigh, interview by Mary Laura Philpott, "Fracking—This Time It's Personal: Jennifer Haigh's Compelling New Novel," *Musing* (blog), Parnassus Books, May 10, 2016, https://parnassusmusing.net/2016/05/10/jennifer-haigh-heat-and-light/.
81. Fox, *Gasland*.
82. Mike Soraghan, "Groundtruthing Academy Award Nominee 'Gasland,'" *New York Times*, February 24, 2011, https://archive.nytimes.com/www.nytimes.com/gwire/2011/02/24/24greenwire-groundtruthing-academy-award-nominee-gasland-33228.html.
83. Fox, *Gasland*.
84. Haigh, "Fracking—This Time It's Personal."
85. Jaqueline Yahn argues that ideologies of American exceptionalism driving coal development in northern Appalachia have rendered the region vulnerable to exploitation by the natural gas industry. See Yahn, "Frackonomics," 139-154.
86. Haigh, *Heat and Light*, 426. For a history of energy in Appalachia, see Black and Ladson, "Legacy of Extraction."
87. Haigh, *Heat and Light*, 10, italics in original.
88. Haigh, *Heat and Light*, 260.

89. Haigh, *Heat and Light*, 326. SMCLs are secondary maximum contaminant levels.
90. Haigh, *Heat and Light*, 325, italics in original.
91. Haigh, *Heat and Light*, 77.
92. Haigh, *Heat and Light*, 81.
93. Haigh, *Heat and Light*, 319–20.
94. Hurd, "Foreword," xiii.
95. Szeman and the Petrocultures Research Group, *After Oil*, 41.
96. Reece, "Reclaiming a Toxic Legacy through Art and Science."
97. Personal communication, March 18, 2019.
98. Comp, "Science," 66–67.
99. Comp, "Liability to Asset," 420.
100. Sabraw, "Current Body of Work."
101. John Sabraw (@johnsabraw), "Toxic Art: The Proof Is in the Paint," Medium, March 30, 2018, https://medium.com/@johnsabraw/toxic-art-the-proof-is-in-the-paint-fcf90183a484.
102. Sabraw, personal phone conversation, May 2018.
103. Newell, Robin, and Wehner, "Introduction."
104. Young, "Counter-Monument," 271.
105. Young, "Counter-Monument," 270; 295.
106. Comp, "Science," 64.
107. Comp, "Liability to Asset," 416.
108. Comp, "Science," 63–64.
109. Comp, "Liability to Asset," 418–19.
110. Comp, "Liability to Asset," 416.
111. Sabraw, Personal Interview.
112. For more information about Appalshop, including a list of past and current projects visit, https://www.appalshop.org/about-us/.
113. *Queer Appalachia*, "About Us."

## 4. On the Wrong Side of the Levee

1. Headlines, in fact, tended to distort this claim a bit. The report actually argues that in order for countries to reduce carbon emissions enough by 2050 to prevent an increase of more than 1.5° C, significant progress would need to be made prior to 2030 to reach that target. See, e.g., Bob Berwyn, "What Does '12 Years to Act on Climate Change' (Now 11 Years) Really Mean?" *Inside Climate News*, August 27, 2019, https://insideclimatenews.org/news/27082019/12-years-climate-change-explained-ipcc-science-solutions.

2. Mason-Delmotte et al., eds., *Global Warming of 1.5°C*.
3. Pörtner et al., eds., *Report on the Ocean and Cryosphere*.
4. David Roberts, "The Green New Deal, Explained," *Vox*, March 30, 2019, https://www.vox.com/energy-and-environment/2018/12/21/18144138/green-new-deal-alexandria-ocasio-cortez.
5. Brian Kahn, "More than 600 Environmental Groups Just Backed Ocasio-Cortez's Green New Deal," *Gizmodo*, January 1, 2019, https://earther.gizmodo.com/more-than-600-environmental-groups-just-backed-ocasio-c-1831640541; Gustafson et al., *Green New Deal Has Strong Bipartisan Support*.
6. U.S. Congress, House, *Duty of the Government to create a Green New Deal*.
7. Marianne Lavelle, "Where Is the Green New Deal Headed in 2020?" *Inside Climate News*, January 2, 2020, https://insideclimatenews.org/news/02012020/green-new-deal-future-2020-election-climate-change-sanders-ocasio-cortez/.
8. Zoya Teirstein, "The Group that Pushed the Green New Deal Sets Its Sights on 2020 and Beyond," *Grist*, June 19, 2019, https://grist.org/article/for-the-sunrise-movement-2020-is-just-the-beginning/.
9. Because of their exploration of climate-related issues, *New York 2140* and *Beasts of the Southern Wild* have both been described as climate fiction, a subgenre of literary fiction that engages with expected and ongoing biophysical and sociocultural effects of climate change. Yet because both the novel and the film are deeply engaged with questions of social justice, this designation is perhaps overly narrow. Many texts that fall under the nebulous heading of climate fiction are not as clearly focused on issues of social justice as they are characterized by the repetition of several key tropes derived from a long tradition of speculative and science fiction or early environmentalist rhetoric, imagine apocalyptic or postapocalyptic futures, and emphasize the grand scales of climate change (Ziser and Sze, "Climate Change," 385–87; Stephen Siperstein, "Climate Change Fiction: Radical Hope from an Emerging Genre," *Dragonfly.eco* (blog), September 25, 2014, https://dragonfly.eco/climate-change-fiction-radical-hope-from-an-emerging-genre/). These themes animate some of the most oft-cited examples of cli-fi, including Margaret Atwood's MaddAddam trilogy, Cormac McCarthy's *The Road (2006)*, Nathaniel Rich's *Odds against Tomorrow (2013)*, Paolo Bacigalupi's *The Windup Girl (2009)* and *The Water Knife (2015)*; and films like *Waterworld (Kevin Reynolds, dir., 1985)*, *The Day after Tomorrow (Roland Emmerich, dir., 2004)*, and *Mad Max: Fury Road* (George Miller, dir., 2005).
10. Hardy, Milligan, and Heynan, "Racial Coastal Formation."

11. G. Johnson, "Introduction"; and Hartnell, *After Katrina*. Johnson and Hartnell have written extensively on the many ways in which neoliberal economic policies in New Orleans have contributed to racialized inequality, uneven development, gentrification, and the privatization of public assets, all of which have converged to render the city uniquely vulnerable to climate risk.
12. Ian Liberty, "The (In)Equities of Superstorm Recovery," *Rugers CLiME*, September 20, 2013, https://www.clime.rutgers.edu/publications-filtered/the-inequities-of-superstorm-recovery?rq=superstorm%20recovery; Ben Taub, "Inequality and Hurricane Harvey," *New Yorker*, September 6, 2017, https://www.newyorker.com/news/news-desk/inequality-and-hurricane-harvey.
13. Coral Davenport and Campbell Robertson, "Resettling the First American 'Climate Refugees,'" *New York Times*, May 3, 2016, https://www.nytimes.com/2016/05/03/us/resettling-the-first-american-climate-refugees.html.
14. von Mossner, "Cinematic Landscapes in *Beasts of the Southern Wild*," 64
15. U.S. Congress, House, *Duty of the Government to create a Green New Deal*.
16. Warren Democrats, "We Need a Blue New Deal."
17. Michael Grunwald, "The Trouble With the 'Green New Deal,'" *Politico Magazine*, January 15, 2019, https://www.politico.com/magazine/story/2019/01/15/the-trouble-with-the-green-new-deal-223977.
18. Parr, *Wrath of Capital*, 3.
19. Molly Crabapple, Naomi Klein, and Alexandria Ocasio-Cortez, "A Message from the Future with Alexandria Ocasio-Cortez," *Intercept*, April 17, 2019, https://theintercept.com/2019/04/17/green-new-deal-short-film-alexandria-ocasio-cortez/.
20. Kate Aronoff, "With a Green New Deal, Here's What the World Could Look Like for the Next Generation," *Intercept*, December 5, 2018, https://theintercept.com/2018/12/05/green-new-deal-proposal-impacts/.
21. Raj Patel and Jim Goodman, "A Green New Deal for Agriculture," *Jacobin*, April 4, 2019, https://jacobinmag.com/2019/04/green-new-deal-agriculture-farm-workers.
22. Rothstein, *Color of Law*, 17–38.
23. Lipsitz, *Possessive Investment in Whiteness*, 18.
24. For overviews of the racial disparities in New Deal–era federal housing policy, see Lipsitz, *Possessive Investment in Whiteness*, 1–23; and Rothstein, *Color of Law*.
25. Whyte, "Settler Colonialism," 135. For more on the mixed legacies of the Indian Reorganization Act, which did permit tribes access to federal funds and support that aided them in developing economies, infrastructure, and social services, see Estes, *Our History Is the Future*.

26. Aronoff et al., *Planet to Win*, 183. See also Klein, *On Fire*; and Chomsky and Pollin, *Climate Crisis and the Global Green New Deal*.
27. Joseph Aldy, "What Green New Deal Advocates Can Learn From the 2009 Economic Stimulus Act," *Conversation*, February 15, 2019, https://theconversation.com/what-green-new-deal-advocates-can-learn-from-the-2009-economic-stimulus-act-111577; and Grunwald, "Trouble With the 'Green New Deal.'"
28. Mark Hertsgaard, "A Global Green Deal," *Nation*, February 1, 1999, https://www.thenation.com/article/archive/a-global-green-deal/.
29. Thomas L. Friedman, "Opinion: The Power of Green," *New York Times*, April 15, 2007, https://www.nytimes.com/2007/04/15/opinion/15iht-web-0415edgreen-full.5291830.html.
30. See, e.g., Greg Ip, "Only the Markets Can Make the Green New Deal Real," *Wall Street Journal*, May 3, 2019, https://www.wsj.com/articles/only-markets-can-make-the-green-new-deal-real-11556900131.
31. There is a broad body of work documenting the correlation between neoliberal economic policies and human inequality according to a variety of indicators. I examine some of these studies in this chapter. For further reading, see Harvey, *Brief History of Neoliberalism*; Piketty, *Capital in the Twenty-First Century*; Piketty and Saez, "Income Inequality in the United States, 1913–1988."
32. Fieldman, "Neoliberalism, The Production of Vulnerability and the Hobbled State."
33. See, e.g., Foster, *Ecological Rift*; Moore, *Capitalism in the Web of Life*; Malm, *Fossil Capital*; and Ervine, *Carbon*.
34. Larry Elliot, "Capitalism Can Crack Climate Change. But Only If It Takes Risks," *Guardian*, August 16, 2018, https://www.theguardian.com/commentisfree/2018/aug/16/capitalism-climate-change-risks-profits-china.
35. See, e.g., Bell, "Can the Capitalist System Deliver Environmental Justice?"
36. Parr, *Wrath of Capital*, 5–6.
37. Koch, *Capitalism and Climate Change*, 155–177.
38. Marianne Lavelle, "A Key Climate Justice Question at COP25: What Role Should Carbon Markets Play in Meeting Paris Goals?" *Inside Climate News*, December 6, 2019, https://insideclimatenews.org/news/05122019/cop25-un-climate-talks-environmental-justice-pollution-carbon-markets-article-6.
39. See, e.g., Rogers, *Green Gone Wrong*.
40. Omi and Winant, *Racial Formation in the United States*, 105–36.
41. Hardy, Milligan, and Heynan, "Racial Coastal Formation."

42. Joey Eschrich, "Climate Change and Real Estate Speculation . . . in 2140," *ASU Now*, September 12, 2017, https://asunow.asu.edu/20170912-creativity-climate-chaos-and-real-estate-speculation%C2%A0-2140.
43. Robinson, *New York 2140*, 139.
44. Robinson, *New York 2140*, 34.
45. Buck, "On the Possibility of a Charming Anthropocene."
46. Moore, *Capitalism in the Web of Life*, 173.
47. Robinson, *New York 2140*, 205.
48. Robinson, *New York 2140*, 144–45.
49. Robinson, *New York 2140*, 160.
50. Moore, *Capitalism in the Web of Life*, 170.
51. Moore, "Cheap Nature," 89.
52. World-ecology can be described as an ecologically focused fusion of Marxist cultural geography and world-systems theory. In terms of the former, Moore's thoughts on the coconstitution of capitalism and nature resemble those of Marxist geographer David Harvey, who has argued that "ecosystems tend to both instantiate and reflect . . . the social systems that gave rise to them" (*Justice*, 27). With regard to the latter, as an origin story Moore's Capitalocene syncs with the timeline favored by world-systems theorists to describe the emergence of the "capitalist world-economy" (Wallerstein, *World-Systems Analysis*, 23). World-ecology, in short, takes a structurally and temporally open-ended view of capitalism, whereby relations between labor, power, production, and more-than-human nature, considered in dialectical unity, provide a means of thinking through the current global climate crisis as a historical process.
53. Moore, *Capitalism in the Web of Life*, 2.
54. Moore, *Capitalism in the Web of Life*, 3.
55. Robinson, *New York 2140*, 32, 318.
56. Patel and Moore, *History of the World*.
57. Moore, *Capitalism in the Web of Life*, 68.
58. Patel and Moore, *History of the World*, 180–201.
59. Sophie Sapp Moore, Monique Allewaert, Pablo F. Gómez, and Gregg Mitman, "Plantation Legacies," *Edge Effects*, May 15, 2021, https://edgeeffects.net/plantation-legacies-plantationocene/.
60. Vergès, "Racial Capitalocene," 80–99.
61. Robinson, *New York 2140*, 88.
62. Ortiz, "Financialization, Climate Change, and the Future of the Capitalist World Ecology," 267.
63. Robinson, *New York 2140*, 117.
64. Robinson, *New York 2140*, 16–19.

65. Robinson, *New York 2140*, 123.
66. Robinson, *New York 2140*, 118.
67. Sassen, "Predatory Formations Dressed in Wall Street Suits," 4.
68. Yusoff, *Billion Black Anthropocenes*, 2.
69. Yusoff, *Billion Black Anthropocenes*, 1–22.
70. Chris Mooney, "Katrina. Sandy. Harvey. The Debate Over Climate and Hurricanes is Getting Louder and Louder," *Washington Post*, August 30, 2017, https://www.washingtonpost.com/news/energy-environment/wp/2017/08/30/katrina-sandy-harvey-the-debate-over-climate-and-hurricanes-is-getting-louder-and-louder. Several scholars have explored the intersections between race and environmental justice in Louisiana and the Gulf Coast in the wake of Hurricane Katrina. See, e.g., Bullard, *Race, Place, and Environmental Justice*; and Julie Sze, "Toxic Soup Redux: Why Environmental Racism and Environmental Justice Matter after Katrina," *items: Insights from the Social Sciences* (blog), Social Science Research Council, June 11, 2006, https://items.ssrc.org/understanding-katrina/toxic-soup-redux-why-environmental-racism-and-environmental-justice-matter-after-katrina/.
71. Robinson, *New York 2140*, 151.
72. Piketty, *Capital in the Twenty-First Century*, 271.
73. Piketty, *Capital in the Twenty-First Century*, 20.
74. Piketty, *Capital in the Twenty-First Century*, 663–99; Michelle Fox, "Why We Need a Global Wealth Tax: Piketty," CNBC, March 10, 2015, https://www.cnbc.com/2015/03/10/why-we-need-a-global-wealth-tax-piketty.html.
75. Parr, *Wrath of Capital*, 113.
76. Parr, *Wrath of Capital*, 112–29.
77. Robinson, *New York 2140*, 122.
78. Robinson, *New York 2140*, 209.
79. Robinson, *New York 2140*, 279.
80. For an extended discussion on gentrification and urban "greening" initiatives in Brooklyn that primarily serve to benefit New York's affluent classes and attract capital investments, see Gould and Lewis.
81. See Dawson, *Extreme Cities*, 153–63.
82. Evan Rawn, "Spotlight: Bjarke Engels," *ArchDaily*, October 2, 2019, https://www.archdaily.com/553064/spotlight-bjarke-ingels.
83. Dawson, *Extreme Cities*, 153–63.
84. VIA 57 West, "Availability."
85. Robinson, *New York 2140*, 501.
86. Robinson, *New York 2140*, 511.

87. Historian Michael Denning views the Marxian term *lumpenproletariat* as a conceptual precursor to what he calls *wageless life*, a global underclass that, because of neoliberal economic policies, resides outside of normative economic conceptions of employment and unemployment. As he explains, Marx used the designation "as part of a family of terms—the lumpenproletariat, the mob, *I lazzarone, la bohéme*, the poor whites" that constituted "an unproductive and parasitic layer of society" ("Wageless Life," 87). While Frantz Fanon resuscitated the term to describe disenfranchised masses with radical political potential within the context of anticolonial struggles in the 1960s, Robinson clearly remains—in line with the overall theme of *New York 2140*—largely focused on political economy over antiracist and decolonial struggles.

88. Robinson, *New York 2140*, 398. Such a proposal reflects modes of Keynesian interventionism ascribed to the brief period of postwar prosperity and growth in the United States. In 1935, in the midst of the Great Depression, John Maynard Keynes wrote in *The General Theory of Employment, Interest, and Money* of extreme inequality and the dangers it poses to the capitalist system: "The outstanding faults of the economic society in which we live are its failure to provide for full employment and its arbitrary and inequitable distribution of wealth and incomes" (372). Broadly, Keynesian economics has become synonymous with state-interventionist economic policies, including lowering taxes and increasing government spending, in the form of fiscal stimulus packages and bailouts, to stave off economic crises such as recessions.

89. Keynes, *General Theory*, 376. As of 2010—the upper limit of Piketty's datasets—this has obviously not come to fruition; in the United States, the value of private capital exceeded national income by 400 percent (Piketty, *Capital in the Twenty-First Century*, 171).

90. Robinson, *New York 2140*, 602.

91. Summers is infamous for his comments on what he viewed as the economic necessity of toxic waste dumping in the poorest regions of the Global South (Nixon, *Slow Violence*, 1-2). In *Stress Test: Reflections on Financial Crises* (2014), former secretary of the treasury Timothy Geithner, who served in the Obama administration, details internal debates over bank nationalization in the wake of the 2008 financial crisis, an idea to which Summers was allegedly and remarkably open.

92. Manoj Singh, "The 2007-08 Financial Crisis in Review," *Investopedia*, November 27, 2021, https://www.investopedia.com/articles/economics/09/financial-crisis-review.asp.

93. See, e.g., Steil et al., "Social Structure of Mortgage Discrimination"; Rugh and Massey, "Racial Segregation and Foreclosure"; and Taylor, *Race for Profit*.

94. Burd-Sharps and Rasch, *Impact of the US Housing Crisis*.

95. Robinson, *New York 2140*, 131.

96. Alexander C. Kaufman, "The King of Climate Fiction Makes the Left's Case for Geoengineering," *Huffington Post*, July 28, 2018, https://www.huffpost.com/entry/climate-geoengineering-kim-stanley-robinson_n_5b4e54bde4b0de86f487b0b9.

97. Several reviewers drew parallels between the film's depiction of hurricane-induced flooding in the Bathtub and the inundation of the Lower Ninth Ward. See, e.g., Steve Pond, "*Beasts of the Southern Wild* Rips through Sundance," *Reuters*, January 22, 2012, https://www.reuters.com/article/us-sundance-beasts/beasts-of-the-southern-wild-rips-through-sundance-idUSTRE80L0TU20120122; and Franz Lidz, "How Benh Zeitlin Made *Beasts of the Southern Wild*," *Smithsonian Magazine*, December 2012, https://www.smithsonianmag.com/arts-culture/how-benh-zeitlin-made-beasts-of-the-southern-wild-135132724/. For digitized, multivariable data sets and maps of New Orleans and the disproportionate impacts of Hurricane Katrina on poor and minority neighborhoods, see the Katrina Project, developed and maintained by sociologist John Logan and the Spatial Structures in the Social Sciences (S4) initiative at Brown University.

98. Campanella, *Bienville's Dilemma*, 210–13.

99. Landphair, "Forgotten People of New Orleans," 837.

100. Lloyd, "Creaturely, Throwaway Life after Katrina," 246.

101. von Mossner, "Cinematic Landscapes in *Beasts of the Southern Wild*," 64, 66.

102. See, e.g., Brox, "Monster of Representation"; and Yaeger, "*Beasts of the Southern Wild* and Dirty Ecology."

103. C. Johnson, "Introduction," *xxv–xliii*.

104. C. Johnson, "Charming Accommodations," 188.

105. Whyte, "Is It Colonial Déjà Vu?"

106. Julie Dermansky, "The True Story Behind the Set of 'Beasts of the Southern Wild,'" *Earth Island Journal*, January 16, 2013, https://www.earthisland.org/journal/index.php/articles/entry/true_story_behind_beasts_of_the_southern_wild/.

107. Maldonado et al., "Impact of Climate Change," 602–3; Davenport and Robinson, "Resettling the First American 'Climate Refugees.'"

108. Davis, *Planet of Slums*, 121, 22.

109. Davis, *Planet of Slums*, 121–50.

110. Hartnell, "Writing the Liquid City," 936.
111. Hartnell, "Writing the Liquid City," 934–36.
112. Thomas Hackett, "The Racism of 'Beasts of the Southern Wild,'" *New Republic*, February 18, 2013, https://newrepublic.com/article/112407/racism-beasts-southern-wild.
113. bell hooks, "No Love in the Wild," *NewBlackMan (in Exile)* (blog), September 5, 2013, https://www.newblackmaninexile.net/2012/09/bell-hooks-no-love-in-wild.html.
114. Dyson, *Come Hell or High Water*.
115. Gotham, "Disaster, Inc."
116. C. Johnson, "Charming Accommodations," 187–89.
117. C. Johnson, "Charming Accommodations," 188, 189.
118. C. Johnson, "Charming Accommodations," 188.
119. Hartnell, "Writing the Liquid City," 942.
120. Hartnell, "Writing the Liquid City," 942–43; Kelly Candaele, "The Problematic Political Messages of 'Beasts of the Southern Wild'," *Los Angeles Review of Books*, August 9, 2012, https://lareviewofbooks.org/article/the-problematic-political-messages-of-beasts-of-the-southern-wild/.
121. Davenport and Robinson, "Resettling the First American 'Climate Refugees.'"
122. Biloxi-Chitimacha-Choctaw, "The Island."
123. Babs Roaming Buffalo Bagwell, "Life on the Edge of Climate Change: An Up-Close Look at Being Climate Refugees," *Huffington Post*, October 23, 2013, https://www.huffpost.com/entry/life-on-the-edge-of-climate_b_4136709.
124. Maldonado et al., "Impact of Climate Change," 602–3.
125. Burke, "*Beasts of the Southern Wild* and Indigenous Communities," 61.
126. van Vuure, *Retracing the Aurochs*, 72–78. It is unclear why Zeitlin chose to depict aurochs in his film that is decidedly rooted in North American cultures and ecologies.
127. See Brox, "Monster of Representation"; and Yaeger, "*Beasts of the Southern Wild* and Dirty Ecology."
128. Burke, "*Beasts of the Southern Wild* and Indigenous Communities," 68.
129. Burke, "*Beasts of the Southern Wild* and Indigenous Communities," 7.
130. Burke, "*Beasts of the Southern Wild* and Indigenous Communities," 6.
131. State of Louisiana, *Master Plan*; Maldonado et al., "Impact of Climate Change," 606.
132. Dan Barry, "In Louisiana, a Sinking Island Wars with Water and the Government," *New York Times*, June 18, 2006, https://www.nytimes.com/2006/06/19/us/19road.html.

133. Cain Burdeau, "Louisiana Indian Village Holds Out Against Plea to Move," *Indian Country Today,* December 18, 2009, https://indiancountrytoday.com/archive/louisiana-indian-village-holds-out-against-plea-to-move.
134. Davenport and Robinson, "Resettling the First American 'Climate Refugees.'"
135. Burke, "*Beasts of the Southern Wild* and Indigenous Communities," 14.
136. Tristan Baurick, "How Lessons from Isle de Jean Charles Could Guide Federal Climate Migration Planning," NOLA.com, August 16, 2020, https://www.nola.com/news/environment/article_8f6c9338-de68-11ea-9f99-534747c43bd0.html.
137. Isle de Jean Charles, "Tribal Resettlement."
138. For coverage of the resettlement plan, see Michael Isaac Stein, "How to Save a Town from Rising Waters," *Wired,* January 25, 2018, https://www.wired.com/story/how-to-save-a-town-from-rising-waters/; Mark Schleifstein, "State Is Buying Isle de Jean Charles Relocation Site for $11.7 Million," *Times-Picayune,* March 20, 2018, https://www.nola.com/environment/index.ssf/2018/03/state_is_buying_isle_de_jean_c.html; and Kezia Setyawan, "Isle de Jean Charles Residents View Future Homes for First Time," *Houma Today,* April 7, 2021, https://www.houmatoday.com/story/news/2021/04/07/isle-de-jean-charles-residents-view-future-homes-first-time/4822656001/.
139. U.S. Congress, House, *Duty of the Government to create a Green New Deal.*
140. Climate Justice Alliance, "A Green New Deal Must Be Rooted in a Just Transition for Workers and Communities Most Impacted by Climate Change," press release, December 11, 2018, https://climatejusticealliance.org/green-new-deal-must-rooted-just-transition-workers-communities-impacted-climate-change/.
141. Climate Justice Alliance (@CJAOurPower), "Check out this message from Rep. Alexandria Ocasio-Cortez," Twitter post, January 10, 2019, https://twitter.com/CJAOurPower/status/1083475684767514624.
142. Hakim Bishara, "Congresswoman Alexandria Ocasio-Cortez Unveils a Series of Green New Deal Art Posters," *Hyperallergic,* August 20, 2019, https://hyperallergic.com/515449/congresswoman-alexandria-ocasio-cortez-unveils-a-series-of-green-new-deal-art-posters/.
143. Amanda Kolson Hurley, "What's the Deal with AOC's Retro-Style GND Posters?" *Bloomberg,* August 30, 2019, https://www.bloomberg.com/news/articles/2019-08-30/no-aoc-s-posters-aren-t-based-on-soviet-art.
144. Bishara, "Green New Deal Art Posters."

## Conclusion

1. Sze, *Environmental Justice in a Moment of Danger,* 76.

2. Dustin Bleizeffer, "Wyo Residents Observe a Changing Climate and Quality of Life," *Climate Portal* (blog), MIT, November 4, 2021, https://climate.mit.edu/posts/wyo-residents-observe-changing-climate-and-quality-life.
3. U.S. Energy Information Administration, "Wyoming: Profile Analysis."
4. Wyoming Department of Revenue, *2019 Annual Report*.
5. Wyoming Taxpayers Association, "Direct Tax Collections."
6. Camille Erickson, "Looking Back: The Bankruptcy that Rocked Wyoming Coal Country in 2019," *Casper Star Tribune*, December 4, 2020, https://trib.com/business/energy/looking-back-the-bankruptcy-that-rocked-wyoming-coal-country-in-2019/article_2e10380c-0d53-5ad3-b7f0-63c4c2622d50.html.
7. Brad Handler, Matthew S. Henry, and Morgan Bazilian, "It's Time for States That Grew Rich from Oil, Gas, and Coal to Figure Out What's Next," *Conversation*, September 23, 2020, https://theconversation.com/its-time-for-states-that-grew-rich-from-oil-gas-and-coal-to-figure-out-whats-next-145295.While economic forecasts have improved modestly to match an uptick in oil and gas production and a broader economic recovery, long-term reliance on a volatile energy industry remains a risky bet.
8. Andrew Graham, "In Budget Talks, Gov Highlights Cuts to Programs for Vulnerable," *WyoFile*, July 14, 2020, https://www.wyofile.com/in-budget-talks-gov-highlights-cuts-to-programs-for-vulnerable/.
9. Cha, "Just Transition for Whom?"
10. See Western, *Pushed Off the Mountain*.
11. Lockwood, *Behind the Carbon Curtain*, 4.
12. Leigh Paterson, "In Wyoming, Coal Culture Runs Deep," *Inside Energy*, August 1, 2014, http://insideenergy.org/2014/08/01/in-wyoming-coal-culture-runs-deep/.
13. Western, *Pushed Off the Mountain*, 10.
14. Andrew Van Dam, "Why People Really Want to Move to Idaho but Are Fleeing Its Neighbor, Wyoming," *Washington Post*, December 26, 2017, https://www.washingtonpost.com/news/wonk/wp/2017/12/26/2017s-fastest-and-slowest-growing-states-are-neighbors-heres-why-their-paths-diverged/.
15. Paul Krza, "Wyoming is 'Open for Business,'" *High Country News*, July 7, 1997, https://www.hcn.org/issues/105/3283.
16. Van Dam, "Why People Really Want to Move to Idaho."
17. Dustin Bleizeffer, "One State Still Craves Coal," *Casper Star Tribune*, December 20, 2020, https://trib.com/opinion/columns/bleizeffer-one-state-still-craves-coal/article_e6ce51a1-832c-541c-9536-2c30d01e8c9b.html.
18. Andrew Graham, "Economic, Existential Angst Mark Start of Utility Inves-

tigation," *WyoFile*, February 4, 2020, https://www.wyofile.com/economic-existential-angst-mark-start-of-utility-investigation/.
19. Andrew Graham, "The Wyoming PSC's Uncomfortable Moment in the Spotlight," *WyoFile*, November 29, 2019, https://www.wyofile.com/the-wyoming-pscs-uncomfortable-moment-in-the-spotlight/.
20. Cooper McKim, "Carbon Capture Storage Project Gets Funding for Next Stage," *Wyoming Public Media*, April 28, 2020, https://www.wyomingpublicmedia.org/post/carbon-capture-storage-project-gets-funding-next-stage#stream/0.
21. Victor, "City Punts on Backing Tie Siding Wind Farm," *Laramie Boomerang*, April 10, 2020, https://www.laramieboomerang.com/news/local_news/city-punts-on-backing-tie-siding-wind-farm/article_f3ca5f7f-aeae-5ee6-b961-2b3fde020f5c.html.
22. In the spirit of full disclosure, part of my salary is paid by the School of Energy Resources at the University of Wyoming, where I have conducted research on the sociocultural dynamics of energy transitions since 2019.
23. For a detailed accounting of the Carbon Sink controversy, see Lockwood, *Behind the Carbon Curtain*, 19–55. Lockwood, a professor of creative writing at the University of Wyoming, was a vocal advocate of the sculpture and artistic freedom of expression during the controversy.
24. Howe et al., "Geographic variation in opinions."
25. Western and Gerace, *Social License for Wyoming's Energy Future*.
26. Dustin Bleizeffer, "Portraits of Wyo Youth: Six Visions of a Future in the State," *WyoFile*, April 30, 2021, https://wyofile.com/portraits-of-wyo-youth-six-visions-of-a-future-in-the-state/.
27. Jeff Victor, "Albany County Unanimously Approves Rail Tie Wind Project," *Wyoming Public Media*, July 14, 2021, https://www.wyomingpublicmedia.org/natural-resources-energy/2021-07-14/albany-county-commission-unanimously-approves-rail-tie-wind-project.
28. See, e.g., Dustin Bleizeffer and Mason Adams, "Survival Is Anything but Certain for Coal Country," *Energy News Network*, August 25, 2020, https://energynews.us/2020/08/25/west/survival-is-anything-but-certain-for-coal-country/.

# Bibliography

Adamson, Joni. *American Indian Literature, Ecocriticism, and Environmental Justice: The Middle Place.* Tucson: University of Arizona Press, 2001.
———. "Campaign for a Just Transition." In *The Oxford Encyclopedia of Latinos and Latinas in the United States.* 2nd ed. Edited by Suzanne Oboler and Deena Gonzalez. New York: Oxford University Press, 2005 (2011).
———. "Humanities." In *Keywords for Environmental Studies*, edited by Joni Adamson, Mei William A. Gleason, and David N. Pellow, 135-39. New York: NYU Press, 2016.
———"Integrating Knowledge, Forging New Constellations of Practice in the Environmental Humanities." In *Humanities for the Environment: Integrating Knowledge, Forging New Constellations of Practice*, edited by Joni Adamson and Michael Davis, 1-18. New York: Routledge, 2016.
———. "Medicine Food: Critical Environmental Justice Studies, Native North American Literature, and the Movement for Food Sovereignty." *Environmental Justice* 4, no. 4 (2011): 213-19.
Adamson, Joni, Mei Mei Evans, and Rachel Stein. "Introduction: Environmental Justice Politics, Poetics, and Pedagogy." In *The Environmental Justice Reader*, edited by Joni Adamson, Mei Mei Evans, and Rachel Stein, 3-14. Tucson: University of Arizona Press, 2002.
Adamson, Joni, William A. Gleason, and David N. Pellow, eds. *Keywords for Environmental Studies.* New York: NYU Press, 2016.
Adamson, Joni, and Kimberly Ruffin, eds. *The Environmental Justice Reader.* Tucson: University of Arizona Press, 2002.
———. "Introduction." In *American Studies, Ecocriticism, and Citizenship: Thinking and Acting in the Local and Global Commons*, edited by Joni Adamson and Kimberly Ruffin, 1-17. New York: Routledge, 2013.
AghaKouchak, Amir. "Water and Climate: Recognize Anthropogenic Drought." *Nature* 524 (2015): 409-11.
Amer, Muhammed, Tugrul U. Daim, and Antonie Jetter. "A Review of Scenario Planning." *Futures* 46 (2013): 23-40.
*Appalachian Voices.* "A New Economy for Appalachia." Accessed December 13, 2021. https://appvoices.org/new-economy/.

Apter, Andrew. *The Pan-African Nation: Oil and the Spectacle of Culture in Nigeria*. Chicago: University of Chicago Press, 2008.

Arizona Department of Water Resources. *Phoenix Active Management Area Water Demand and Supply Assessment: 1985–2025*. Phoenix: Arizona Department of Water Resources, 2011. http://www.azwater.gov/recharge/documents/PhxAMA_AssessmentSummarySheet.pdf.

Arizona State University. "ASU's Future H$_2$O." Accessed March 17, 2020. https://futureh2o.asu.edu/#section-program-areas.

Aronoff, Kate, Alyssa Battistoni, Daniel Aldana Cohen, and Thea Riofrancos. *A Planet to Win: Why We Need a Green New Deal*. New York: Verso, 2019.

August, Jack L. "A Vision in the Desert: Charles Trumbull Hayden, Salt River Pioneer." *Journal of Arizona History* 36, no. 2 (1995): 109–34.

Bacigalupi, Paolo. *The Water Knife*. New York: Knopf, 2015.

Baglia, Jay, and Elissa Foster. "Performing the 'Really' Real: Cultural Criticism, Representation, and Commodification in *The Laramie Project*." *Journal of Dramatic Theory and Criticism* 19, no. 2 (2005): 127–35.

Baichwal, Jennifer, and Edward Burtynksy, dir. *Watermark*. Montreal: Sixth Wave Productions, 2013.

Bark, Rosalind H., and Katherine L. Jacobs. "Indian Water Rights Settlements and Water Management Innovations: The Role of the Arizona Water Settlements Act." *Water Resources Research* 45, no. 5 (2009).

Barlow, Maude, and Tony Clarke. *Blue Gold: The Fight to Stop the Corporate Theft of the World's Water*. New York: New Press, 2002.

Barrett, Ross, and Daniel Worden, eds. *Oil Culture*. Minneapolis: University of Minnesota Press, 2014.

Barry, Joyce M. *Standing Our Ground: Women, Environmental Justice, and the Fight to End Mountaintop Removal*. Athens: Ohio University Press, 2012.

Bell, Karen. "Can the Capitalist Economic System Deliver Environmental Justice?." *Environmental Research Letters* 10 (2015). https://iopscience.iop.org/article/10.1088/1748-9326/10/12/125017/meta.

Belmecheri, Soumaya, Flurin Babst, Eugene R. Wahl, David W. Stahle, and Valerie Trouet. "Multi-Century Evaluation of Sierra Nevada Snowpack." *Nature Climate Change* 6, no. 1 (2016): 2–3.

Biloxi-Chitimacha-Choctaw. "The Island." Accessed April 12, 2022. http://www.isledejeancharles.com/island#.

Black, Brian, and Marcy Ladson. "The Legacy of Extraction: Reading Ethics and Patterns in Pennsylvania's Landscape of Energy." *Pennsylvania History: A Journal of Mid-Atlantic Studies* 79, no. 4 (Autumn 2012): 377–94.

Boast, Hannah. *Hydrofictions: Water, Power and Politics in Israeli and Palestinian Literature*. Edinburgh: Edinburgh University Press, 2020.

Brown, Jovana. "When Our Water Returns: Gila River Indian Community and Diabetes," *Enduring Legacies Native Cases*. Olympia WA: Evergreen State College, 2009. http://nativecases.evergreen.edu/sites/nativecases.evergreen.edu/files/case-studies/When_Our_Water_returns_10-25-09.pdf.

Brox, Ali. "The Monster of Representation: Climate Change and Magical Realism in *Beasts of the Southern Wild*." *Journal of the Midwest Modern Language Association* 49, no. 1 (2016): 139–55.

Buck, Holly Jean. "On the Possibilities of a Charming Anthropocene." *Annals of the Association of American Geographers* 105, no. 2 (2014): 369–77.

Buell, Lawrence. *The Future of Environmental Criticism*. Malden: Blackwell, 2005.

———. "Toxic Discourse." *Critical Inquiry* 24, no. 3 (Spring 1998): 639–65.

Bullard, Robert D. *Race, Place, and Environmental Justice after Hurricane Katrina: Struggles to Reclaim, Rebuild, and Revitalize New Orleans and the Gulf Coast*. New York: Routledge, 2009.

Burd-Sharps, Sarah, and Rebecca Rasch. *Impact of the US Housing Crisis on the Racial Wealth Gap Across Generations*. Brooklyn: Social Science Research Council, American Civil Liberties Union, 2015.

Burke, Brianna. "*Beasts of the Southern Wild* and Indigenous Communities in the Age of the Sixth Extinction," *Resilience: A Journal of the Environmental Humanities* 6, no. 1 (Winter 2019): 61–85.

Burns, Shirley Stewart. *Bringing Down the Mountains: The Impact of Mountaintop Removal on Southern West Virginia Communities*. Morgantown: West Virginia University Press, 2007.

Burtynsky, Edward, Wade Davis, and Russell Lord. *Water*. Steidl: Gottingen, 2013.

Caminero-Santangelo, Byron. "Witnessing the Nature of Violence: Resource Extraction and Political Ecologies in the Contemporary African Novel." In *Global Ecologies and the Environmental Humanities: Postcolonial Approaches*, edited by Elizabeth DeLoughrey, Jill Didur, and Anthony Carrigan, 226–42. New York: Routledge, 2015.

Campanella, Richard. *Bienville's Dilemma: A Historical Geography of New Orleans*. Lafayette: University of Louisiana at Lafayette Press, 2008.

Canal Convergence. "Su:dagi Haicu A:ga (Water's Story)." Scottsdale Arts. Accessed April 12, 2022. https://canalconvergence.com/work/sudagi-haicu-aga/.

Casas, José. *Flint*. Unpublished script, 2019.

———. "Flint by José Casas (2019)-University of Michigan School of Music, Theatre, and Dance." David Forsee, October 5, 2019, video, 1:57:56. https://vimeo.com/364522804.

Caylor, Ann. "'A Promise Long Deferred': Federal Reclamation on the Colorado River Indian Reservation." *Pacific Historical Review* 69, no. 2 (May 2000): 193–215.

Central Arizona Project. "Agua Fria." Accessed December 26, 2020. https://www.cap-az.com/public/blog/2-uncategorised/189-agua-fria.

Cha, J. Mijin. "A Just Transition for Whom? Politics, Contestation, and Social Identity in the Disruption of Coal in the Powder River Basin." *Energy Research and Social Science* 69 (2020). https://doi.org/10.1016/j.erss.2020.101657.

Cherniack, Martin. *The Hawk's Nest Incident: America's Worst Industrial Disaster*. New Haven CT: Yale University Press, 1986.

Chomsky, Noam, and Robert Pollin. *Climate Crisis and the Global Green New Deal: The Political Economy of Saving the Planet*. New York: Verso, 2020.

Churchill, Ward. "A Breach of Trust: The Radioactive Colonization of Native North America." *American Indian Culture and Research Journal* 23, no. 4 (1999): 23–69.

Clark, Anna. *The Poisoned City: Flint's Water and the American Urban Tragedy*. New York: Metropolitan, 2018.

Colborn, Theo, Carol Kwiatkowski, Kim Schultz, and Mary Bachran. "Natural Gas Operations from a Public Health Perspective." *Human and Ecological Risk Assessment* 17, no. 5 (2011): 1039–56.

Commoner, Barry. *Making Peace with the Planet*. New York: New Press, 1992.

Comp, T. Allan. "From Environmental Liability to Community Asset: Mined Land Reclamation." In *Proceedings of the Eighth International Conference on Mine Closure, Australian Centre for Geomechanics, Cornwall, UK, 2013*, edited by Mark Tibbett, Andy B. Fourie, and Caroline Digby, 415–22. https://papers.acg.uwa.edu.au/p/1352_34_Comp/.

———. "Science, Art, and Environmental Reclamation: Three Projects and a Few Thoughts." In *Designing the Reclaimed Landscape*, edited by Alan M. Berger, 63–76. New York: Taylor and Francis, 2008.

Cook, Benjamin I., Toby R. Ault, and Jason E. Smerdon. "Unprecedented 21st Century Drought Risk in the American Southwest and Central Plains." *Science Advances* 1, no. 1 (2015).

Croom, Natasha N., and Tyson E. Marsh, eds. *Envisioning Critical Race Praxis in Higher Education through Counter-Storytelling*, Charlotte NC: IAP, 2016.

Cultural Coalition. "Portal to the Past at the Pueblo Grande Museum." Accessed March 17, 2020. https://culturalcoalition.com/water-heritage-collective/.

Cunsolo, Ashlee, and Neville R. Ellis. "Ecological Grief as a Mental Health Response to Climate Change-Related Loss." *Nature Climate Change* 8 (2018): 275–81.

Data USA. "East Porterville, California." Accessed March 17, 2020. https://datausa.io/profile/geo/east-porterville-ca/.

Davis, Mike. *Planet of Slums*. New York: Verso, 2006.

Dawson, Ashley. *Extreme Cities: The Peril and Promise of Urban Life in the Age of Climate Change*. New York: Verso, 2019.

Deckard, Sharae. "Ghost Mountains and Stone Maidens: Ecological Materialism, Compound Catastrophe, and the Post-Soviety Ecogothic." In *Global Ecologies and the Environmental Humanities: Postcolonial Approaches*, edited by Elizabeth DeLoughrey, Jill Didur, and Anthony Carrigan, 286-306. New York: Routledge, 2015.

———. "Trains, Stones, and Energetics: African Resource Culture and the Neoliberal World-Ecology." In *World Literature, Neoliberalism, and the Culture of Discontent*, edited by Sharae Deckard and Stephen Shapiro, 239-62. Cham, Switzerland: Palgrave MacMillan, 2019.

———. "Water Shocks: Neoliberal Hydrofiction and the Crisis of 'Cheap Water.'" *Atlantic Studies* 16, no. 1 (2019): 108-25.

Deemer, Bridget, John A. Harrison, Siyue Li, Jake J. Beaulieu, Tonya DelSontro, Nathan Barros, José F. Bezerra-Neto, Stephen M. Powers, Marco A. dos Santos, and J. Arie Vonk. "Greenhouse Gas Emissions from Reservoir Water Sources: A New Global Synthesis." *BioScience* 66, no. 11 (2016): 949-64.

DeJong, David. *Stealing the Gila: The Pima Agricultural Economy and Water Deprivation, 1848-1921*. Tucson: University of Arizona Press, 2016.

Delgado, Richard. "On Telling Stories in School: A Reply to Farber and Sherry." *Vanderbilt Law Review* 46 (1993): 665-76.

———. "Storytelling for Oppositionists and Others: A Plea for Narrative." *Michigan Law Review* 87, no. 8 (1987): 2411-41.

DeLoughrey, Elizabeth, Jill Didur, and Anthony Carrigan, eds. *Global Ecologies and the Environmental Humanities: Postcolonial Approaches*. New York: Routledge, 2015.

———. "Introduction: A Postcolonial Environmental Humanities." In *Global Ecologies and the Environmental Humanities: Postcolonial Approaches*, edited by Elizabeth DeLoughrey, Jill Didur, and Anthony Carrigan, 1-32. New York: Routledge, 2015.

Denning, Michael. "Wageless Life." *New Left Review* 66 (2010): 79-97.

Di Chiro, Giovanna. "Environmental Justice and the Anthropocene Meme." In *The Oxford Handbook of Environmental Political Theory*, edited by Teena Gabrielson, Cheryl Hall, John M. Meyer, and David Schlosberg, 362-78. Oxford: Oxford University Press, 2016.

———. "Seaweed, 'Soul'-ar Panels, and Other Entanglements." In *Humanities for the Environment: Integrating Knowledge, Forging New Constellations of*

*Practice*, edited by Joni Adamson and Michael Davis, 70-87. New York: Routledge, 2016.

Dig Deep and the U.S. Water Alliance. *Closing the Water Access Gap in the United States: A National Action Plan*. Oakland CA: U.S. Water Alliance, 2019. http://uswateralliance.org/sites/uswateralliance.org/files/publications/Closing%20the%20Water%20Access%20Gap%20in%20the%20United%20States_DIGITAL.pdf.

Dimianti, Jeff, and Brent Ryan Bellamy. "Editors Introduction: Envisioning the Energy Humanities." *Reviews in Cultural Theory* 6, no. 3 (2016): 1-4.

Dunar, Andrew J., and Dennis McBride. *Building Hoover Dam: An Oral History of the Great Depression*. Reno: University of Nevada Press, 1993.

Dyson, Michael Erik. *Come Hell or High Water: Hurricane Katrina and the Color of Disaster*. New York: Basic Civitas, 2006.

Ervine, Kate. *Carbon*. Cambridge, UK: Polity, 2018.

Estes, Nick. *Our History Is the Future: Standing Rock Versus the Dakota Access Pipeline, and the Long Tradition of Indigenous Resistance*. New York: Verso, 2019.

EXTRACTION. "Decolonial Visual Cultures in the Age of the Capitalocene." Accessed November 20, 2018. https://extraction.sites.ucsc.edu/.

Faber, Jacob William. "Superstorm Sandy and the Demographics of Flood Risk in New York City." *Human Ecology* 43, no. 3 (2015): 363-78.

Fieldman, Glenn. "Neoliberalism, the Production of Vulnerability and the Hobbled State: Systemic Barriers to Climate Adaptation." *Climate and Development* 3, no. 2 (2011): 159-74.

Fitzpatrick, Kevin M., and Matthew L. Spialek. *Hurricane Harvey's Aftermath: Place, Race, and Inequality in Disaster Recovery*. New York: NYU Press, 2020.

Flint Public Art Project. "Free City." Accessed December 6, 2020. https://flintpublicartproject.com/freecity/.

———. "Mission and Vision." Accessed December 6, 2020. https://flintpublicartproject.com/mission-vision/.

Foster, John Bellamy, Brett Clark, and Richard York. *The Ecological Rift: Capitalism's War on the Earth*. New York: Monthly Review, 2010.

Fox, Josh, dir. *GasLand*. New York: HBO Documentary Films, 2010.

Fox, William L. "The Art of the Anthropocene." In *Curating the Future: Museums, Communities, and Climate Change*, edited by Jennifer Newell, Libby Robin, and Kirsten Wehner, 194-205. New York: Routledge, 2017.

Garrard, Greg, ed. *The Oxford Handbook of Ecocriticism*. Oxford: Oxford University Press, 2014.

Gómez-Barris, Macarena. *The Extractive Zone: Social Ecologies and Decolonial Perspectives*. Durham NC: Duke University Press, 2017.

Gotham, Kevin Fox. "Disaster, Inc.: Privatization and Post-Katrina Rebuilding in New Orleans." *Perspectives on Politics* 10, no. 3 (2012): 633–46.

Gould, Kenneth A., and Tammy L. Lewis, *Green Gentrification: Urban Sustainability and the Struggle for Environmental Justice*. New York: Routledge, 2016.

Griffin, Daniel, and Kevin J. Anchukaitis. "How Unusual Is the 2012–2014 California Drought?." *Geophysical Research Letters* 41, no. 24 (2014): 9017–23.

Griffith, Jane. "Hoover Dam: Land, Labor, and Settler Colonial Production." *Cultural Studies—Critical Methodologies* 17, no. 1 (2017): 30–40.

———. "Law, Literature, and Leslie Marmon Silko: Competing Narratives of Water." *Studies in American Indian Literature* 29, no. 2 (Summer 2017): 26–48.

Grossman, Daniel S., and David J. G. Slusky. "The Impact of the Flint Water Crisis on Fertility." *Demography* 56 (2019): 2005–31.

Guerrero, Zarco. "Zarco Guerrero Biography." Zarmask. Last modified 2017. https://zarkmask.com/zarco-guerrero-biography/.

Gustafson, Abel, Seth Rosenthal, Anthony Leiserowitz, Edward Maibach, John Kotcher, Matthew Ballew, and Matthew Goldberg. *The Green New Deal Has Strong Bipartisan Support*. Yale University and George Mason University. New Haven CT: Yale Program on Climate Communication, 2018. https://climatecommunication.yale.edu/publications/the-green-new-deal-has-strong-bipartisan-support/.

Haddeland, Ingjerd, Jens Heinke, Hester Biemans, Stephanie Eisner, Martina Flörke, Naota Hanasaki, Markus Konzmann, et al. "Global Water Resources Affected by Human Interventions and Climate Change." *Proceedings of the National Academy of Sciences* 111, no. 9 (2014): 3251–56.

Haigh, Jennifer. *Heat and Light*. New York: Harper Collins, 2016.

Harding, Stephan, and Lynn Margulis. "Water Gaia: 3.5 Thousand Million Years of Wetness on Planet Earth." In *Gaia in Turmoil: Climate Change, Biodepletion, and Earth Ethics in an Age of Crisis*, edited by Eileen Crist and H. Bruce Rinker, 41–60. Cambridge MA: MIT Press, 2010.

Hardy, R. Dean, Richard A. Milligan, and Nik Heynan. "Racial Coastal Formation: The Environmental Injustice of Colorblind Adaptation Planning for Sea-Level Rise." *Geoforum* 87 (2017): 62–72.

Harris, Leila M., Scott McKenzie, Lucy Rodina, Sameer H. Shah, and Nicole J. Wilson. "Water Justice: Key Concepts, Debates, and Research Agendas." In *The Routledge Handbook of Environmental Justice*, edited by Ryan

Holifield, Jayajit Chakraborty, and Gordon Walker, 338–49. New York: Routledge, 2018.

Hartnell, Anna. *After Katrina: Race, Neoliberalism, and the End of the American Century*. Albany: SUNY Press, 2017.

———. "Writing the Liquid City: Excavating Urban Ecologies after Katrina." *Textual Practice* 31, no. 5 (2017): 933–45.

Harvey, David. *A Brief History of Neoliberalism*. Oxford: Oxford University Press, 2005.

———. *Justice, Nature, and the Geography of Difference*. Cambridge MA: Blackwell, 1996.

Hecht, Gabrielle. *Being Nuclear: Africans and the Global Uranium Trade*. Cambridge MA: MIT Press, 2012.

Heise, Ursula K., Jon Christensen, and Michelle Niemann, eds. *The Routledge Companion to the Environmental Humanities*. New York: Routledge, 2016.

Henry, Matthew S., Morgan Bazilian, and Chris Markuson. "Just Transitions: Histories and Futures in a Post-COVID World." *Energy Research & Social Science* 68 (October 2020).

Hess, Christoph, Ernst Emil, and Wagner Costa Ribiero. "Energy and Environmental Justice: Closing the Gap." *Environmental Justice* 9, no. 5 (October 2016): 153–58.

Hia-Ced Hemajakam LLC. "Our History." Accessed March 17, 2020. http://hiaced.com/history.html.

Highsmith, Andrew R. *Demolition Means Progress: Flint, Michigan, and the Fate of the American Metropolis*. Chicago: University of Chicago Press, 2015.

Holm, Poul, Joni Adamson, Hsinya Huang, Lars Kirdan, Sally Kitch, Iain McCalman, James Ogude, et al. "Humanities for the Environment—A Manifesto for Research and Action." *Humanities* 4, no. 4 (2015): 977–92.

Houser, Heather. "Knowledge Work in the Commons in Barbara Kingsolver's and Ann Pancake's Appalachia." *MFS: Modern Fiction Studies* 63, no. 1 (Spring 2017): 95–115.

Howe, Peter D., Matto Mildenberger, Jennifer R. Marlon, and Anthony Leiserowitz. "Geographic Variation in Opinions on Climate Change at State and Local Scales in the USA." *Nature Climate Change* 5, no. 6 (June 2015): 596–603. https://doi.org/10.1038/nclimate2583.

Humphreys, Macartan, Jeffrey D. Sachs, and Joseph E. Stiglitz. *Escaping the Resource Curse*. New York: Columbia University Press, 2007.

Hundley, Norris, Jr. *Water in the West: The Colorado River Compact and the Politics of Water in the American West*. Berkeley: University of California Press, 2009.

Hurd, Barbara. Foreword to *Shale Play: Poems and Photographs from the Fracking Fields*, by Julia Spicher Kasdorf and Stephen Rubin, i-xiii. State College PA: Penn State University Press, 2018.

Inayatullah, Sohail. "Six Pillars: Futures Thinking for Transforming." *Foresight* 10 (2008): 4-21.

Indigenous Environmental Network. *Indigenous Principles of a Just Transition*. Accessed March 1, 2022. http://www.ienearth.org/wp-content/uploads/2017/10/IENJustTransitionPrinciples.pdf.

Iovino, Serenella, and Serpil Opperman. "Introduction: The Environmental Humanities and the Challenges of the Anthropocene." In *Environmental Humanities: Voices of the Anthropocene*, edited by Serenella Iovino and Serpil Opperman, 1-21. New York: Rowman and Littlefield, 2016.

Isle de Jean Charles. "Tribal Resettlement." Accessed December 20, 2020. http://www.isledejeancharles.com/our-resettlement.

Jackson, Robert B., Avner Vengosh, Thomas H. Darrah, and Jonathon D. Karr. "Increased Stray Gas Abundance in a Subset of Drinking Water Wells Near Marcellus Shale Gas Extraction." *Proceedings of the National Academy of Sciences* 110, no. 28 (July 9, 2013): 11250-55.

Jarva, Vuokko. "Introduction to Narrative for Futures Studies." *Journal of Futures Studies* 18, no. 3 (2014): 5-26.

Johnson, Cedric. "Charming Accommodations: Progressive Urbanism Meets Privatization in Brad Pitt's Make it Right Foundation." In *The Neoliberal Deluge: Hurricane Katrina, Late Capitalism, and the Remaking of New Orleans*, edited by Cedric Johnson, xvii-xlix. Minneapolis: University of Minnesota Press, 2011.

———. "Introduction: The Neoliberal Deluge." In *The Neoliberal Deluge: Hurricane Katrina, Late Capitalism, and the Remaking of New Orleans*, edited by Cedric Johnson, 187-224. Minneapolis: University of Minnesota Press, 2011.

———, ed. *The Neoliberal Deluge: Hurricane Katrina, Late Capitalism, and the Remaking of New Orleans*. Minneapolis: University of Minnesota Press, 2011.

Johnson, Gaye Theresa, and Alex Lubin, eds. *Futures of Black Radicalism*. New York: Verso, 2017.

———. "Introduction." In *Futures of Black Radicalism*, edited by Gaye Theresa Johnson and Alex Lubin, 17-27. New York: Verso, 2017.

Jones, Christopher. "Petromyopia: Oil and the Energy Humanities." *Humanities* 5, no. 2 (2016).

———. *Routes of Power: Energy and Modern America*. Cambridge MA: Harvard University Press, 2014.

Kasdorf, Julie Spicher, and Steven Rubin. *Shale Play: Poetry and Photographs from the Fracking Fields*. State College PA: Penn State University Press, 2018.

Katrina Project. "Hurricane Katrina." Brown University, Spatial Structures in the Social Sciences (S4). Accessed August 18, 2018. https://s4.ad.brown.edu/Projects/Hurricane/katrina.html.

Kelley, Robin D. G. *Freedom Dreams: The Radical Black Imagination*. Boston: Beacon, 2002.

Keynes, John Maynard. *The General Theory of Employment, Interest, and Money*. Cambridge, UK: Harcourt, Brace, and World, 1936; rpt. Palgrave MacMillan, 2018.

Klare, Michael. *Resource Wars: The New Landscape of Global Conflict*. New York: Henry Holt, 2001.

Klein, Naomi. *On Fire: The (Burning) Case for a Green New Deal*. New York: Simon and Schuster, 2019.

———. *This Changes Everything: Capitalism vs. the Climate*. New York: Simon and Schuster, 2014.

Koch, Max. *Capitalism and Climate Change*. New York: Palgrave, 2012.

Kuletz, Valerie. *The Tainted Desert: Environmental Ruin in the American West*. New York: Routledge, 1998.

Landphair, Juliette. "'The Forgotten People of New Orleans': Community, Vulnerability, and the Lower Ninth Ward." *Journal of American History* 94, no. 3 (2007): 837–45.

Latimer, Jeff, Craig Dowden, and Danielle Muise. "The Effectiveness of Restorative Justice Practices: A Meta-Analysis." *Prison Journal* 85, no. 2 (2005): 127–44.

Lawson, Raneta J. "Critical Race Theory as Praxis: A View from Outside the Outside." *Howard Law Journal* 38, no. 2 (1995): 353–70.

LeMenager, Stephanie. *Living Oil: Petroleum Culture in the American Century*. Oxford: Oxford University Press, 2014.

———. *Manifest and Other Destinies: Territorial Fictions of the Nineteenth-Century United States*. Lincoln: University of Nebraska Press, 2004.

Leopold, Les. *The Man Who Hated Work and Loved Labor: The Life and Times of Tony Mazzocchi*. White River Junction VT: Chelsea Green, 2007.

Levy, Stacy. "Acid Mine Drainage and Art." Accessed April 30, 2018. https://www.stacylevy.com/amd-art.

Lipsitz, George. *The Possessive Investment in Whiteness*. Philadelphia: Temple University Press, 2006.

———. "What Is This Black in the Black Radical Tradition?." In *Futures of Black Radicalism*, edited by Gaye Theresa Johnson and Alex Lubin, 108–19. New York: Verso, 2017.

Lloyd, Christopher. "Creaturely, Throwaway Life After Katrina." *South: A Scholarly Journal* 48, no. 2 (Spring 2016): 246–64.

Lockwood, Jeffrey A. *Behind the Carbon Curtain: The Energy Industry, Political Censorship, and Free Speech.* Albuquerque: University of New Mexico Press, 2017.

Lowe, Lisa. *The Intimacies of Four Continents.* Durham NC: Duke University Press, 2015.

Macdonald, Graeme. "'Monstrous Transformer:' Petrofiction and World Literature." *Journal of Postcolonial Writing* 53, no. 3 (2017): 289–302.

Maldonado, Julie Koppel, Christine Shearer, Robin Bronen, Kristina Peterson, and Heather Lazrus. "The Impact of Climate Change on Tribal Communities in the US: Displacement, Relocation, and Human Rights." *Climatic Change* 120 (2013): 601–14.

Malin, Stephanie A., and Kathryn Teigen DeMaster. "A Devil's Bargain: Rural Environmental Injustices and Hydraulic Fracturing on Pennsylvania's Farms." *Journal of Rural Studies* 47 (2016): 278–90.

Malm, Andreas. *Fossil Capital: The Rise of Steam Power and the Roots of Global Warming.* New York: Verso, 2016.

Malm, Andreas, and Alf Hornborg. "The Geology of Mankind? A Critique of the Anthropocene Narrative." *Anthropocene Review* 1, no. 1 (2014): 62–69.

Mann, Michael E., and Peter H. Gleick. "Climate Change and California Drought in the 21st Century." *Proceedings of the National Academy of Sciences* 112, no. 13 (2015): 3858–59.

Martin, Carol. *Theatre of the Real.* New York: Palgrave, 2013.

Martin-Alier, Joan. *The Environmentalism of the Poor: A Study of Ecological Conflicts and Valuation.* Northampton, UK: Edward Elgar, 2003.

Mason-Delmotte, Valérie, Panmao Zhai, Hans-Otto Pörtner, Debra Roberts, Jim Skea, Priyadarshi R. Shukla, Anna Pirani, et al., eds. *Global Warming of 1.5°C. An IPCC Special Report on the impacts of global warming of 1.5°C above pre-industrial levels and related global greenhouse gas emission pathways, in the context of strengthening the global response to the threat of climate change, sustainable development, and efforts to eradicate poverty.* Geneva: Intergovernmental Panel on Climate Change, 2018. https://www.ipcc.ch/sr15/.

Matz, Jacob, and Daniel Renfrew. "Selling 'Fracking': Energy in Depth and the Marcellus Shale." *Environmental Communication* 9, no. 3 (2015): 288–306.

Mays, Kyle T. *Hip Hop Beats, Indigenous Rhymes: Modernity and Hip Hop in Indigenous North America.* Albany NY: SUNY Press, 2018.

Mazzocchi, Anthony. "A Superfund for Workers," *Earth Island Journal* 9, no. 1 (Winter 1993-4): 40–41.

———. "An Answer to the Jobs-Environment Conflict?." *Green Left* 114 (September 8, 1993). https://www.greenleft.org.au/content/answer-jobs-environment-conflict.

McCauley, Darren, and Raphael Heffron. "Just Transition: Integrating Climate, Energy, and Environmental Justice." *Energy Policy* 119 (2018): 1–7.

Melamed, Jodi. "Racial Capitalism." *Critical Ethnic Studies* 1, no. 1 (2015): 76–85.

———. *Represent and Destroy: Rationalizing Violence in the New Racial Capitalism*. Minneapolis: University of Minnesota Press, 2011.

Mienczakowski, Jim. "The Theatre of Ethnography: The Reconstruction of Ethnography into Theatre with Emancipatory Potential." *Qualitative Inquiry* 1, no. 3 (1995): 360–75.

Mitchell, Timothy. *Carbon Democracy: Political Power in the Age of Oil*. New York: Verso, 2011.

Moore, Jason W. *Capitalism in the Web of Life: Ecology and the Accumulation of Capital*. New York: Verso, 2015.

Movement for Black Lives. "Reparations." Accessed December 4, 2020. https://m4bl.org/policy-platforms/reparations/.

Muehlmann, Shaylih. *Where the River Ends: Contested Indigeneity in the Mexican Colorado Delta*. Durham NC: Duke University Press, 2013.

Nabhan, Gary Paul. "The Ecology of Floodwater Farming in Arid Southwestern North America." *Agro-Ecosystems* 5 (1979): 245–55.

———. *Gathering the Desert*. Tucson: University of Arizona Press, 1985.

Nabhan, Gary Paul, Wendy Hodgson, and Frances Fellows. "A Meager Living on Lava and Sand? Hia Ced O'odham Food Resources and Habitat Diversity in Oral and Documentary Histories." *Journal of the Southwest* 31, no. 4 (Winter 1989): 508–33.

Nash, Roderick Frazier. *Wilderness and the American Mind*. 4th ed. New Haven CT: Yale University Press, 2001. First published 1967.

National Academy of Sciences. "Rehabilitation Potential of Western Coal Lands: A Report to the Energy Policy Project of the Ford Foundation." Cambridge MA: Ballinger, 1974.

National Park Service. "California: Parker Dam." Last modified January 13, 2017. https://www.nps.gov/articles/california-parker-dam.htm.

Nestlé. "Facts and Figures: *2019 Annual Report*." Accessed October 15, 2020. https://www.nestle.com/investors/annual-report/facts-figures.

Newell, Jennifer, Libby Robin, and Kirsten Wehner, eds. *Curating the Future: Museums, Communities, and Climate Change*. New York: Routledge, 2017.

———. "Introduction: Curating Connections in a Climate-Changed World." In *Curating the Future: Museums, Communities, and Climate Change*, edited by Jennifer Newell, Libby Robin, and Kirsten Wehner, 1-16. New York: Routledge, 2017.

Niblett, Michael. "Oil on Sugar: Commodity Frontiers and Peripheral Aesthetics." In In *Global Ecologies and the Environmental Humanities: Postcolonial Approaches*, edited by Elizabeth DeLoughrey, Jill Didur, and Anthony Carrigan, 268-85. New York: Routledge, 2015.

———. "World-Economy, World-Ecology, World Literature." *Green Letters: Studies in Ecocriticism* 16, no. 1 (2012): 15-30.

Nixon, Rob. *Slow Violence and the Environmentalism of the Poor*. Cambridge: Harvard University Press, 2011.

Norton, Wayne. "Desertscapes." Photography Exhibit. Pueblo Grande Museum and Archaeological Park. Phoenix AZ, March 2016.

Ogneva-Himmelberger, Yelena, and Liyao Huang. "Spatial Distribution of Unconventional Gas Wells and Human Populations in the Marcellus Shale in the United States: Vulnerability Analysis." *Applied Geography* 60 (2015): 165-74.

Oliver-Smith, Anthony. "Theorizing Vulnerability in a Globalized World: A Political Ecological Perspective." In *Mapping Vulnerability: Disasters, Development, and People*, edited by Greg Bankoff, Dorothea Hilhorst, and George Ferks, 10-24. New York: Taylor and Francis, 2004.

Omi, Michael, and Howard Winant. *Racial Formation in the United States*. New York: Routledge, 2015.

Ortiz, Roberto J. "Financialization, Climate Change, and the Future of the Capitalist World Ecology: On Kim Stanley Robinson's *New York 2140*." *Soundings: An Interdisciplinary Journal* 103, no. 2 (2020): 264-85.

Osborn, Stephen G., Avner Vengosh, Nathaniel R. Warner, and Robert B. Jackson. "Methane contamination of drinking water accompanying gas-well drilling and hydraulic fracturing." *Proceedings of the National Academy of Sciences* 108, no. 20 (May 17, 2011): 8172-6.

Pancake, Ann. *Strange as This Weather Has Been*. Berkeley: Shoemaker and Hoard, 2007.

Parr, Adrian. *The Wrath of Capital: Neoliberalism and Climate Change Politics*. New York: Columbia University Press, 2012.

Paschen, Jana-Axinja, and Ray Ison. "Narrative Research in Climate Change Adaptation—Exploring a Complementary Paradigm for Research and Governance." *Research Policy* 43, no. 6 (2014): 1083-92.

Patel, Raj, and Jason W. Moore. *A History of the World in Seven Cheap Things: A*

*Guide to Capitalism, Nature, and the Future of the Planet.* Berkeley: University of California Press, 2017.

Petras, James, and Henry Veltmeyer. *Extractive Imperialism in the Americas: Capitalism's New Frontier.* Leiden: Brill, 2014.

Piketty, Thomas. *Capital in the Twenty-First Century.* Translated by Arthur Goldhammer. Cambridge MA: Belknap, 2014.

Piketty, Thomas, and Emmanuel Saez. "Income Inequality in the United States, 1913–1988." *Quarterly Journal of Economics* 118, no. 1 (2003): 1–39.

Pima-Maricopa Irrigation Project. *History of the Gila River Water Settlement Act of 2004.* Self published. Accessed March 16, 202.0 https://www.gilariver.com/settlement.htm.

Pörtner, Hans-Otto, Debra C. Roberts, Valérie Masson-Delmotte, Panmao Zhai, Melinda Tignor, Elvira Poloczanska, Katja Mintenbeck, et al. *Special Report on the Ocean and Cryosphere in a Changing Climate.* Geneva: Intergovernmental Panel on Climate Change, 2018. https://www.ipcc.ch/srocc/.

Powell, John Wesley. "From Savagery to Barbarism. Annual Address of the President, J. W. Powell, Delivered February 3, 1885." *Transactions of the Anthropological Society of Washington* 3 (1883): 173–96.

———. *Report on the Lands of the Arid Region of the United States.* Washington DC: GPO, 1879.

Preston, Jen. "Racial Extractivism and White Settler Colonialism: An Examination of the Canadian Tar Sands Mega-Projects." *Cultural Studies* 31, no. 2–3 (2017): 353–75.

Prud'homme, Alex. *Hydrofracking: What Everyone Needs to Know.* Oxford: Oxford University Press, 2014.

Pulido, Laura. "Flint, Environmental Racism, and Racial Capitalism." *Capitalism Nature Socialism* 27, no. 3 (2016): 1–16.

———. "Geographies of Race and Ethnicity 2: Environmental Racism, Racial Capitalism, and State-Sanctioned Violence." *Progress in Human Geography* 41, no. 4 (2017): 524–33.

Purdy, Jedediah. "The Long Environmental Justice Movement." *Ecology Law Quarterly* 44, no. 809 (2017): 850–54.

Queens Museum, "Flint Fit." Accessed December 4, 2020. http://www.queensmuseum.org/flint-fit/.

Queer Appalachia. "About Us." Accessed August 30, 2018. https://www.queerappalachia.com/about.

Reece, Erik. "Reclaiming a Toxic Legacy through Art and Science," *Orion Magazine*, November-December 2007.

Reisner, Marc. *Cadillac Desert: The American West and its Disappearing Water.* Rev. ed. New York: Penguin, 1993 (1986).

Robertson, Sarah. "Gothic Appalachia." In *The Palgrave Handbook of Southern Gothic*, edited by Susan Castillo Street and Charles L. Crow, 109-20. New York: Springer, 2016.

Robinson, Cedric. *Black Marxism and the Making of the Black Radical Tradition*. Chapel Hill: University of North Carolina Press, 1983.

Robinson, Kim Stanley. *New York 2140*. New York: Orbit, 2017.

Rodell, Matthew, J. S. Famiglietti, D. N. Weise, J. T. Reager, H. K. Beaudoing, F. W. Landerer, and M.-H. Lo. "Emerging Trends in Global Freshwater Availability." *Nature* 557 (May 31, 2018): 651-59.

Rogers, Heather. *Green Gone Wrong: Dispatches from the Front Lines of Eco-Capitalism*. New York: Verso, 2010.

Ross, Andrew. *Bird on Fire: Lessons from the World's Least Sustainable City*. Oxford: Oxford University Press, 2011.

Ross, Michael. *The Oil Curse: How Petroleum Wealth Shapes the Development of Nations*. Princeton NJ: Princeton University Press, 2012.

Rothstein, Richard. *The Color of Law*. New York: Liveright, 2017.

Rugh, Jacob S., and Douglas Massey. "Racial Segregation and the American Foreclosure Crisis." *American Sociological Review* 75, no. 5 (2010): 629-51.

Rust, Stephen, Salma Monani, and Sean Cubitt, eds. *Ecocinema Theory and Practice*. New York: Routledge, 2013.

Ryan, Terre. "The Nineteenth-Century Garden: Imperialism, Subsistence, and Subversion in Leslie Marmon Silko's *Gardens in the Dunes*." *Studies in American Indian Literatures* 2, no. 19 (2007): 115-32.

Sabo, John, Tushar Sinha, Laura C. Bowling, Gerrit H. W. Schoups, Wesley W. Wallender, Michael E. Campana, Keith A. Cherkauer, et al. "Reclaiming Freshwater Sustainability in the Cadillac Desert." *Proceedings of the National Academy of Sciences* 107, no. 50 (2010): 21263-70.

Sabraw, John. "Current Body of Work: Unearthed Topographies." Accessed March 21, 2018. http://www.johnsabraw.com/studio.

Salt River Project. "A History of Canals in Arizona." Accessed April 12, 2022. https://www.srpnet.com/water/canals/history.aspx.

Sassen, Saskia. *The Global City: New York, London, Tokyo*. 2nd ed. Princeton NJ: Princeton University Press, 2001.

———. "Predatory Formations Dressed in Wall Street Suits and Algorithmic Math." *Science, Technology, and Society* 22, no. 1 (2017): 1-15.

Scanlan, Stephen J. "The Theoretical Roots and Sociology of Environmental Justice in Appalachia." In *Mountains of Injustice: Social and Environmental Justice in Appalachia*, edited by Michele Morrone, Geoffrey L. Buckley, Donald Edward Davis, and Jedediah Purdy, 3-31. Athens: Ohio University Press, 2011.

Schneider-Mayerson, Matthew. "The Influence of Climate Fiction: An Empirical Survey of Readers." *Environmental Humanities* 10, no. 2 (2018): 473–500.

———. "'Just as in the Book'? The Influence of Literature on Readers' Awareness of Climate Injustice and Perception of Climate Migrants." *ISLE: Interdisciplinary Studies in Literature and the Environment* 27, no. 2 (2020): 337–64.

Schneider-Mayerson, Matthew, Alexa Weik von Mossner, and W. P. Maiecki. "Empirical Ecocriticism: Environmental Texts and Empirical Methods." *ISLE: Interdisciplinary Studies in Literature and the Environment* 27, no. 2 (2020): 327–36.

Scott, Rebecca R. *Removing Mountains: Extracting Nature and Identity in the Appalachian Coalfields*. Minneapolis: University of Minnesota Press, 2010.

Sheridan, Thomas E. *Arizona: A History*. Rev. ed. Tucson: University of Arizona Press, 2012.

Shiva, Vandana. *Water Wars: Privatization, Pollution, and Profit*. London: Pluto, 2002.

Silko, Leslie Marmon. *Gardens in the Dunes*. New York: Simon and Schuster, 1999.

Solarzano, Daniel G., and Tara J. Yosso. "Critical Race and LatCrit Theory and Method: Counter-Storytelling." *International Journal of Qualitative Studies in Education* 14, no. 4 (2001): 471–95.

Star, Jonathan, Erika J. Rowland, Mary E. Black, Carolyn A. F. Enquist, Gregg Garfin, Catherine Hawkins Hoffman, Holly Hartmann, Katherine L. Jacobs, Richard H. Moss, and Anne M. Waple. "Supporting Adaptation Decisions through Scenario Planning: Enabling the Effective Use of Multiple Methods." *Climate Risk Management* 13 (2016): 88–94.

State of Louisiana. *Louisiana's Comprehensive Master Plan for a Sustainable Coast*. Baton Rouge LA: OTS-State Printing, 2017. http://coastal.la.gov/wp-content/uploads/2017/04/2017-Coastal-Master-Plan_Web-Book_CFinal-with-Effective-Date-06092017.pdf.

Steil, Justin P., Len Albright, Jacob S. Rugh, and Douglas S. Massey. "The Social Structure of Mortgage Discrimination." *Housing Studies* 33, no. 5 (2018): 759–76.

Stern, Gerald. *The Buffalo Creek Disaster: The Story of the Survivors' Unprecedented Lawsuit*. New York: Random House, 1976.

Stovall, David. "Forging Community in Race and Class: Critical Race Theory and the Quest for Social Justice in Education." *Race Ethnicity and Education* 9, no. 3 (2006): 243–59.

Summitt, April. *Contested Waters: An Environmental History of the Colorado River*. Boulder: University Press of Colorado, 2013.

Sze, Julie. "Environmental Justice Anthropocene Narratives: Sweet Art, Recognition, and Representation." *Resilience: A Journal of the Environmental Humanities* 2, no. 2 (2015).

———. *Environmental Justice in a Moment of Danger*. Berkeley: University of California Press, 2020.

———. "From Environmental Justice Literature to the Literature of Environmental Justice." In *The Environmental Justice Reader*, edited by Joni Adamson, Mei Mei Evans, and Rachel Stein, 163–80. Tucson: University of Arizona Press, 2002.

Szeman, Imre, and Dominic Boyer. "Introduction." In *Energy Humanities: An Anthology*, edited by Imre Szeman and Dominic Boyer, 1–13. Baltimore MD: Johns Hopkins University Press, 2017.

Szeman, Imre, and Jeff Dimianti, eds. *Energy Culture: Art and Theory on Oil and Beyond*. Morgantown: West Virginia University Press, 2019.

Szeman, Imre, and the Petrocultures Research Group. *After Oil*. Alberta: University of Alberta Press, 2016.

Taylor, Keeanga-Yamahtta. *Race for Profit*. Chapel Hill: University of North Carolina Press, 2019.

Trexler, Adam. *Anthropocene Fictions: The Novel in a Time of Climate Change*. Charlottesville: University of Virginia Press, 2015.

Trumka, Richard. "We'll Either Have a Just Transition or No Transition at All." Speech given at Ceres Global Investor Summit, virtual. May 20, 2020. https://aflcio.org/speeches/trumka-well-either-have-just-transition-or-no-transition-all.

Tsing, Anna L. *Friction: An Ethnography of Global Connection*. Princeton NJ: Princeton University Press, 2005.

Tyrell, Ian. *Crisis of the Wasteful Nation: Empire and Conservation in Theodore Roosevelt's America*. Chicago: University of Chicago Press, 2015.

University of Michigan School of Music, Theatre & Dance. "'Flint:' A New Play by José Casas, Asst. Professor of Theatre & Drama." April 2, 2019. Video, 3:43. https://www.youtube.com/watch?v=3qpUa4FuLqM.

U.S. Bureau of Reclamation. "About Us—Fact Sheet." Last modified May 6, 2021. https://www.usbr.gov/main/about/fact.html.

———. *Colorado River Basin Ten Tribes Partnership Water Study*. Washington DC: U.S. Department of the Interior, December 2018. https://www.usbr.gov/lc/region/programs/crbstudy/tws/finalreport.html.

U.S. Climate Data. "Climate Phoenix—Arizona." Accessed March 17, 2020. https://www.usclimatedata.com/climate/phoenix/arizona/united-states/usaz0166.

U.S. Congress. House of Representatives. *Recognizing the duty of the Federal Government to create a Green New Deal*. 116th Cong., 1st sess., H.R. Res. 109, introduced February 7, 2019. https://www.congress.gov/bill/116th-congress/house-resolution/109/text.

———. Energy Policy Act of 2005. Pub. L. No. 109.58. https://www.gsa.gov/cdnstatic/PLAW-109publ58.pdf.

U.S. Energy Information Administration. *Annual Coal Report 2020*. Washington DC: U.S. Department of Energy, 2021. https://www.eia.gov/coal/annual/pdf/acr.pdf.

———. "Wyoming: Profile Analysis." Last modified April 21, 2022. https://www.eia.gov/state/analysis.php?sid=WY.

van Loon, Anne F., Tom Gleeson, Julian Clark, Albert I. J. M. van Dijk, Kerstin Stahl, Jamie Hannaford, Giuliano Di Baldassarre, et al. "Drought in the Anthropocene." *Nature Geoscience* 9 (2016): 89–91.

———. "Drought in a Human-Modified World: Reframing Drought Definitions, Understanding, and Analysis Approaches." *Hydrology and Earth Systems Sciences* 20 (2016): 3631–50.

van Vuure, Cis. *Retracing the Aurochs: History, Morphology and Ecology of an Extinct Wild Ox*. Sofia, Bulgaria: Pensoft, 2005.

Vergès, Françoise. "Racial Capitalocene." In *Futures of Black Radicalism*, edited by Gaye Theresa Johnson and Alex Lubin, 80–99. New York: Verso, 2017.

VIA57 West. "Availability." Accessed August 3, 2018. https://www.via57west.com/.

Vizenor, Gerald. *Manifest Manners: Narratives on Postindian Survivance*. Lincoln: University of Nebraska Press.

von Mossner, Alexa Weik. "Cinematic Landscapes in *Beasts of the Southern Wild*." *Topos: The International Review of Landscape Architecture and Urban Design* no. 88 (2014): 62–64.

Vörösmarty, C. J., P. B. McIntyre, M. O. Gessner, D. Dudgeon, A. Prusevich, P. Green, S. Glidden, et al. "Global Threats to Human Water Security and River Biodiversity." *Nature* 467 (2010): 555–61.

Wallerstein, Immanuel. *World-Systems Analysis*. Durham NC: Duke University Press, 2004.

Walsh, F. Rall, III, and Mark D. Zoback. "Oklahoma's Recent Earthquakes and Saltwater Disposal." *Science Advances* 1, no. 5 (18 June 2015).

Wang, Jackie. *Carceral Capitalism*. Boston: MIT Press, 2018.

Water Education Foundation. "Aquapedia Background—Colorado River." Accessed March 16, 2020. https://www.watereducation.org/aquapedia/colorado-river.

Watkins, Clare Vaye. *Gold Fame Citrus*. New York: Riverhead, 2016.
Watts, Michael. "Oil Frontiers: The Niger Delta and the Gulf of Mexico." In *Oil Culture*, edited by Ross Barrett and Daniel Worden, 189–210. Minneapolis: University of Minnesota Press, 2014.
Warren Democrats. "We Need a Blue New Deal for Our Oceans." Accessed December 6, 2020. https://elizabethwarren.com/plans/blue-new-deal.
Wenzel, Jennifer. "Petro-Magic Realism: Toward a Political Ecology of Nigerian Literature." *Postcolonial Studies* 9, no. 4 (2006): 449–64.
———. "Turning over a New Leaf: Fanonian Humanism and Environmental Justice." In *The Routledge Companion to the Environmental Humanities*, edited by Ursula K. Heise, Jon Christensen, and Michelle Niemann, 165–73. New York: Routledge, 2016.
Western, Jessica, and Selena Gerace. *Social License for Wyoming's Energy Future: What Do Residents Want?* Laramie: University of Wyoming School of Energy Resources and the Ruckelshaus Institute of Environment and Natural Resources, November 2020. http://www.uwyo.edu/haub/_files/_docs/ruckelshaus/pubs/2020-wyomings-energy-social-license-report.pdf.
Western, Samuel. *Pushed Off the Mountain, Sold Down the River: Wyoming's Search for Its Soul*. Moose WY: Homestead, 2002.
Whyte, Kyle Powys. "The Dakota Access Pipeline, Environmental Justice, and U.S. Colonialism." RED INK: *An International Journal of Indigenous Literature, Arts, & Humanities* 19, no. 1 (2017): 154–69.
———. "Indigenous Climate Change Studies: Indigenizing Futures, Decolonizing the Anthropocene." *English Language Notes* 55, no. 1–2 (2017): 153–62.
———. "Is It Colonial Déjà Vu? Indigenous Peoples and Climate Injustice." In *Humanities for the Environment: Integrating Knowledge, Forging New Constellations of Practice*, edited by Joni Adamson and Michael Davis, 88–104. New York: Routledge, 2016.
———. "Our Ancestors' Dystopia Now: Indigenous Conservation and the Anthropocene." In *The Routledge Companion to the Environmental Humanities*, edited by Ursula K. Heise, Jon Christensen, and Michelle Niemann, 206–15. New York: Routledge, 2016.
———. "Settler Colonialism, Ecology, and Collective Continuance." *Environment and Society: Advances in Research* 9 (2018): 125–44.
Wilson, Sheena, Adam Carlson, and Imre Szeman, eds. *Petrocultures: Oil, Politics, Culture*. Montreal: McGill-Queens University Press, 2017.
Wiseman, John, Che Biggs, Lauren Rickards, and Taegen Edwards. *Scenarios for Climate Adaptation: Guidebook for Practitioners*. Victorian Centre for Climate Change Adaptation Research, University of Victoria, 2011.

Witt, Joseph D. *Religion and Resistance: Faith and the Fight against Mountaintop Removal Coal Mining*. Lexington: University Press of Kentucky, 2016.

Wolfe, Patrick. "Settler Colonialism and the Elimination of the Native." *Journal of Genocide Research* 8, no. 4 (2006): 387–409.

Wright, John, dir. *Beyond All Boundaries*. Los Angeles: Jux Media, 2016.

Wyoming Department of Revenue. *2019 Annual Report*. Cheyenne: State of Wyoming, 2020. https://revenue.wyo.gov/about-us/dor-annual-reports.

Wyoming Taxpayers Association. "Direct Tax Collections and Public Service Costs 2019." December 12, 2020. http://wyotax.org/wp-content/uploads/2020/12/Cost-of-Services-2019.pdf.

Yaeger, Patricia. "*Beasts of the Southern Wild* and Dirty Ecology." *Southern Spaces* (February 13, 2013). https://southernspaces.org/2013/beasts-southern-wild-and-dirty-ecology.

Yahn, Jacqueline. "Frackanomics." In *Appalachia Revisited: New Perspectives on Place, Tradition, and Progress*, edited by Rebecca Schumann and William Adkins Fletcher, 139–54. Lexington: University of Kentucky Press, 2016.

Young, James E. "The Counter-Monument: Memory against Itself in Germany Today." *Critical Inquiry* 18, no. 2 (1992): 267–96.

Yusoff, Kathryn. *A Billion Black Anthropocenes or None*. Minneapolis: University of Minnesota Press, 2018.

Zeitlin, Benh, dir. *Beasts of the Southern Wild*. Los Angeles: Fox Searchlight, 2012.

Ziser, Michael. "Ecomedia." In *Keywords for Environmental Studies*, edited by Joni Adamson, William A. Gleason, and David N. Pellow, 75–76. New York: NYU Press, 2016.

Ziser, Michael, and Julie Sze. "Climate Change, Environmental Aesthetics, and Global Environmental Justice Cultural Studies." *Discourse* 29, no. 2–3 (2007): 384–410.

# Index

*Page numbers in italics indicate illustrations.*

Afrodiasporic studies, 125
*After Oil (Petrocultures Research Group)*, 16, 106
Alliance for Appalachia, 10
amaranth, 39-41, 43
American Federation of Labor and Congress of Industrial Organizations (AFL-CIO), 9
Anishinaabes, 2, 20, 28-29
Anthropocene, 12, 123-26
anthropocentrism, 12
Appalachia, 3, 10, 17, 21-22, 85, 87-88, 90-91, 93-97, 99, 101, 103-6, 110-11, 147, 149, 156, 175n3, 178n85
aridity, 30-31, 34, 40, 52, 167n34
Arizona, 20, 25-31, 35, 37-39, 42, 47-55, 71, 165n3, 169n87
Army Corps of Engineers, 32-33
Aronoff, Kate, 118
aurochs, 139-40, 187n126

Baltimore MD, 2-3
the Bathtub, 133-35, 137-38, 141-42, 186n97
*Beasts of the Southern Wild* (Zeitlin), 23, 114, 116, 133-36, 138-40, 142, 180n9
Black Lives Matter, 1, 64-65, 81
*Black Marxism* (Robinson), 5, 60-61. See also Robinson, Cedric

Blackness, 17, 71
BlueGreen Alliance, 8
Blue New Deal, 11, 117
Buffalo Creek flood, 86, 95
Bureau of Reclamation (USBR), 30-34, 39

*Cadillac Desert* (Reisner), 32, 34-36
canals, 4, 25-26, 39, 45-48, 50, 52-53, 123, 134, 136, 139
capital accumulation, 5, 17, 62-65, 121
capitalism, 4-6, 12, 15, 19, 121, 124-25, 128, 132, 183n52; extractive, 6-7, 19, 85-86, 88-91, 93, 105, 111, 126, 161n26; free-market, 12, 22; frontier, 89; green, 125; neoliberal, 62, 126; petroleum-driven, 90; racial, 5, 17, 21, 28, 57-66, 68, 70, 72, 74-77, 79, 83, 125-26, 147, 161n26, 171n16
Capitalocene, 62, 121-25, 127, 137, 183n52
captivity narrative, 43, 167n34
carbon energy regimes, 120
catastrophe, 6, 104, 113, 127, 138-39, 141
Central Valley CA, 2
citizenship, 13, 33, 77
class, 10, 13, 19, 23, 60-64, 67, 77, 89, 101-2, 111, 119, 121, 123, 126-31, 184n80, 185n87

211

Clean Air Act, 11, 91
Clean Water Act, 11, 21, 92
climate adaptation, 3, 14–15, 122, 143, 163n62
climate change, 167n33; and adaptation, 14; and capitalism, 124; and climate denial, 151–52; cultural representations of, 137; experiences of, 140, 150, 180n9; and extraction, 89; and fiction, 13, 22, 36, 44, 85, 126, 134–35, 180n9; and geoengineering, 123; global, 3, 16, 139; and Green New Deal (GND), 121; and impacted communities, 6, 150, 180n9; and magical realism, 134; narratives, 122; and public engagement, 47, 151–52; and topography, 139; and transition principles, 9
climate equity, 132
Climate Justice Alliance (CJA), 10, 58, 66, 133, 143
coal, 3, 17, 21–23, 85–88, 91–98, 101, 103, 105–6, 108–11, 148–52, 156, 160n20, 175nn2–3, 176n12, 178n85
coastal futures, 126
collective continuance, 20, 25, 28–29, 38–42, 44, 46–48, 52–54, 119, 140, 147, 157
colonialism, 5, 12, 33, 37, 40, 43, 61–62, 87, 93, 111, 125, 161n26
Colorado River Basin, 11, 17, 20, 25, 27, 29–31, 36–39, 44–45, 48, 52, 54, 169n87
Colorado River Drought Contingency Plan (DCP), 2, 20, 25
Colorado River Indian Tribes (CRIT), 27, 38–39, 44, 53–54
Commoner, Barry, 8

counternarratives, 6, 12, 16–17, 28, 38
cultural sovereignty, 10, 55, 142
cultural studies, 12, 18–19

Dakota Access Pipeline (DAPL), 1–2, 5, 7, 33
dams, 2–3, 17, 19, 30–34, 36, 39, 47–48, 50, 85–86, 92, 135, 168n65; megadams, 5
decolonization, 10, 28, 53–54
desert, 32, 40–45, 47, 52–54
Desert Land Act (1877), 33
Detroit MI, 1–2, 66, 78, 157
Detroit River, 59, 63–64
drilling, 86, 97–100, 103–5
drought, 2, 17, 19, 29, 31, 36–41, 45, 55, 118, 147–48, 167n33; and climate change, 47; and colonialism, 30; decolonize, 25, 28, 53; management, 11; and megadrought, 20, 35, 48

ecological regimes, 19
economic equity, 9, 71, 117
energy development, 88–90, 103
energy economy, 22, 87, 103, 105, 111
energy humanities, 3, 16, 18, 90
Energy Justice Network, 10
energy studies, 17, 87, 106
environmental humanities, 12–15, 19, 90, 162n51, 163n62
Environmental Protection Agency (EPA), 3, 86
environmental studies, 4, 19
equitable futures, 16–17, 58, 60, 105, 148, 156–57
equity, 14, 76, 88, 113, 116
exclusion, 4–6, 15, 19, 23, 28–29, 32, 43, 61, 116, 122, 135, 137, 139, 147

extraction, 22, 85–89; coal, 85, 88, 93, 95–96, 103; culture, 91, 94–96, 101, 103, 105, 110–11, 149; and energy, 89, 152; of fossil fuel, 3, 9, 21, 85, 89, 147, 151, 157; of gas, 98, 102, 156; of groundwater, 31; of minerals, 149; of natural resources, 4–5; oil, 139; post-, 22, 85, 88, 97, 105–6, 111, 157; pre-, 97; of raw material, 4, 18, 86, 90; of water, 33, 43, 55, 72–73

films, 6, 15, 22–23, 28, 37, 53–54, 102, 111, 114, 116, 118, 127, 133–34, 137, 139–42, 144, 147, 154, 162n51, 180n9, 187n126

Flint MI, 1, 17, 57, 147, 149; and abandonment, 21; and environmental justice, 77; Fit, 21, 60, 67, 78–80, 83; *Flint*, 21, 60, 66–71, 74–78, 83, 172n41; Flint Lives Matter, 60, 67, 81; *Flint Town*, 68; and *Greetings from Flint*, 81–82; and hip-hop, 1–2; Public Art Project, 21, 60, 67, 83; and reparations, 58; River, 1, 59, 64, 79, 81; and water activism, 2, 18, 60, 64, 75; water crisis, 5, 57–60, 63, 66–67, 70–73, 81, 86, 115, 137; water system, 17; water transition, 7

flood control, 23, 33, 135, 138

Fort Laramie Treaty (1868), 7, 33

fossil fuels, 3, 7, 9, 16–17, 21–22, 85, 88, 90, 101, 103, 106, 110, 116, 118, 120–21, 147–52, 157; and fossil fuel regimes, 121

freedom, 65–66, 133, 138, 141, 147, 190n23

freedom dreams, 60, 66–67, 77, 79, 83

futures studies, 14

*Gardens in the Dunes* (Silko), 20, 28, 38–44, 47–48, 55

gender, 10, 13, 61–62, 71–72, 121

Gila River, 25, 45, 52, 165n6

Gila River Indian Community, 20, 25–27, 35, 44, 165n2, 165n5

global food systems, 3

Global South, 5, 87, 136, 185n91

governance, 4, 21, 41, 61–62, 64, 119, 142, 157

Great Depression, 11, 114, 128, 185n88

greenhouse gases, 3, 31, 116

Green New Deal (GND), 11, 22, 113–14, 118–19, 142–43, 145–46, 157

groundwater, 21, 31, 38, 42, 72–73, 97, 106, 113, 167n33

*Heat and Light* (Haigh), 22, 87, 101–2, 104

hip-hop, 1–2

Homestead Act, 26, 30, 32–33, 52

Hoover Dam, 34, 41

Hopis, 34

Hualapais, 34

human agency, 12, 123

Hurricane Harvey, 3, 115, 160n11

Hurricane Katrina, 3, 115, 123, 126–27, 130, 134–35, 137–38, 184n70, 186n97

Hurricane Maria, 3

hydropower, 3, 19, 30, 33, 39, 99

inclusive futures, 65

Indigeneity, 17, 96–97

Indigenous Environmental Network (IEN), 1, 10

*213*

Indigenous people, xi, 96–97; and the Amazon, 19; and climate change, 3, 115–16, 133; and collective continuance, 29, 39–40, 46, 48, 54, 157; and dams, 5; and dispossession, 35–37, 46, 119, 139–40, 165n6, 167n41; and erasure, 5–6, 17, 20, 27, 32, 47; and infrastructure, 23, 43; and knowledge, 10, 28, 40, 53–54, 118; and land use, 32–33; and lifeways, 48, 140; and music, 2; oppression of, 11, 23, 89, 116, 125, 142, 147, 157, 160n20; and resistance, 39, 143–44, 156; and sovereignty, xi, 44, 117; and water, 1, 32–32, 34–35, 47, 73, 168n57

inequality, 5, 11, 22, 64, 74, 114, 119, 121, 123, 126–28, 130, 143, 161n23, 181n11, 182n31, 185n88

injustice, 6–7, 16, 38, 48, 54, 144, 147, 156; economic, 94; environmental, 7, 13, 29, 91, 157, 176n17; food, 51, 165n8; social, 4, 54, 89, 94, 157; systemic, 7; water, 6, 11, 18–19

Intergovernmental Panel on Climate Change (IPCC), 113

irrigation, 4, 26, 30–33, 39–41, 45–46, 48, 50, 52–53, 170n113

justice, 1, 14, 60, 75–76, 116; climate, 6, 10–12, 23, 114, 120, 127, 130, 133–34; economic, 11, 13; energy, 156; environmental, 2, 6–10, 13, 19, 23, 39, 49, 58, 60, 62–63, 77, 85, 125, 143, 156, 161n35, 184n70; food, 76, 111; racial, 9, 58, 133; redistributive, 127; reparative, 57, 66, 75, 78, 83, 119–20, 122, 131, 142; restorative, 8, 58, 116, 161n35; and 17 Principles of Environmental Justice, 9; social, 10, 12, 66, 69, 132, 180n9; theories of, 7; water, 2, 5, 18, 147, 159n4

just transition, 6–12, 15–16, 21–23, 28, 37, 44, 57–62, 64–66, 76, 78–79, 83, 105, 116–17, 122, 132–33, 139, 142–43, 147–49, 151, 153, 157, 163n62

Just Transition Fund, 88, 156, 176n12

just water, 6–7, 16, 19–20, 37, 40, 54–55, 57, 81, 115, 147

Kasdorf, Julia Spicher, 22, 87, 99

Lake Oahe, 1
Lakotas, 1–2, 5, 20, 28, 33
land privatization, 5
land reclamation, 32–33, 46, 55, 79, 89, 109–10, 118, 169n73
land reclamation art, xii, 22, 88, 105, 147
landscape architecture, 6
land theft, 2, 5, 43, 62
Lead and Copper Rule, 3, 57
levees, 18, 23, 115–16, 133–42
literary fiction, 6, 15, 18, 37, 54, 147, 180n9
literary studies, 15, 162n51
Los Angeles CA, 31, 35–36, 39, 42, 69
Louisiana, 23, 115, 118, 134, 139, 141, 184n70
Louisiana Bayou, 23, 136, 140–41

Mazzocchi, Tony, 8
media studies, 15
methane, 31, 97, 100, 102–3
Missouri River, 1, 33
modernity, 3, 18, 41, 61, 79, 90, 136

Mohaves, 34, 39, 54
mountaintop removal (MTR) coal mining, 22, 91–93, 95, 97–98, 105
museum exhibits, 6, 48, 54–55, 81, 106, 147
museum studies, 46, 162n51
music, 6, 67, 81, 111, 147, 154

NAACP, 9
National Environmental Policy Act (NEPA), 8
National Flood Insurance Program, 11
National Resources Defense Council (NRDC), 3
natural gas, 17, 85, 87, 97, 99, 101–2, 104, 150, 178n85
neoliberal governance, 135, 139
neoliberal hydrological regime, 19, 115
neoliberalism, 5, 19, 22, 62–63, 72–73, 115–17, 120–21, 126–29, 131, 135, 138–39, 141, 161n26, 181n11, 182n31, 185n87
neoliberalization, 21, 115, 134, 137–38, 147
Nestlé, 72–75, 79
Newark NJ, 2
New Deal (1930s), 11, 23, 114, 119–21, 143, 181n24
Newlands Reclamation Act (1902), 30, 35, 53
New Orleans LA, 3, 115, 127, 134–39, 181n11, 186n97
*New York 2140* (Robinson), 23, 114–16, 122, 124–25, 127, 129–33, 142, 144, 180n9, 185nn87–88
New York NY, 23, 115, 122–23, 142
North American Free Trade Agreement (NAFTA), 9

Ocasio-Cortez, Alexandria, 11, 114, 118, 127, 131, 143–44
oil, 18, 21, 102, 148, 150, 152, 156; crash, 163n62, 186n7; and exploitation, 98, 100; industry, 135; and oil-centricity, 17; prospectors, 90; tankers, 139; tough, 38; wells, 87; workers, 118
Oil, Chemical, and Atomic Workers (OCAW), 8
oppression, 2, 7, 10–11, 19, 61, 65, 70, 83, 116, 144

Pancake, Ann, 22, 85, 87, 91, 94–95, 102–5. See also *Strange as This Weather Has Been* (Pancake)
Parker Dam, 38–41, 43–44, 169n87
participatory governance, 14–15, 20, 27, 29, 113
Pennsylvania, 22, 87–88, 97–99, 101–5
Phoenix AZ, 20, 26–28, 31, 35–36, 44–49, 52–53, 71, 109
photography, 6, 15, 22, 87, 99–100, 105, 108, 141, 147, 178n72
policy studies, 15
post-extraction futures, 22, 88–89, 105–11, 157
Potawatomis, 5, 20, 27
Powell, John Wesley, 20, 30–31
public art, 6, 15, 20–21, 28, 48, 54–55, 60–67, 79, 81–83, 118
Pueblo Grande Museum, 20, 28, 46–49, 52–53, 55
Puerto Rico, 3

race, 2, 9–10, 12, 21, 28, 33, 60–62, 70–71, 89, 111, 121–22, 137, 161n26, 184n70
racial difference, 5

racial equity, 9, 118
racial extractivism, 5, 33, 161n26
racism, 5, 12, 61, 68, 89, 119, 144; environmental, 21, 58-60, 62-63, 65-66, 68, 77-78, 81, 119, 156; scientific, 125; systemic, 67-68, 122, 126-27, 143
religious studies, 12
reparation ecology, 7-8, 58
reparations, 7, 10-11, 58, 65-66, 77, 79, 83, 143-44, 157
reservoirs, 3, 31, 36, 47, 51, 167n33
resource governance, 27, 31, 33, 57, 147
resource regimes, 20, 30, 48, 54
Robinson, Cedric, 5, 21, 60-61, 65
Robinson, Kim-Stanley, 23, 114-15, 122-23, 125-27, 130-33. See also *New York 2140* (Robinson)
Roosevelt, Franklin Delano, 11, 43, 114
Rubin, Steven, 22, 87, 99-100, 105

Salt River, 35, 45-46, 48, 51-53
Sand Lizard people, 38-44
settler colonialism, 1, 5, 17, 20, 27, 29, 39, 42, 44, 51, 54, 125, 135, 139-40, 161n26, 167n35
Silko, Leslie Marmon, 20, 28, 38-42, 47, 55, 169n87. See also *Gardens in the Dunes* (Silko)
Sister Salt, 38-40, 42-44
slow violence, 13, 98
social equity, 6, 9
solidarity, 2, 6, 147
Sonoran Desert, 40, 52-53
Soufy, 2
Southern Paiutes, 34
Standing Rock Committee, 1

Standing Rock ND, 1-2, 5, 18, 33, 65
storytelling, 2, 6-8, 15-16, 19, 21, 58-60, 65, 68, 70, 88, 144, 147-48, 151, 156-57, 163n62; material, 47-48, 109
*Strange as This Weather Has Been* (Pancake), 22, 85-86, 91, 101
sustainability, 6, 9, 54, 74, 88, 129-30
sustainable futures, 67, 109

technology studies, 18
traditional lands, xi, 1, 34
trauma, 6-7, 10, 70-71, 76, 78, 95
tribal sovereignty, 7, 54, 119
Tucson AZ, 31, 40, 45

United Church of Christ Commission on Racial Justice, 9
urban reclamation, 124, 138

Verde River, 35, 45
Vergès, Françoise, 62, 125
violence, 6, 13, 15, 19, 27-29, 33-34, 37-38, 42-43, 54, 62-65, 70, 77, 86-87, 93, 98, 100-101, 105, 116, 125

Warren, Elizabeth, 11, 117
water futures, 6, 54
water governance, 28, 33, 40, 44, 48
Water Is Life Expo, 1
*The Water Knife* (Bacigalupi), 36
Water Protectors, 1, 7
water systems, 17-18, 20, 38, 48, 57, 72, 86, 115, 147
wealth inequality, 5, 128
western lands, 30, 167n34
western United States, 20, 27-33, 35, 37, 46-48, 55, 147, 150-51, 160n20

western water, 29, 34, 167n57
West Virginia, 3, 85–88, 91–92, 95, 99–100, 175n2
white supremacy, 2, 5, 74, 125, 140
Whyte, Kyle, 5, 20, 27–29, 37, 119
World War I, 92
World War II, 8, 128
Wyoming, 23, 30, 69, 148–51, 153–57

Yale School for Climate Change Communication, 114
YoNasDa LoneWolf, 1

Zeitlin, Benh, 23, 114, 116, 133, 135, 137, 140, 187n126
Zunis, 34

Printed in the USA
CPSIA information can be obtained
at www.ICGtesting.com
CBHW022324290424
7768CB00002B/203